THE AGONY OF SHOPPING AND OTHER PLAYS

By

Constantino Vincent Riccardi

WIPF & STOCK · Eugene, Oregon

Wipf and Stock Publishers
199 W 8th Ave, Suite 3
Eugene, OR 97401

The Agony of Shopping and Other Plays
By Riccardi, Constantino Vincent
Copyright©1994 by Riccardi, Constantino Vincent
ISBN 13: 978-1-5326-1733-1
Publication date 1/24/2017
Previously published by Contra Mundum Productions, 1994

PREFACE

THE AGONY OF SHOPPING AND OTHER PLAYS has developed over the past twenty-five years through a diversity of experiences. In my idealistic youth I studied philosophy and theology in such strange places as a Jesuit college in Rome, Italy and a Protestant seminary in Berkeley, California. That was the 1960's.

In the 1970's I discovered that the final bloom of "the flower children" had faded. It was a time to make a buck. I became a business broker selling liquor stores, beer joints, and cocktail lounges.

In the 1980's the corporate ladder rose upward. An acquisition and merger company hired me. I began to understand "the market system" and what it could offer. I also began to understand what it could not offer.

In the 1990's I have come to the conclusion that the corporate ladder is not Jacob's Ladder. Some men and women may have millions of dollars, but few of us have a hundred years.

To remind myself and others that there still remain spiritual resources despite the gasping and grasping over Mammon, I have decided to bring forth a series of plays.

THE AGONY OF SHOPPING is a trilogy. In the first play spoiled women are bitching about what they do not have. In the second play, YES! . . . BUT WE STILL HAVE SLUMS, men are trying to analyze spoiled women and the value of money. In the final play, THE AUCTION, a psychological and spiritual audit is made on modern American values.

THOMAS THE SKEPTIC is the story of Doubting Thomas and the age old struggle for faith.

SOREN KIERKEGAARD deals with the life and thought of one of history's most profound thinkers.

RUNNING FOX is the story of greed and the United States' exploitation of Native Americans which led to the

Sand Creek Massacre of 1864.

EGMONT AND THE THEOLOGIAN poetically portrays the last prison days of Dietrich Bonhoeffer, the German theologian who was hanged by the Nazis.

REMEMBER TORRES! traces the life and thought of Camilo Torres, a Colombian priest who fought and died for social justice.

MOSES McNUTT is a satire on consumerism and modern American society.

Since the dramas have many voices within them, I will say no more except to wish the reader the very best.

Vince Riccardi

CONTENTS

Preface 3
The Agony of Shopping: A Trilogy 7
Part 1: The Agony of Shopping 9
Part 2: Yes! . . . But We Still Have Slums 35
Part 3: The Auction 73

Thomas the Skeptic 91

Soren Kierkegaard 111

Running Fox 153

Egmont and the Theologian 211

Remember Torres! 247

Moses McNutt 289

THE AGONY OF SHOPPING:
A TRILOGY

THE AGONY OF SHOPPING

YES! . . . BUT WE STILL HAVE SLUMS

THE AUCTION

THE AGONY OF SHOPPING

CHARACTERS

MONTE WEST
ANGELINA CAVALCANTI, Monte's daughter
2 WAITRESSES

[A bar/restaurant in Palm Springs, California. It is November, 1985. Two tables of glass and chrome are surrounded by chrome chairs with vermilion velour backs and seats. The chrome tables and chairs are so bright as to be glaring. Ferns and tennis racquets as well as pictures of tennis stars hang from the walls. In the background an actual tennis court can be seen through a large glass window. The name of the bar/restaurant is "The Singles." Its logo of two crossed racquets with the words "The Singles," should be arranged in such a way that the logo can be seen as well as the tennis court in the background. At one of the tables, a sixty-five year old, thirty pounds over-weight, bloated and puffy woman named Monte West is seated at a table. She is wearing large sunglasses and a multicolored black and red turban around her head. None of her hair can be seen. With the turban covering her head and the huge sunglasses, she has the look of an immense insect. She is smoking a cigarette. On the table in front of her are five empty martini glasses. Despite her flab and her deterioration caused by massive quantities of alcohol, the woman still has traces of her once great, youthful beauty. As the scene begins, Monte, in a very whining voice, is complaining to the waitress. The waitress is twenty-five with exceptionally pretty legs and is dressed in a white blouse with very short white tennis shorts. All the hatred and envy of the fading beauty for the blooming beauty should be evident in the older woman's voice.]

Monte [imperiously]: Waitress, waitress . . .

Waitress: Yes, ma'am. What is it that I can do for you?

Monte [pointing to an ice bucket]: The wine . . . it is not chilled enough. [raging] What is wrong with this place? Don't you people know how to chill a good bottle of wine?

Waitress [matter of factly]: But excuse me, ma'am. You ordered the wine, and it has been sitting in the ice bucket for an hour. You have been drinking martinis for an hour. The wine is still unopened.

Monte [screaming in a vicious, vixen's manner]: Don't contradict me. I am the customer, and you are the waitress! Do you hear me? Do you hear me? Now, why wasn't the wine chilled?

Waitress [patiently]: The wine was and is chilled, ma'am. It's just that ... well, maybe you've had too much to drink, and ...

Monte [furiously]: I'LL TELL YOU WHEN I'VE HAD TOO MUCH TO DRINK! YOU'RE NOT TO TELL ME! Do you know who I am?!! Do you know who I know?!! Just because you're young with pretty legs, you can't make fun of me. Why, I've married four men, and they all loved me and my legs! I was young once, you know.

Waitress [uneasily]: Ma'am, I think that you've had too much to drink. Maybe I'd better get you a cab. You've had all that liquor and nothing to eat.

Monte [screaming]: WHY WASN'T THE WINE CHILLED?!! WHY WASN'T THE WINE CHILLED?!!

Waitress [quietly]: But ma'am, the wine has not been opened.

Monte [screaming]: DON'T CONTRADICT ME! DON'T ARGUE WITH ME! I'm the customer ... [slurring her words] ... and the cus-toom-er is-ss always r-i-g-h-t. [There is a brief silence and then Monte drops her turbaned and sunglassed head onto the serving dish. There is another brief silence. Monte begins snoring with her head on the serving dish. A few grunts are heard from Monte as the waitress, chuckling to herself, moves off stage. A few moments pass and snores, gasps, wheezing, and belching are heard from Monte. Finally, it appears that Monte has arrived at that peace known only to a contented cow. As the older woman is belching and grunting, a young woman, age thirty-five, enters. She is very attractive and is wearing a tweed business suit with one of those ties worn by career women in which the tie is formed into a loose looped bow. Her hair is perfectly arranged. She has a look of exhaustion on her face.]

Angelina: Mother! [becoming irritated] Mother! [becoming exasperated] Mother! [She begins pushing her mother's shoulders up and down.] Mother, it's me, Angelina! Mother, wake up! Mother, sober up! Oh, my God! [She sits down next to her mother and begins weeping.] Mother, for the love of God, what are you doing?

Monte [slurring her words]: I w-a-as o-n-l-y t-r-y-ing to g-e-t-t a glass of w-i-i-ne and . . . and . . . and they p-o-u-rred all those martinis into meeee! They shouldn't haaave d-oone that! [Soon Monte's sloppy effusiveness begins to overcome her slurring.] Oh, Angelina, is it you? Is it really you? God, my guardian angel is here! You're here at last, you're finally here at last! What kept you, my angel? Where have you been?

Angelina: The flight from San Francisco was late. Besides, I had a Chapter 11 proceeding in the bankruptcy court. I am sorry, but things just didn't work out for me to get here earlier.

Monte [whining]: Oh. Angelina, if only you had been here. They wouldn't have given me so much to drink.

Angelina [furiously]: Mother, look at yourself! You're dead drunk! You're supposed to be down here to dry out! You're supposed to be at the Betty Ford Detoxification Center! And look at yourself! Drunk as a derelict! My God!

Monte [becoming furious]: Oh, shut up! Who is Betty Ford and who are you? Don't get high and mighty with me. Why Betty Ford only became the First Lady because Nixon was a lying crook! And her husband, why her husband, Jerry Ford, had no more right to become President than a mule has the right to become a racehorse. My God, that woman goes around trying to convert drunks after she's had her booze and lived in the White House! She's no damn good, I tell you! No goddamn good!

Angelina [pleading]: Mother, please, please. You should be drying out.

Monte [raging]: WITH BETTY FORD? THAT MISERABLE BITCH! WHY SHOULD I DRY OUT? TO MAKE BETTY HAPPY? TO MAKE YOU HAPPY? GO TO HELL, ALL OF YOU! I'LL DO IT MY WAY! [She begins humming the popular song "I Did It My Way." She then belches, swallows, and continues to rage.] I DID IT MY WAY! THAT'S WHAT I DID! I DID IT MY WAY! MY OWN GODDAMN WAY!

Angelina [sternly]: Mother, you did it drunk. Please, lower your voice and try to get a grip on yourself.

Monte [with subdued fury]: Who in the hell are you to tell me what to do?

Angelina: I am your daughter. Please, please, calm down.

Monte [quietly]: Okay, but I need a drink.

Angelina: You don't need a drink.

Monte: Goddamit, I need a drink. Waitress! Waitress! [The waitress appears. Angelina bows her head. Monte looks at Angelina and stops for a moment.] Waitress, perhaps you should open the bottle of wine. [Both the waitress and Angelina look relieved. The waitress opens the bottle and pours a preliminary taste into Monte's glass. Monte swirls the wine around her glass and takes a sip.] Excellent. Now that's a well-chilled wine. [The waitress smiles, pours the wine into Angelina's glass and then fills Monte's. She places the bottle in the bucket and exists.]

Angelina [sipping her wine, pausing, and placing the glass on the table]: Thank you, mother.

Monte [sarcastically]: For what?

Angelina: For trying to control yourself.

Monte [placing her glass down and shrugging her shoulders]: Oh. [There is a brief pause.] So it means something to you, does it?

Angelina: Whenever you try to help yourself, it means something to me.

Monte [quietly]: So, I still mean something to you?

Angelina [bowing her head]: You mean a great deal to me. If only you would dry out.

Monte [viciously]: Oh, why don't you dry up! Look at you, all decked out in your "career girl" yuppie uniform. So you're a lawyer now! So what? I remember when you had to dry out. Not just from booze, but from pills. You remember that, don't you?

Angelina [quietly]: Yes, mother, I remember that. Do we have to . . .

Monte [self-righteously]: Of course we do. You're not coming down here to judge me. Just because you're a big lawyer on Montgomery Street in San Francisco, you're not going to judge me!

Angelina [with deep hatred]: Nobody's here to judge you. I'm here to help you, that's all.

Monte [furiously]: Well, who needs your goddamn help? Why don't you help someone else? Help one of your clients; that's what you should do. I don't need your help.

Angelina [mournfully]: I try to help my clients, and I'm trying to help you. But it's not easy.

Monte [self-righteously]: Oh, shut up and stop sniveling. You're a lawyer now. I saw to that. When your second husband kicked you out the door, who took care of you? I did!

And now look at you! Sitting there and condemning me like a judge. Who are you anyway?

Angelina [quietly]: Mother, please.

Monte [furiously]: Oh, shut up. What kind of law do you practice anyway?

Angelina: Bankruptcy law.

Monte [laughing]: What in God's name do you know about bankruptcy? You were born with a platinum spoon in your mouth. Nick and I saw to that! He was the best husband I ever had. He was . . .

Angelina: He was number three.

Monte [pondering for a moment]: Yes. I guess he was number three.

Angelina [quietly]: And you left him for another man when he went bankrupt.

Monte [sipping her wine]: I left him . . . I left him, but it wasn't so simple. I was turning fifty, and he was out of money. I'd rather be miserable and rich than miserable and poor. I'm not used to misery. It doesn't agree with me. Besides, you were getting your first divorce... and . . . and . . .

Angelina [outraged]: Oh, c'mon, mother, you left him. Don't blame it on age or on me. Blame it on the drink and your appalling self-pity. [There is a brief silence. Angelina stares at Monte who has a blank look on her face. Angelina grins.] Mother, what does a rich woman make for dinner?

Monte [Sipping her wine, she speaks indifferently.]: How the hell should I know.

Angelina [laughing]: Well, mother, you should know. What a rich woman makes for dinner is reservations. You're good at that! So shut up and stop feeling sorry for yourself! You're just an old, dying, termite queen! That's what you are! You've gnawed through men, and you've gnawed through homes! You'll probably go through more men and more homes until the final reservations are made, and you become dinner for worms!

Monte [aghast]: What a terrible thing to say.

Angelina [laughing demoniacally]: What a terrible woman you are! You old, dying, termite queen!

Monte [Reflecting a few moments, her tone changes to one of absolute fury.]: Well, who in the hell are you? Now that you've got your law degree! How do you make your money?

Angelina [self-righteously]: By defending the needy! Those facing bankruptcy! That's how I make my living!

Monte [viciously]: Is that right?

Angelina [with the greatest self-righteousness]: That's right!

Monte [snarling]: And what do you charge your clients?

Angelina [furiously]: What do you mean?

Monte [viciously]: If someone is facing bankruptcy, what do you charge them up front?

Angelina [sheepishly]: You know, mother.

Monte [with great glee]: Oh, c'mon, out with it! What do you charge up front?

Angelina [bowing her head]: Oh, stop it, mother.

Monte [in mockery]: Oh c'mon, Angelina. Tell mommy what Angelina charges up front to defend the poor and the downtrodden? C'mon, Angelina. What's your price?

Angelina [quietly]: You know, mother. $5,000 up front.

Monte [laughing demoniacally]: What a bitch you are! And you call me a termite queen! Why you're nothing more than a call girl with a law degree! $5,000 a trick and I bet you know all the tricks! [yelling hysterically] Waitress . . . waitress! Waitress, come over here quick. I want you to meet my daughter, the call girl! Waitress . . . waitress . . . A Double Martini UP! My God, where is she?

[The waitress appears somewhat confused.]

Waitress: I think you had better go.

Angelina [viciously]: Why should we go? There's no one here? We have our rights!

Monte [laughing]: You tell 'em honey! You're right we have our rights! [to the waitress] You'd better not push her around. She's a lawyer and a call girl!

Waitress: But . . .

Angelina [laughing]: But nothing. We're going to get blown away, aren't we, mother? We're going to get mapped, drunk, smashed! Right, mother?

Monte [with great dignity]: Yes, we are!

[The waitress looks around helplessly and then leaves.]

Monte [pulling the bottle of wine out of the bucket]: Here, have a drink. It'll do you good. [Monte fills Angelina's glass.]

Angelina [indignantly]: Who does that babe think she is? Just because she has great legs, she doesn't own the world.

Monte [morosely sipping her wine]: The bitch!

Angelina [laughing uproariously]: Stop it, mother! We're both envious, and you know it.

Monte [shrugging her shoulders indifferently and gulping more wine]: Yeah, we're envious.

Angelina [smiling]: But we have each other.

Monte [laughing]: Yeah, the termite queen and the call girl. [Both laugh. There is a silence.]

Angelina [compassionately]: Mother, why don't you dry out?

Monte [Pouring herself another glass of wine, she hisses viciously at Angelina.]: Why don't you dry up!

Angelina [helplessly]: Okay . . . okay. [There is a silence. Monte bows her head. Sluggishly, she begins to speak.]

Monte: I came down here to dry out. Drove all the way from Beverly Hills. Went to the spa. Had the seaweed facial, the underarm wax, and the body wrap. And then the shopping began . . . [weeping] . . . and then the shopping began.

Angelina [laughing]: Oh, stop it. Jesus! The seaweed facial and [laughing] and the shopping. Mother, you were always good at shopping.

Monte [sadly staring into her wine glass]: Shopping has cost me a lot.

Angelina [laughing]: And it has cost your four husbands a lot, too.

Monte [quietly]: You don't understand.

Angelina [sternly and laughing]: And neither will most of the human race.

Monte [gulping more wine]: To hell with the human race. [quietly] You don't understand.

Angelina [in a bored manner]: Understand what, mother?

Monte [wearily]: Understand what it means to be just a dressed up little doll all your life. That is why I divorced your father . . . Nick gave me everything, One day I came home from shopping. I went into the bedroom. I unwrapped everything. I sat on the bed, and I began weeping. Surrounded by all the beautiful things, I sat down and wept. The next day I filed for divorce.

Angelina [somewhat startled]: I thought you divorced him because he went broke.

Monte [bowing her head]: Well, that was part of it. But there was something else. I was tired of always being the pretty, dressed up, little doll. But I was unable to be anything else. Besides, Nick, your father, couldn't bear the thought of not being top dog all the time. He wanted me to go shopping all the time despite the fact that he was broke. Male ego, I guess. We had been fighting a lot before the divorce. His wheel business was failing. He had lost a lot of money. The bankers were closing in. It was hell.

Angelina [coldly]: But you didn't stay with him.

Monte [sadly]: I couldn't. [wearily] I was tired of being the dressed up doll, but then I was also afraid of struggle. [smiling] You, know, I am not used to struggle. Anyway, I thought I could always find a richer man. When you turn fifty . . . [reflecting] . . . It was fifteen years ago. You were in your early twenties . . . Well, when you're fifty you get scared. Life is passing you by. You start to want a new life. Time closes in on you just as the bankers did on Nick. So . . . so I looked for a richer man and a new life. Maybe some day you'll understand.

Angelina [bowing her head]: Oh, I think I understand, mother. I understand. You see I've been having an affair with a married man who's forty-five.

Monte [sadly]: Oh, Angelina, whatever possessed you to do such a thing.

Angelina [sadly]: Loneliness, mother, loneliness. It's just the work and the loneliness. Going back to the same apartment. Seeing the shattered souls struggling to keep their businesses and possessions away from the arms of the octopus called greed – in that animal kingdom of get or be gotten. It all gets to you, mother. And there he was. Handsome. Successful. Powerful. Warm arms in the cold. It's nothing new, mother.

Monte [despairingly]: Oh, God.

Angelina [quietly]: Well, it's just about over. He won't divorce his wife. He has three children. He's decided it's finished, and so have I. But the torment! To be alone at night and think of him with his wife! To be the second woman! To be there for an afternoon now and then . . . and then he's gone back to her. No . . . I couldn't take it any more. I just couldn't.

Monte [indignantly]: You shouldn't.

Angelina [sadly]: But I would, if he would call me again. But he won't. He's too tired. Too . . . too tired of the deception . . . the torment . . . [There is a silence.] I guess we're all tormented, mother. Tormented with greed, tormented with love, tormented with life.

Monte [bowing her head]: Is it any wonder that we drink?

Angelina [self-righteously]: It's no excuse, mother.

Monte [furiously]: Okay, you self-righteous bitch, is it excusable that you go to bed with a married man?

Angelina [bowing her head and weeping]: Oh, stop it, Mother. [There is a long silence.]

Monte [staring at her]: Then you stop it, okay?

Angelina [quietly]: Okay. Okay. I'll stop it, if you do.

Monte [changing the subject]: Do you see your father . . . do you see Nick now and then?

Angelina: We go to lunch now and then. On the holidays we get together. He recently joined a small bank. He seems to like it.

Monte [laughing]: Nick? A banker? You've got to be kidding? Why, he's hated bankers all his life. They were always ruining some deal he had. I remember what it was like to live with him before he bought that wheel company. He used to be a business broker. He sold all sorts of companies and he made a lot of money . . . so much money that, like a stupid idiot, he bought that wheel company. Oh, God, if he had only remained a broker, we would probably still be married today. [She bows her head and begins sobbing.] You know, at times, I miss him terribly.

Angelina [grinning satanically]: Well, mother, I assure you of one thing – he doesn't miss you!!! He refuses to speak of you whenever I mention your name. He only tells me to shut up. He snarls at me, and tells me to shut up!!! [viciously] My God, what did you do to him?

Monte [whining]: What did I do to him? What did I do to him? What did he do to me? Is a woman supposed to be thrown on the dunghill of poverty at the age of fifty? God, do you know how the world treats the old and the poor? Do you know anything? You with your law degree and your cute little looped tie! Wait until you're my age and the crows' feet appear around the eyes! Then you'll understand!

[There is a silence. Both then stare at each other.]

Angelina [pleading]: Mother, why couldn't you struggle with Nick? Most women do that. Why couldn't the two of you have stayed together, struggled together, loved together? It would have been something. It would have meant something.

Monte [screaming]: Waitress! Waitress! Oh, my God! Where is she?

Angelina [quietly]: I don't think she can help you, mother.

[The waitress appears.]

Waitress [matter-of-factly]: My shift is just about over. Another girl will be here to help you soon. Perhaps you want me to close out your tab.

Monte [muttering to herself]: Close out . . . close in . . . What difference does it make? God. I suppose you want your tip now?

Waitress [furiously]: Look, lady, keep your goddamn tip. I don't want a goddamn thing from either you or that YUPPIE bitch you're sitting with! Pick on the next girl who waits on you! I'm leaving. [She walks off the stage with great fury and great dignity. A few moments pass. Monte looks at Angelina. Both are shocked.]

Monte [a little confused]: Well, what do you expect today? No service and no respect. People are overpaid, underworked, and they don't know their places.

Angelina [laughing wildly]: Mother, you're such a bitch! What is that young woman's place? To serve you? Too many people have served you! Who in the hell are you that anyone should take your abuse?

Monte [viciously]: What are you a women's libber or something? She insulted you, didn't she? She called you a YUPPIE, didn't she? You're a lawyer, goddamit! Are you going to take that? Sue the bitch, I tell you! Sue the restaurant! Sue the city! Sue the state! Sue the President! Sue the country! Sue the universe! Sue God! Goddamit! Sue everybody! Sue everything! I'll not be spoken to that way! Why I'm Mrs. . . . Mrs. . . . Mrs. . . . Mrs. . . . [In the emotional exhaustion she drops her head on the table, burping and belching.] Why, I'm Mrs. . . .

Angelina [with a satanic grin]: Mrs. Termite Queen.

Monte [raising her head and speaking furiously]: Why you bankruptcy slut, don't you dare say that!!! Honor your father and mother, you miserable slut. How could I have ever had a daughter like you?

Angelina [maliciously]: Why, mother, you're quoting the Bible. Mother! Queen of the Termites! Don't you dare yell at me! I'm NOT one of your husbands! I'm NOT some wimp who's going to roll over and die to make "THE PRECIOUS ONE" happy! Just pour some more booze down your throat and shut up!!! [There is a long silence. Both women glare at each other. Each bows her head and looks at the glasses before them. A new waitress appears who is just as attractive as the one who left.]

Waitress [cheerfully]: Would you like another drink?

Monte [relieved]: I sure would! A double martini up.

Angelina [anxiously]: Mother!

Monte [furiously]: Oh, shut up, you slut!

[The waitress is taken aback and then tries to hide her smile.]

Waitress [looking at Angelina]: And you, miss?

Angelina [annoyed]: It's Ms.

Monte [viciously]: Yeah, she's also a call girl.

Angelina [indignantly]: Shut up, mother. Waitress, I'll have a Perrier. [The waitress bows, smiles confusedly, and leaves.]

Monte [in a bored tone]: What is a Perrier?

Angelina [annoyed]: It's mineral water.

Monte [pontificating]: Why in the hell are you drinking mineral water? Is it that time of the month or something? My God, you're too young to drink mineral water! Have some gin or some scotch or something worth drinking.

Angelina [disgusted]: Shut up, mother.

Monte [furious]: You shut up!

Angelina [matching her in fury]: No, you shut up!

Monte: No, you!

Angelina: No, you!

[There is a brief silence.]

Angelina [seriously]: Okay, I'll shut up, if you'll only answer one question. Why didn't you struggle with Nick when he went bankrupt? You should have stood by him.

Monte [annoyed and arrogant]: I've already explained myself. What are you, some type of avenging angel to come down here from San Francisco and judge me? It's none of your damn business what I do! None of your business! [yawning and belching] Just drink your mineral water. God! Mineral water! Drink owl piss for all I care.

Angelina [disgusted]: Okay, mother, that's enough. Why can't you struggle for anything?

Monte [quietly bowing her head]: Because I don't know how. I've always been taken care of. Some man was always there to take care of me, to amuse me, to loan me money, to give me money, to let me be a little girl in the department stores . . . [speaking self righteously] How is someone like me to know how to struggle? That's for other people!

Angelina [laughing]: Yes, mother. Let those poor husbands struggle. It will build character in them. God, what a bloodsucking vampire you are! Feeding off the labor, blood and time of others! Sitting here and getting smashed and living off the blood of others!

Monte [furious]: Yeah, well you take your $5,000 dollars up front and call me a vampire! You legalistic cannibal! You, who feeds off the woes of others! You devourer of putrid flesh! Sure, judge! Go ahead and judge! [somberly] What difference does it make?

[The waitress arrives with the martini and mineral water. She quickly leaves as though she were avoiding the plague.]

Angelina [bitterly]: It doesn't make any difference, mother. So let's just yell at each other until we're dead. We're good at that! God, why did I ever come down here to talk with you? Drink yourself to death! Get it over with!

Monte [viciously]: So you want to see me dead? Is that it? Will that make you happy? Well, I'll tell you something! When you see me dead and in my coffin, you'll be sorry for this day!

Angelina [laughing]: Oh, stop it, mother. You've been using that line ever since I was a little girl. You'll never die. There are too many men to marry. Multitudes of men to marry. Maybe you should move to China; they have one billion men. That would keep you busy. You wouldn't get bored there. Go to China, mother! Or, go to hell! [viciously sipping her mineral water] Go find your goddamn coffin and get it over with!

[Both stare at each other in absolute fury.]

Monte [exhausted]: Okay, Angelina, that's enough. I'm sorry. I don't need any more of this. You've won. I can't take any more of it. I'm tired. [yawning] I need sleep. I need rest. I need someone to love me . . . me . . . me . . . Monte West for what I am. You don't love me, Angelina. No one loves me . . . me . . . Monte West. [sobbing] I'm just an old dying woman who needs a little solace before the final curtain. [She drifts off into an alcoholic reverie. She begins humming the popular song "I Did It My Way." She controls her sobbing and begins singing softly.] "The final curtain . . . I did it my way."

Angelina [laughing]: Yeah, well you did a mighty poor job! God, you remind me of Mimi von Bora. You remember Mimi, don't you? Mimi's been married five times. Mimi's doing great, mother. You should give her a call. You could both drink yourselves to death.

Monte [relapsing into a childish whine of one reflecting on forgotten dreams]: Oh Mimi! Oh, my darling Mimi! Oh, how could I forget you? How is my Mimi? What is she doing? Oh, she has had such a hard life . . . such a hard, hard life! We used to have so much fun when we were young. The men, the parties, the glamour spots of the world . . . [Sighing] Oh, Mimi, my precious Mimi, what has become of you?

Angelina [laughing]: There is nothing precious about Mimi, mother. Well, maybe there is. She is the talk of San Francisco. What a bitch! Mimi's got a divorce settlement from her fifth husband! Yes, it was Mimi's fifth. [laughing sarcastically] Mother, you like to drink. Just remember that a fifth is very close to a quart and four quarts make a gallon. Well, your precious Mimi has gallons of gold. Mimi's done just fine. Better than you!

Monte [shocked]: What do you mean?

Angelina [laughing hysterically]: Oh, mother, you're such a baby. Mimi's in out of the cold! She got her divorce settlement! She did! Mimi settled for $100,000 a month until her death! That's what her ex-husband is paying! Your "precious Mimi" has it made!

Monte [shocked and furious]: She got what?

Angelina [laughing]: She got everything, mother! And her fifth husband, well, he's got big bills. Very, very big bills! Oh, God! It is the talk of San Francisco!

Monte [outraged]: What? What are you saying?

Angelina: Mother, she got one of the biggest divorce settlements in history! $100,000 per month until her death or until she remarries. I am sure she will learn to remain unmarried and, how shall we say, enjoy herself! That's your "precious Mimi"! She can see the woods for the trees!

Monte [outraged]: The bitch!

Angelina [laughing]: Now don't be envious, mother!

Monte [venomously]: The slut!

Angelina [laughing]: Stop it, mother!

Monte [with absolute wrath]: The whore! Lying on her back for that kind of money. Why, why, she's worse than you!

Angelina [with great indignation and hate]: No, mother! She's worse than you!

Monte [boiling over]: And you! Look what you charge! You bitch! You slut! You whore! God, why did I ever bring you into the world?

Angelina [laughing with vicious hysteria]: Because you made so much money, and so many men on your back! Oh, stop it, mother! Don't become self-righteous! You're one of them! Screw your brains out, and take your money! You know the deal! You're part of the deal! My God what an elevated slut you are! Supporting yourself on your back! [laughing uproariously] What a slut you are!

Monte [furious for a moment and then weeping]: Angelina. Angelina! How can you say that to your mother? You know what I am! You know that I love you! How can you say that to me? [whining] You don't love me, Angelina. No one loves me.

Angelina [mercilessly]: Oh, stop it, mother. No one loves you? Why should they? You're just a pretty little slut who goes shopping! You're just like a whole host of others who do the same . . . until they get cancer or they get old, or their husbands find younger women . . . Yes, mother, we are a people doomed to shop and lie about being happy little girls . . . or professional people . . . or dead people. That is what we are! That is what we are!

Monte [shocked]: You're terrible, Angelina, terrible. Just

because I still don't know my place in life . . . just because . . .

Angelina [howling with laughter]: "Just because you still don't know your place in life?" Why, that's hilarious! You remind me of a bumper sticker I saw on a Rolls Royce when I was coming in from the airport. The sticker read, "A woman's place is in the shopping mall." That's your place, mother! That's your only place! The shopping mall, the bedroom, the bar, or the grave! You've found your place, mother. You've found your place.

Monte [whining]: How can you say that to your mother?

Angelina [laughing demoniacally]: Okay, your place is on your back!!!!

Monte [holding her ears with the palms of her hands]: Stop it, Angelina, stop it!!

Angelina [still laughing demoniacally]: Sure, mother. I'll stop it. I'll stop it when you stop drinking. [beaming] Have you seen the bumper sticker which says: "Whoever dies with the most toys, wins?" The truth is: "Whoever dies with the most toys, dies"! And you're dead, mother! You died in the shopping mall; you died at the wedding altar; you died in the bedroom; you died in the bar! You're dead, dead, dead! [Angelina sighs ecstatically.] You're dead, mother.

Monte [with a type of morbid grief founded upon envy]: Well, Mimi isn't dead. Goddamn it, she's got it made. $100,000 a month. Who can pay her that kind of money?

Angelina [laughing]: Her fifth ex-husband is one of the biggest slumlords in San Francisco. It came out at the divorce trial that his income is six million dollars per year! Six million dollars! That's his income, not his net worth! He can afford her, the son of a bitch! Imagine taking that kind of money from the poor! And now Mimi's taking it from him!

Monte [whining with envy]: The bitch!

Angelina [laughing hysterically]: Not only that, Mimi's starting a foundation – a tax exempt foundation so that she can shelter her alimony with "good works." It's called CHILDREN AGAINST POVERTY! Think of it! Your precious Mimi wants to "save" children from poverty while her husband throws them out on to the streets! That's Mimi; that's her slumlord husband; that's life! [She laughs for a few moments, and then takes a sip of her drink. She speaks softly.] That's life. [A few seconds pass. An uncomfortable silence ensues. Angelina speaks matter-of-factly.] Well, mother, let's understand one thing: Mimi's in out of the cold, and that's all we want to be! In out of the cold. That's the human race, mother. That's what we are. We're in out of the cold. Me with my law practice. Mimi with her quart [laughing] . . . I mean her fifth. You with Mr. West. That's your name, isn't it? Monte West. That's your name now. Well, Monte, I love you despite what you are. Monte West, the drinker. Monte West, the goddess of times gone by. You're okay, mother. You're okay, despite what you have become.

Monte [sloppily]: Angelina, Angelina. I love you! I've always wanted you to say that! That I mean something to you! I don't mean anything to anyone.

Angelina [bored]: Oh, mother, don't get sloppy! We're all too sloppy! You're a bitch, mother, and so am I. We need money, mother, and we'll do anything for it! We will! You know we will. We're human beings with stomachs. So we'll lie on our backs, or plead in the courts . . . we'll do anything we have to. That's what we'll do, mother. That's what we'll do.

Monte [sobbing]: It's not fair, Angelina. It's just not fair. Why should we go through such pain? Why should we?

Angelina [snarling]: Mother, what pain are we going through? We're not going through anything! We're living off other people's money and other people's problems! Your husband, what's his name?

Monte [quietly]: You mean Tom West.

Angelina [furiously]: Yes, I mean Tom West, if that's his name. What does Tom care for the poor, or the broken, or the bankrupt? What does Tom care? He doesn't care! Why should he? Tom's got you, and he's got money! He's finally got some upper middle-class power! And he's got you! And, he's got nothing! That's what he's got: you and nothing! What a slut you are!

Monte [furiously]: Don't talk that way to your mother, you little whore! You have no right! How dare you say that to me! Why, I picked you up out of the gutter when your husband left you, and now you talk that way to me! Why, you're nothing! Nothing! Nothing, I tell you! Nothing!

Angelina [viciously]: Oh stop telling me that you pulled me out of the gutter! Who put me in the gutter in the first place? You did! You with your upper middle-class lies about success and "making it" when all you've done is make men for money! You dying prostitute! You copulating booze bag! Why don't you go to hell! You pulled me out of the gutter? Very well! But I was standing on your whore-like shoulders! You bitch!

Monte [attempting to become angry, but fighting exhaustion]: Okay, Angelina, okay. I've told you before, you've won. Leave me in peace. Please, leave me in peace.

Angelina [looking heavenward]:
May she rest in peace!
May she rest in peace!
She took her money, and she took her men!
Others have paid for her shopping sins!

Monte [quietly bowing her head]: Okay . . . okay, you've won. [There is a brief moment of silence. Monte then begins to hiss like a snake and snarl like a she-wolf] You've won, goddamn you! You've won. But I pulled you out of the gutter! I did! And this is how you treat me! God, what have I produced?

Angelina [demoniacally]: You've produced a lot of shopping bills and a lot of marriage certificates! You're a real producer, mother, a real producer! Do you deserve a medal for helping your daughter out just because I discovered that my first husband was bisexual? Is it my fault that he liked men more than me? Was I supposed to know that? As for being pulled out of the gutter, all that I did was come home! Being around you is like being around the gutter! I left you as soon as I could get my law degree and support myself.

Monte [self-righteously]: So it's all right to judge me after I've slaved for you all these years.

Angelina [howling with laughter]: Mother, the only thing you know about slavery is the men you've enslaved!!! Either that or your slavery to shopping! God! You gave me Nick's money to go to law school. You didn't earn it! You just spent it! So, shut up!

Monte [Starting to fall off to sleep, she belches and yawns. She grunts a few times. She speaks in a very languid voice while she yawns.]: I need another drink. Maybe only some wine. I'll go to the Betty Ford whorehouse in the morning. I will . . . I'll talk to the madam. I'll go to the happy hunting ground for the spoiled and the rich. I'll sober up so that I can die of boredom. God, why was I born? Maybe I lived at another time. Shirley MacLaine, the movie actress and dancer . . . she believes that we have had former lives. You should read her book, DANCING IN THE LIGHT, or have you read it?

Angelina [disgusted and annoyed]: No mother, I haven't read DANCING IN THE LIGHT. Why should I? It seems that we're only raging in the dark, and so is the greater part of humanity. No, mother, I haven't read Shirley's book, but I would like to take Shirley and her kind into a bankruptcy court, and then ask her how many people she sees "dancing in the light"?!!! Most of us are just raging in the dark . . . that is all we are doing.

Monte [in a puppishly cute way]: Oh, Angelina, why must you be so negative? Maybe we have had former lives. Maybe I was a queen once. Maybe I was Marie Antoinette. Do you think I could have been Marie Antoinette? Marie Antoinette with her pretty little apron, and her palace, and her milk pails, playing the fresh country lass . . . [sighing] Yes, I must have been Marie Antoinette in a former life.

Angelina [staring venomously at Monte]: Yes, mother, she was a real queen. When she was told that the people were starving to death and that the people had no bread, she said, "Let them eat cake!" Yes, mother, you certainly could have been Marie Antoinette. You certainly could have.

Monte [in a conceited reverie]: Oh, thank you, my precious Angelina. Thank you. You are, indeed, my angel.

Angelina [with great disgust and contempt]: Well, mother, around you there is only one angel that I want to be – the angel of death! What a bitch you are! God, I can't believe your ego! If I had a former life, I would want to be a revolutionary who destroyed the rich and the spoiled! I would stick your goddamn spoiled head on the guillotine and cut it off! I would! It's your kind of slime that has degraded this world for centuries! You're no good, and you deserve death! I would have beheaded you in public if we both had "former lives." [Angelina laughs maliciously to herself. She then stares at Monte. Monte has a very frightened and pathetic look on her face. Angelina laughs for a few seconds, and then looks away from Monte. She speaks to herself as much as to her mother with great bitterness.] Okay, mother, I've won, but I didn't really want to win . . . I've won enough, and I've lost enough. I've won in the courtroom, but I've lost in the bedroom. [quietly] I guess it's over for me already. I'm thirty-five and morally and emotionally bankrupt. God, what a life.

Monte [compassionately]: Oh. Angelina, don't say that. You're still young. There will be other men.

Angelina [sadly, with the tears welling up in her eyes]: But I don't want another man. I only want him. But I can't have him. So, I'll just go back to the office, and go to the courtroom . . . I suppose in the end, I'll just go to hell. That's about it, mother.

Monte [wearily anxious]: But Angelina, what will I do with MY time? What will happen to ME?

Angelina [bored and exhausted]: You're condemned to shop, mother. That is all you can do. Maybe you'll die at the perfume counter, spraying yourself with expensive cologne. Maybe you'll die at the lingerie counter dreaming of all the men you've slept with. Maybe you'll die trying to stuff your booze bloated body into a pair of tennis shorts, Mother, shop until your liver swells up with booze . . . until you swell up with booze. Swell and shop, Mother. Shop and swell. You have sentenced yourself, and this is your sentence:
"Thou shalt drink and shop until thy death.
May Almighty God have mercy
on your husband's cash flow."
It is your sentence, mother. It is the sentence of many a rich woman. May God have mercy on your spoiled and twisted soul. [Both glare at each other and slowly bow their heads as the lights fall.]

YES! . . . BUT WE STILL HAVE SLUMS

CHARACTERS

NICK CAVALCANTI
JACOB FRANK
MALCOLM HUNTINGTON
A WAITER

[The Capital Club is located on the seventy-seventh floor of the Universal Bank Building in San Francisco, California. It is November of 1985. The stage background is a panoramic view of the north part of the San Francisco Bay. Marin County and the Golden Gate Bridge are stage right. The top of the Transamerica Pyramid Building is stage center. The Bay Bridge and Oakland are stage left. The Capital Club is wood-paneled where there are no panoramic windows. Three tables should be set with the white table cloths and highly polished silverware. On each table is a silver bud vase in which a red rose is placed. As the conversation begins, Nick Cavalcanti is seated at the center table with Jacob Frank. Nick is sixty years old with gray hair. He is in excellent physical condition and has a sun tan. Although once handsome, life's struggles have so stained him that there is an air of viciousness about him – a viciousness similar to that of a panther which has had to defend itself in the jungle's night. Next to Nick is Jacob Frank, a German born Jew of seventy-five. Jacob is over six feet tall and is also in excellent physical condition. His demeanor is one of respectful melancholia as though some secret ballast of suffering has taught him to measure his words and deeds.]

Nick [annoyed]: Well, he's supposed to be here, but he isn't here. A typical goddamn big-time banker. He's so used to having everyone come to him that he can't keep his own appointments. Jesus, it makes me sick.

Jacob [smiling good-naturedly]: It's really not that important. It's been many years since I've seen you. We'll have more time together. How's your wife?

Nick [morosely]: Monte and I have been divorced for many years. [smiling] The happiest years of my life.

Jacob [not really knowing what so say]: Oh. I didn't know.

Nick [laughing]: Don't feel bad. I went broke, and she divorced me. After twenty years of marriage, she divorced me. She said she couldn't live in poverty. After several years of being divorced I've come to understand one thing – being in poverty morally and spiritually was being married to her! And could she spend money! She could spend money before it was printed! God, what an albatross when she was around my neck! Well, she left me, and I count my blessings.

Jacob [reflecting]: I guess it has been longer than I thought. Why, it's been almost twenty years since you and Jim McClain sold my uniform manufacturing business. I would see you on the street now and then, but I'm really glad you invited me to lunch. Now and then I'd call McClain and ask about you. Most of the time he didn't know where you were. Anyway, thanks for lunch.

Nick [good-naturedly]: Oh it was a pleasure. [absentmindedly] After I went broke . . . when I used to be a business broker with McClain, we would talk about the word "broker." [laughing] I am sure it means someone who goes broke sooner or later. McClain was just a tough Calvinistic Scotsman who didn't seem to care if he went broke or not. He would just work all the time, and he was twenty years younger than I. But we sold a lot of businesses together, and we made a lot of money. [Nick looks around for a waiter. The waiter appears.] What'll you have Jacob?

Jacob: White wine.

Nick: I'll have a Gin Mary. [The waiter bows and leaves.]

Jacob [smiling]: What is a Gin Mary?

Nick: That's a Bloody Mary with gin.

Jacob [laughing]: Does it make any difference to you?

Nick: Not really. I just got in the habit.

Jacob: Vodka's supposed to be better for you.

Nick [lighting a cigarette]: Jacob, I've already gotten rid of Monte and . . .

Jacob [laughing]: And who needs me to tell you that vodka's better than gin, or that you shouldn't smoke.

Nick [absentmindedly]: You've got it.

Jacob [laughing]: You'll never change. Do you still drink the way you used to?

Nick [smiling]: Not since I got rid of Monte. Boy, that woman could drink! She could drink and shop. She had it down! And she's gotten remarried. It's her fourth. The poor bastard.

Jacob: You said that she divorced you because you went broke when you were a broker?

Nick [laughing]: No. I went broke after I was a broker. I bought the controlling interest in an automobile wheel company. Just before the recession or what some called a depression. Man, was it depressing! The company made $300,000 per year for twenty years. Plus there was a $150,000 officer's salary. And then I bought it! It was one of the best companies I had ever seen! I was finally going to get rich. [shrugging his shoulders] What's the old saying among lawyers . . . He who defends himself has an idiot for a client and a fool for a lawyer . . . or something like that. Well when a business broker buys a company, he's got a jackass for a buyer! That's all I can say. So, I bought the company, and then the automotive industry went bust. The company had previously supplied wheels to Chrysler, General Motors, and Ford. And what happened? Soon there were no orders to speak of. Wrong time, wrong business, wrong man. And that was it. I held out for about a year and a half, and then they padlocked the place. I had to start over. That's hard to start over when you're over fifty, you know. Very hard. [The waiter appears with the drinks. He places them on the table. Nick sighs and takes a gulp of his drink. Jacob stares at him for a few seconds.]

Jacob [somberly]: Yes, I know how hard that is. It happened to me, or I should say that it happened to us, a whole people. When Hitler came to power in the 30's things began to be pretty bad for us German Jews. It had been hard in the 20's, too, for all the Germans. In the 20's my father owned a butcher shop in Frankfort. We paid the butchers three times a day! There was so much useless paper money on the floor that we couldn't even sweep it up! Then Hitler came to power. Most of the Germans thought things were better. The economy improved. There were public works projects – new roads, new buildings, new weapons . . . and then it began against us. The terror and the concentration camps. [looking sternly into space] . . . And so we had to leave everything . . . those of us who could. I saw what was happening. My mother and father were imprisoned, but in the early 30's you could still pay off some of the Nazis under the table. We got out just in time. Some were not so lucky.

Nick [looking at the ceiling]: Well, I never had to go through that.

Jacob [as if speaking to himself]: Recently I met with my old friend, Hans Greenberg. He escaped Germany, but his parents were not so fortunate. His father owned three metal fabrication plants in Germany. He was of the Jewish elite. He told me that, before Hitler, his normal course in life would have been to get a classical education, a law degree, and sooner or later become a judge or a banker. Things didn't work out that way. Instead, the Nazis imprisoned his parents, and then they approached Hans. They said if he wanted to see his parents alive again, he had best sell one of the factories. Hans sold one of the factories and raised the equivalent of $500,000. The Nazis released his parents . . . for a few weeks. They were then imprisoned again. The Nazis then got ahold of Hans and said if he wanted to see his parents alive, he must sell another factory. This went on until he and his family were penniless. The Nazis then took his parents to the death camps. Hans barely escaped with his life.

Nick [shaking his head]: Terrible . . . ghastly.

Jacob [thoughtfully]: Yes. Terrible, ghastly and worse. That was many years ago. Hans has done well in this country being the owner of a metal fabrication company. However, and this is something you should know, Hans has a strange outlook on money. He told me something that is really worthwhile. He said, "If you have a problem for which you can write a check, then you have no problem. But when they stick a machine gun at your head and say you're going to a death camp, then you have a problem." [There is a silence.]

Nick [reflecting]: A problem indeed.

Jacob [raising his eyebrows]: Yes, a real problem. [another silence]

Nick [smiling, attempting to overcome the silence]: Well, that makes my problem seem a little small.

Jacob [sternly]: Nonsense, a problem is a problem. No one wants to see a company go under. How many out there know what it is like to make a payroll? How many have workers depending on them? What is it really like to face the unknown?

Nick [quietly]: Well, you've done it. Your friends have done it. I guess I've done it in a small way.

Jacob [quietly]: You certainly have. I guess the whole thing is finding the courage to get up again, even though there is a terrible ballast in the soul which weighs you down – a terrible weight that can crush you.

Nick [quietly]: Yes, I know. [There is a silence.]

Jacob [attempting to carry on the conversation]: So what do you do now?

Nick [reflecting]: Well, after the divorce, I tried a lot of things.

Even taught philosophy and the history of religions at a community college.

Jacob [very pleased]: Really! Why that's wonderful. At least, I think it would be wonderful. How was it?

Nick [elated]: It was very good. I had taken degrees in philosophy and religion prior to my selling businesses. [laughing] In fact, I studied philosophy and religion for seven years after college. But then, you know, I ran out of money. I looked in the want-ads under "P" for philosopher and "T" for theologian. Not too much work unless you wanted to go the whole academic route of waiting for a teaching position to open while you starve. So I started to sell businesses. [laughing] I went from the study of Renaissance philosophy, world religions, and Idealism to the selling of liquor stores, cocktail lounges, and beer joints. [still laughing] I guess I'll never be a favorite of The Women's Christian Temperance League. [fiercely taking a sip of his drink.] But then who really gives a damn about The Women's Christian Temperance League?

Jacob [laughing]: Well, at least you made a little money.

Nick [smiling]: I sure did. <u>And</u> . . . I lost a lot of money. It's like my father used to say, "What you lose on the peaches, you make on the bananas."

Jacob [laughing]: Was your father a grocer?

Nick [reflecting]: No, my father was a criminal lawyer. He had one hundred and ten murder trials and not one of his clients was executed. He was also very good at divorce. [laughing] He had to be, he was married four times that we know of. He liked the good life and his own form of justice.

Jacob [interested]: Which form is that?

Nick [somberly]: That we are all innocent until proven guilty.

Jacob [reflecting]: That is a high form of justice.

Nick [frowning]: Well, anyway, I started selling businesses. During that time I read an article in The Wall Street Journal entitled "What Do Philosophers Do?" The article concluded that philosophers do pretty much whatever they want to do. There was a long list of successful businessmen who had been philosophy students in college. Logic, the analysis of arguments, and so forth are good training for the corporate world. One only needs to become "street wise," get cut up a few times, and you're off and running. Besides, there is an old Italian saying: "In Italy only the bad actors are on the stage. The great ones are in the village squares, drinking wine, waving their hands, and making deals!" I guess I'm very Italian.

Jacob [laughing]: You certainly are! Remember that banker who said he would finance the sale of my company, and then, after three months, refused? I thought you were going to kill him! Pounding the desk and telling him that you were going to break his back in the gutter! Telling him that he would rot in hell! God, what a madman you were!

Nick [laughing]: Well, I guess I did get a little carried away. But, we made the deal.

Jacob [raising his glass]: You did very well for yourself.

Nick [also raising his glass]: And, so, I might add, did you! [Both laugh, toast each other, and take a sip from their respective drinks.] So, anyway, I taught school for a while. I even thought about going back and getting a Ph.D.; I only have an M.A. But I was too old for the academic route. Besides I had learned too much in the streets. However, one very positive experience did happen after Monte divorced me. A young woman . . .

Jacob [grinning and raising his eyebrows]: Yessss . . . !

Nick [laughing]: Now, Jacob. I know that you always want to play the matchmaker. No, it's not what you think. Besides, she was only twenty-five.

Jacob [indignant]: What's wrong with twenty-five? You and I should be so lucky! What's wrong with you? A young man your age. I'm disappointed in you.

Nick [laughing]: Oh, c'mon. I was fifty-five. What was I going to do with a woman twenty-five?

Jacob [slyly]: Use your imagination. You could educate her. That's what you could do.

Nick [annoyed]: Look, I've had enough education among the philosophical-religious types, the streets, and Monte. I've decided to become a hermit, a type of this-worldly hermit. It saves energy and time.

Jacob [laughing]: I'm ashamed of you.

Nick [laughing]: Okay, but listen. I was teaching this course one evening, and there was this very pretty young woman, and . . .

Jacob [smiling lustfully]: . . . And the night was meant for love!

Nick [laughing]: No. No. I was delivering a series of lectures on the existence of God and whether or not we have immortal souls. Well, this young woman comes up to me, and she tells me that she has been on drugs for six years, and that she was bored with sex.

Jacob [shaking his head sadly]: That is very unhealthy.

Nick [not paying any attention to Jacob]: She said that because of the lectures she was beginning to believe that maybe she had a higher dignity, and perhaps she had a soul. [Nick smiles and takes a sip of his drink.]

Jacob [perplexed]: And . . . ?

Nick [frowning indignantly]: And what? Isn't that great? My

God, isn't that great!! I thought that I had gone to another place. I felt that I was coming to know God! Mystics talk about revelations and spiritual experiences. I don't know if it was that, or what it was. But it was a very strange apprehension of the mystery of things.

Jacob [laughing]: Oh Nick, you're probably just repressed. That's all. Too much struggle and too much thinking. You've got all these hormones and vital fluids damned up in you. It's bad for the digestion! If this keeps up, you'll become some type of religious nut! Now I know this really beautiful woman who is about forty-five. I mean really beautiful, from France, and she's just gotten a divorce! She's perfect for you! Into reincarnation, religion, poetry and all that crap! She'll solve all your problems! She'll . . .

Nick [laughing]: You're not listening to me, Jacob.

Jacob [with a bored yawn]: Okay, so you met God, and you let her slip through your fingers. I don't know what this world is coming to. Wait 'til you get to be my age, and you feel God breathing down your neck all the time! You won't be so excited about the next world. You'll know that you're going to find out about it soon enough!

Nick [laughing good-naturedly]: Anyway, it was something different. Something very strange. One could almost say something "holy" . . .

Jacob [trying to be congenial]: I'm sure it was. Perhaps you even did some good.

Nick [talking to himself]: Well, anyway, I still teach two nights a week. It is really amazing what is inside some of those students. It's . . . [A distinguished looking man of sixty-five enters. His name is Malcolm Huntington. He is the epitome of the successful, slightly overweight, white Anglo-Saxon Protestant businessman. He wears an expensive suit. His general appearance is impeccable. He is suave to the point of arousing disgust in an observer. He speaks with a warm and phony teddy bear voice.]

Malcolm [unctuously]: Nick, my God, how are you? It's so good to see you after all these years. I am so sorry I was late, but you know, banking is what it is. You've got to go where the money is. It's great to see you!

Nick [snarling under his breath]: Malcolm, you finally made it. I'm well acquainted with what banking is. I'd like you to meet my good friend, Jacob Frank, former owner of J and F Manufacturing Company. Jacob, this is Malcolm Huntington, a banking acquaintance of mine.

Malcolm [vigorously shaking Jacob's hand]: A pleasure to meet you, a real pleasure. [Malcolm is one of those men who is "professionally" enthusiastic. Malcolm sits down and looks for the waiter. The waiter, like a praying mantis, is immediately at the table.] A martini up with Bombay gin. [The waiter bows pompously and exits. Malcolm turns to Nick.] Nick, it's really great to see you. It's been a long, long time. I've missed our conversations. Yes, sir, you certainly were a man who knew how to talk! How is Monte and the baby?

Nick [morosely]: Monte and I are divorced. The "baby" is now a bankruptcy attorney.

Malcolm [quietly, not really knowing what to say]: Oh, sorry to hear that.

Nick [impishly]: Nothing to be sorry about. She's a good bankruptcy lawyer. [Malcolm begins to fidget and to look around. The waiter appears with the martini. The waiter places the drink on the table, bows, and exits. Malcolm takes a heavy draught, sighs, and looks relieved. He then has to concentrate in order to remember what he said.]

Malcolm [with the good-natured, teddy bear demeanor of the "accomplished" man]: No, that isn't what I mean. I'm sure your daughter's a great attorney. She always was smart . . . and good-looking. I mean, I'm sorry about you and Monte.

Nick [laughing sardonically]: Oh, don't worry about Monte.

She's always had her way with men. She's married again. This one is really loaded. He deals in motion pictures. She's down in Beverly Hills with the rest of them. She did fine. Furthermore, I did better. I got rid of her. [Nick laughs out loud for a few moments in a very bitter way. There is an uncomfortable silence.]

Malcolm [trying to make conversation]: And, Mr. Frank, that was your name wasn't it?

Jacob [slyly raising his eyebrows]: It still is.

Malcolm [laughing in his teddy bear way]: Yes, I'm sure it is. Well, Mr. Frank, how did you come to know my good friend, Nick Cavalcanti? [Nick winces at this last statement.]

Jacob [good-naturedly]: Nick sold my uniform manufacturing company some time ago. We became good friends. We used to talk about life and things. It's been a long time. He can talk about a lot of things; he's not so bad at business either.

Malcolm [pontificating]: Yes, Nick is a real Renaissance man. He can wear many hats. He's accustomed to . . .

Nick [quietly interrupting Malcolm]: To many things. [There is a silence.]

Malcolm [uncomfortably]: Yes, to many things. Say Nick, you remember Bambi, don't you?

Nick [as a man in a dream]: Bambi ... you mean the fawn . . . in the Walt Disney movie? . . .

Malcolm [laughing good-naturedly]: Yes. I mean no. Bambi's my daughter. Bambi just got her Ph.D. in process theology at Divinity Tech in Southern California. She's a professor of religion now.

Nick [grimacing in a dreamlike state]: Oh. Divinity Tech. Yes, I know that place well. The institute for process theology. Everything is a process. Everything. Yes, indeed, we are all part of the process. Life, death, suicide, murder, bankruptcy, child pornography, the slums. It's just one big goddamn process. Yes, indeed. [He takes a sip from his drink. He smiles sarcastically.] Did you know that I studied at Divinity Tech a while back?

Malcolm [a little confused]: You did? Well then, maybe you met Bambi. She's tall, thin, a vegetarian, into women's rights, into . . .

Nick [disgusted]: Into the process.

Malcolm [matter-of-factly]: Yes, process theology. She got her Ph.D. in that.

Nick [grinning]: Great. Just as I would expect.

Malcolm [paternally]: We're very proud of her.

Nick [frowning and raising his eyebrows]: You would be.

Malcolm [perplexed]: How is it that you came to study there? I know that once you had acquired some advanced degrees but . . .

Nick [reflecting]: After my divorce from Monte, I decided to study philosophy again. Philosophy and theology. I enrolled at Divinity Tech. I studied for a while, found that very little was being said about real life, and I left. I was offered a job with Green Litter, the investment banking firm. A lot of money. Plenty of money. $150,000 per year in the acquisition and merger department in Beverly Hills. Every benefit known to man. Obviously I took the job. Then one day I was walking down Rodeo Drive, and I saw Monte walking towards me. Her arms were loaded with packages. She had been shopping. [laughing] Her poor husband! She glared at me and I at her. She scowled and walked to the other side of the street. If I could have walked to the other side of the street first, I would have. God, what a bitch! I couldn't stand the thought of ever seeing her again. So, I quit my job, and moved back to San Francisco.

Malcolm [grinning]: You probably got a better offer.

Nick [laughing]: It was one-third the pay. [Both Malcolm and Jacob are startled.]

Malcolm [catching his breath]: My God, Nick! For the kind of money you were making in Beverly Hills I wouldn't care if the Loch Ness Monster lived there.

Nick [laughing]: But she does live there. I tell you! She does live there! And if she lives there, I'm not going to live there! I've been tortured enough by her, and her devouring arms of greed! I can't stand the thought of seeing her again. Let her go down to the depths of acquiring more and more, and surface now and then! Let her find another jugular vein from which to suck the blood of Mammon! [raging] Let her go to hell!!! [Nick grins and takes a sip from his glass.] Sorry, gentlemen, but it's good purgation. Yes, sir, we all need rage mechanisms to get it all out. And rage I have! Thus, I don't have ulcers. Well, anyway, I left Beverly Hills and came back to The City By The Bay with its slums. I work for The Inner City Bank. I like it there.

Malcolm [with a type of disappointment in his teddy hear voice]: But Nick. That's a very small bank. You took that over Green Litter?

Nick [somberly]: I'm sixty years old. I have to do something with my life. Besides. I like it there. It's near the brokerage office McClain and I used to run together. I like it there because it reminds me of a lot of things. And, we have a good time, too. The government and the bank are placing a lot of loans for The Small Business Administration. Loans are being arranged for responsible immigrants and those who have shown that they can make something of the "so-called" free enterprise system. I like it. It gives me some hope.

Jacob [After a brief silence, he speaks somberly.]: Yes, hope is something you really need when you get to be my age.

Malcolm [superficially]: Well, you know, I've talked to Bambi about hope. I'm getting up there in years, too. Bambi gave a great lecture down at Wellington College in Santa Barbara. It was entitled "Hope and the Process." The lecture was well attended by some of the best people with the best blood in town. She put us all at ease. Yes, sir, there is nothing to worry about. [He sips his martini.]

Nick [sardonically]: Well, maybe Bambi and "the best blood" aren't worried, but I am.

Malcolm [startled]: What could you possibly be worried about? We're all part of a great and wondrous natural process. It's part of the hymn of the universe. We're made of matter and psychic stuff. We go back into the elements of nature in the end. It's the beautiful song of life. We're lucky to be part of it. Just accept what we are, that's all.

Nick [furious]: You accept it! Don't tell me what to do! My God, look out the window! Look to the south of this restless city! There are slums, I tell you! People who can't live without money! Prostitution, drug addiction, child pornography! [Nick shakes his head in rage. There is a silence. He speaks quietly.] Oh, hell, I'm sorry. I don't mean to get so excited. I guess that there's just a lot of "bad blood" out there. That's all.

Malcolm [complacently]: You shouldn't get so upset. You see, it's just natural selection. The survival of the fittest. We all studied that in college. [looking at Jacob Frank nervously]. At least I think we all studied that in college . . .

Jacob [grinning sardonically]: I didn't study it at college. I studied it under Hitler before I left Germany. Hitler also believed in a type of natural selection. Nature and history had selected the Aryan race as the master race. Jews were selected as the slave race. [grimacing threateningly at Malcolm] I guess we Jews just have "bad blood" in us. [Nick grins for a moment and then bows his head. Malcolm becomes very uncomfortable. There is a silence.]

Malcolm [nervously]: Excuse me. Mr. . . . ah, Mr. . . .

Jacob [quietly]: Mr. Frank.

Malcolm [nervously]: Mr. Frank, I want you to know that in no way did I mean to say anything against the Jews. What Hitler did to you and your people still makes me sick . . . and a lot of good Americans gave their lives to get rid of him! They did! [Self-righteously, Malcolm leans back in his chair.]

Jacob [quietly]: I know they did. But you can see my hatred for words like "natural selection" and "good blood." I heard such words when I was a boy, I don't want to hear them ever again.

Nick [looking south which would be to the audience and to the slums]: I don't like to hear it either. I think that what we mean by "natural selection" today is a philosophy expounded by those who knew how to select their parents in advance. Their parents, or their grandparents, or their great grandparents got to the real estate first in this place called California. Their ancestors were "naturally selected" to get the first slice of the pie. I might add that in many cases it was a very big slice of pie.

Jacob [laughing]: It was the same thing in Europe. The first man to get to the real estate was later called "king." The king and the princes then "subdivided" the land. It is an old story.

Nick [bitterly]: Yeah, it was part of "The Process"!

Jacob [bitterly]: I spit on the "The Process"!!! [Nick laughs viciously.]

Malcolm [excited and defensive]: Now just a minute, gentlemen. Just a minute. Hitler and the Third Reich happened a long time ago. Look at what this great land called America has been to all nationalities! A fresh start! A home for "free enterprise"! Why just the other day President Reagan gave a speech on "the new patriotism" which is sweeping the country. Gentlemen, what is the past is the past. The "new patriotism" is now!

Nick [laughing sarcastically]: I am not so sure that "the new patriotism" is not simply "the old greed." Some are "selected" to make fortunes, IF they find the opportunities. Others live as wage slaves until death.

Malcolm [aghast]: But that is America and the free enterprise system. It is the very nature of capitalism. Nick, you're a businessman, surely you know that.

Nick [frowning sarcastically]: Oh, sure. I know that. I know that there is capitalism for the poor and socialism for the rich. That is what I know. I remember when Reagan was running for reelection. I got on the subway train and a Reagan supporter was handing out flyers. The flyer read: "While you are going to work, do you know how many people are still in bed living off welfare and your tax dollars?" The flyer then listed all types of questionable statistics. I then asked the young zealot of Reaganism if he knew how many people in Santa Barbara, Hillsborough, Forest Hills and Palm Springs were still in bed living off their inheritances? [laughing] I guess I "selected" the wrong question. He walked away. But I'm right! It's socialism for the rich and capitalism for the poor! [There is a silence.]

Malcolm [shrugging his shoulders]: Nick, I think you've probably been through too much with Monte and all . . .

Nick [laughing]: Oh, God, don't bring her into this! We're talking about the demonic quality of the free enterprise system. Please don't compound it with another devil – a she-devil. My God, one devil at a time, please! One devil at a time! [All three men laugh good-naturedly. Malcolm is relieved that the topic may be changing.]

Malcolm [in a relieved tone]: Look, Nick, now that you're single, I know this great looking divorcee. Plenty of money and she's from a good Santa Barbara family. She has . . .

Nick [interrupting Malcolm and grinning at Jacob]: She has

"good blood" in her! [Jacob smiles. Nick laughs, and Malcolm smiles sheepishly.]

Malcolm [in his teddy bear voice]: Okay, let me apologize for the "blood" business. It was just a figure of speech. That's all. I meant no offense. [Jacob smiles with a look of irony on his face.] I was going to say that she has many wonderful qualities, and she reads a lot. She would be perfect for you.

Nick [laughing]: What does she read?

Malcolm: All sorts of things, literature, philosophy, history. You should get to know her. You really should.

Nick [bored]: Well, I don't know. I really don't know. She sounds like a woman I went out with a few weeks ago. Highly educated and all, she was into astrology. She asked me under which sign I was born. I told her that I was born under the sign of the cross! [sarcastically] She didn't seem to like my joke. A pretty woman, but she lacked cynicism. [yawning] Oh, well. I don't think it's in the cards for me to get involved with a woman again. I think I'll just remain a this-worldly hermit and wait for the ten count.

Malcolm [perplexed]: The ten count?

Nick [smiling]: Sure, you know, the big bang! The launching! The getting out of here! The French poet Baudelaire was once asked where he wanted to live. His answer was. "Anywhere, anywhere but this world!" A cheery thought. When Baudelaire died there was an autopsy and his fellow poets asked what was the cause of his death. The doctor replied that he had dropsy, scurvy, tuberculosis, alcoholism, drug addiction, and syphilis. The doctor said to his friends that they could take their pick of which disease killed him. Any one of the diseases was sufficient to kill him. [laughing and yawning] After Monte left me, I thought about being a first rate decadent. I thought about saying to hell with everything. [yawning] But it would take too much energy. Far too much energy. So, I decided to spend my twilight years screwing around with the federal government and finance. Indeed, it will fill in my hours.

Malcolm [perplexed]: What are you talking about?

Nick [indifferently]: I mean The Inner City Bank and The Small Business Administration, better known as the SBA. We have a good time placing money for those who want a slice of a very cut-up pie. Although Reagan cut a lot of money out of the agency, there's still enough to make it interesting. Besides, I like immigrants, being a second generation Italian myself. I like immigrants, and I hate YUPPIES.

Jacob: YUPPIES?

Nick: Young Urban Professionals. I call them the dust particles in the economic vacuum.

Jacob: The what?

Nick [scowling]: What I mean is that kids, eighteen or nineteen years old, go to business school or law school. Let us say by the age of twenty-three or twenty-four they have their "professional" degrees which allow them to earn seventy thousand dollars a year or charge one-hundred dollars an hour. That's not so bad. What is nauseating is that they begin to pontificate about "risk" and the benefits of the free enterprise system. Many of them really start their law practices with huge quantities of inherited money. Others join corporations and pass away forty of fifty years of their lives under the blanket of corporate security. All of them live in a corporate vacuum mindset. They are divorced from the struggle of the factory worker, the unemployed, and the slum dweller. The YUPPIES act like very spoiled little children who have toys, their homes and automobiles, to clean and polish on the weekends. They live in a vacuum protected from real economic struggle. They live a life that is seldom criticized because the YUPPIES are great consumers of material things and the advertisers want to sell them products. Consequently their life style is extolled. Seldom if ever will they really face the unknown. They will live from the cradle to the grave in complacent financial security. But it is not so much their complacency and lack of social conscience that bothers me. It is their self-righteousness.

Malcolm [irritated]: Oh, for Christ's sake, Nick, what do you want a young man or a young woman to do? Do you want them to take dope or drink cheap wine on the street corner? Do you want them to burn their brains out with drugs? Young people need hope. They need hope in the future. What do you want them to do?

Nick [furiously]: I want them to be able to think about why in the hell we were put on this goddamn planet! That's what I want them to be able to do! My God, the pabulum they're fed makes me sick. They are so full of mortgage rates and cash flow statistics that they can't see that their bodies are mortgaged and that they are all going to flow into the great unknown. What in the hell is going on? What are we producing? What "hope" are we really giving them? What are they supposed to do? Become like us? That's not "hope"; that's hell! [There is a brief silence. Nick speaks quietly.] Talking to YUPPIES is about as exciting as watching worms wrestle. Worms wrestling in the dark! The conqueror worm in the end! All for nothing in the end . . . for nothing in the end. [There is a silence. Nick shrugs his shoulders.] So I work with immigrants . . . it makes me feel good, so I do it.

Malcolm [hoping the subject will soon change]: I think that it is noble what you are doing.

Nick [laughing]: Oh, nonsense. It makes me feel good, that's all. It makes me feel closer to my origins, to my background. As I told you, I am second generation Italian. My father's first job was taking a convicted murderer back to Sicily. He acted as an interpreter when he was fourteen. He fell in love with the law because of that early experience, and later became a lawyer. In those years you could avoid the vacuum. That is, you didn't just go to law school, get a degree, and join a law firm. Instead, you would go to actual trials, work with an experienced attorney, and learn your profession by actually practicing law. That's how my father became an attorney. He defended a lot of Italians, made a lot of money, and . . . [Nick frowns.] He made a lot of enemies. It's a complicated story, but the truth is that he offended some of "the better people" of his day. Malcolm, I guess someone like you would say that he had "bad blood" in him. [Jacob laughs and Nick grins.]

Malcolm [very intimidated by the laughter and the grin]: Now, gentlemen, I wasn't referring to either the Jews or the Italians. I was just . . .

Nick [conciliatory]: Just using a figure of speech.

Malcolm [relieved]: Exactly.

Nick [laughing]: That's okay, Malcolm. I wouldn't want to make you and your "good blood" nervous! [Malcolm frowns. Nick scowls at Malcolm. Nick then speaks as though he was in a trance.] One day my father went into a courtroom to defend an Italian accused of murder. It was an election year . . . a political year . . . a year when not democracy but mobocracy ruled. [Reflecting and sipping his drink.] Did you know that the philosopher, Plato, called democracy "mobocracy" – the lawless rule of the undisciplined herd? Not every man who runs for public office in these great United States is Abe Lincoln. Well, anyway, it was a year in which the district attorney who was over against my father was running for judge. And, well, the judge presiding over the trial was running for the United States Senate. [laughing] Justice may be blind, but so are ambitious men. My father had been a part time prize-fighter before he became a lawyer. In that election year and during the trial, my father saw that both the district attorney and the judge were using his client and the murder trial for publicity. That is, they were trying to convict his client without evidence, tampering with the jury, and using every possible legal trick to send my father's client to his death for their personal, political ambitions. Whatever my father attempted to do legally was quashed by the district attorney and the judge. He watched a conspiracy for political office be used against him and his client. My father was a diplomat, but he was also a hothead. When he saw that all was hopeless, he went over to the district attorney and began hitting him. [laughing] He got in a great many punches before the bailiffs grabbed him and threw him in jail. [laughing out loud] He had broken the district attorney's jaw and blackened one of his eyes. He had also cracked a couple of ribs. But it cost my father six years in the penitentiary for attacking an officer of the court with a deadly weapon. His hands were considered deadly weapons because he had been in the ring. He was also disbarred from ever practicing law again. [smiling] My father was actually able to philosophize about it in the end. You see, he said his client got a new trial because his lawyer, my father, was considered to be incompetent under the law. His client got a new trial which took place when "the election year" was over. His client was found to be innocent. My father was sentenced to ten years but got off in six for good behavior. He later became a great hero in the Italian community for what he had done.

Malcolm [uncomfortably looking at his watch]: Well, this is all very interesting, but, well, I have appointments, and . . .

Nick [raging threateningly]: SHUT UP MALCOLM! YOU'RE NO GODDAMN GOOD! SHUT UP OR I'LL KILL YOU! [A very startled Malcolm looks helplessly at the ceiling. Jacob looks at Malcolm and grins. Nick continues to speak as though in a trance.] My father learned a lot in prison. When he was let out – I was seven years old when I met him – he decided to run a halfway house for prisoners returning to normal life. He would give a man a room and try and find him money and work. It seemed to make him happy, and I got to listen to the ex-prisoners' stories. [Nick takes a sip from his drink and begins to smile.] It all amounts to one statement, and the statement comes from the very great German poet, Goethe. Goethe once said, "With the slightest change in circumstances, there is not a crime I would not commit!" Goethe was a very great man. He was the mayor of Weimar, a friend of Napoleon, a companion of Beethoven. Truly, in every way, Goethe was the universal soul. But if Goethe could make the statement, "With the slightest change, in circumstances, there is not a crime I would not commit!" what can the rest of us say? [Nick laughs. He turns to Jacob.] Jacob, did Goethe have "good blood" in him?

Jacob [sardonically]: Well, it was German blood, but it was better than most German blood.

Nick [grinning]: Indeed, it was. So my father was a convict and a friend to convicts. Because of him and his friends I came to understand a little of Goethe. Indeed, I am the son of a convict, and I am proud of it. [There is a brief silence. Nick, beaming, drinks the rest of his Gin Mary.]

Malcolm [sheepishly looking at his watch]: Well, Nick, you shouldn't be so hard on yourself. I certainly didn't want to offend you or Mr. Frank with my "blood" talk. Besides, you've got a lot to be proud of. How many convicts' sons have done what you have done?

Nick [laughing]: What have I done?

Jacob [furiously]: What's wrong with convicts? This whole country was founded by convicts and the sons of convicts. We Jews were convicts under Hitler because of our "blood"! Whoever grabs the power first makes the rest convicts. It's who grabs the real estate first! And Hitler knew how to grab real estate! Czechoslovakia! Poland! Norway! France! Russia! [morosely] He knew how to grab real estate.

Nick [frowning furiously]: When you talk about Hitler and the rest of them . . . [Nick looks out the window.] Well, all's that I know . . . all's that I can say . . . is that I'd rather be a son of a convict than a son of a bitch!

Jacob [lifting his glass and smiling]: I'll drink to that! [Both laugh and toast each other. Malcolm, confused and embarrassed, sits and watches them. Jacob looks at Malcolm, puts down his glass, and stands up. He goes to the window and looks down. He speaks in a somber tone.] What a city! To the west, the sea. To the north, the beautiful village of Sausalito and the expensive homes of Marin County. To the east, the Bay Bridge. To the south, the slums, the ghettos, and the concentration camps of the inner city. My God, what a world!

Malcolm [defensively]: Don't forget where we are! We're in the financial district! Look at the buildings surrounding us! The bank buildings! The high-rises! The Transamerica Pyramid Building! What buildings!

Nick [sarcastically]: Jim McClain, my old partner, and I used to look at these buildings when we would walk to the bus stop south of Market Street. McClain was a real theologian. He used to say, when the wind picked up and blew dust into his contact lenses, that God had a special purpose for the financial district. According to Jim, God didn't know what to do with Satan after Satan and the other angels fell. God had created Satan the most perfect of creatures, but Satan wanted everything his own way and on his own terms. [laughing] Maybe he wanted a big home in the suburbs and easy cash flow. Anyway, Satan rebelled. So God had to put him somewhere with his band of predators. So God created the financial district to give Satan a home! Yes, sir, that McClain was a real theologian!

Malcolm [annoyed]: Don't speak to me of McClain! That bastard sold me an expensive wine store in Palm Springs. He sold me the store just before Breakaway, the major supermarket chain, opened up a series of wine stores throughout the country. [outraged] As luck would have it, they opened a store one block from my wine shop! We're going broke! [yelling] Don't tell me that Satan lives in the financial district! He lives in the body of Jim McClain! I'm going to sue the bastard! [Nick and Jacob look at each other with faint smiles.]

Nick [indifferently]: Well, good luck, but I'm sure McClain did nothing wrong. Besides, you won't win against him in the courtroom. He's too honest of a man, and he has an excellent reputation for professionalism. He told you to get a lawyer and an accountant to examine the business before you bought it, didn't he?

Malcolm [gruffly]: Well, yes, he did. [furiously] He did.

Nick [sternly]: And did you do that?

Malcolm [furiously quiet]: Yes.

Nick: And what did your accountant and lawyer say?

Malcolm [sheepishly]: Both said that it looked like a good deal. Besides I needed a tax write-off against ordinary income. So I bought the store. It was good at first. [Malcolm smiles.] I would fly down to Palm Springs, hold wine tasting at the store, play golf and tennis, and generally amuse myself. I could even invite Bambi to come and see me. She would take the weekend off and help me with the wine tastings. It was great fun and a tremendous tax write-off. It was great [sadly] . . . until the huge chain store opened up against me. Who can compete against such a monster? Now I've lost over two-hundred-thousand dollars! My God, what a world!

Nick [grinning] It's part of THE PROCESS!

Malcolm [bowing his head]: Yes, I guess it is.

[Nick continues to grin. Jacob, who is still standing, looks at both of them and laughs. He then looks out the window and becomes very serious.]

Jacob [staring at the top of the Transamerica Pyramid Building which is stage center]: You know, they shouldn't have built that pyramid down there.

Malcolm [taken aback]: Why not? It's a beautiful piece of architecture. It's a symbol of finance and industry. Look how it points to the sky, to eternity!

Jacob [quietly]: It's worse than The Tower of Babel.

Malcolm [perplexed]: How can you say that?

Jacob [seriously]: Pharaoh enslaved our people under a pyramid. We were all slaves under a pyramid. [reflecting] Maybe we still are.

Nick [smiling]: Not bad, Jacob. Not bad at all. And where are we going to find a new Moses?

Jacob [quietly]: What is more . . . where are we going to find The God of Moses? [There is a silence. All three men look embarrassed.]

Nick [attempting to break the silence]: Well, the way I see it, we're all going to find Him soon enough, if He's out there. We're all over sixty. [laughing] Yes, sir, we'll find Him soon enough. [There is a profound silence.]

Malcolm [anxiously]: Nick, how can you say such things on such a beautiful day? [He reaches for his martini and sees that his glass is empty. anxiously] Waiter! Waiter! [The pompous waiter appears.] Another martini, Bombay gin. Gentlemen, another round?

Nick [affably]: Sure, another round. [Jacob nods his assent and sits down. The waiter exits.] We all need a few belts of booze when we get serious. [Nick laughs.] So does the whole country. There are ten million alcoholics in this country... [absentmindedly] . . . I wonder what Monte is doing now... probably drinking and shopping . . . You know, an English poet was once asked, "Why do men go to war?" His answer was, "Because their women are watching!" I was once asked, "Why do financiers and men in power . . . why do they not care more for the poor and the destitute?" My answer was simple: "It is because their women are shopping!" [All three men laugh. There is a silence. Nick grins somberly.] What a bitch she was! A beautiful . . . shopping . . . bitch! [The waiter returns and places the drinks on the table. All three take a sip. There is a silence.]

Malcolm [sheepishly]: Well, I know you've had it tough, Nick. And I'm sorry about that wheel company of yours. It probably contributed to your divorce. But The Universal Bank just couldn't extend the loan. I was your banker then, and I tried to do everything I could. I'm sorry I couldn't get the loan committee to go along with me. You and I were good friends before your bankruptcy. . . . But I want you to know I loved you like a brother, like a brother. I tell you that, and I mean it sincerely. [Relieved, he takes another sip of his martini.]

Nick [Nick is very quiet. Then a vicious look of absolute hatred overcomes his face. His voice sounds like an exploding volcano.]: LIKE A BROTHER? LIKE A BROTHER? YOU SON-OF-A-BITCH! YOU LOVED ME LIKE A BROTHER? YEAH, SURE! YOU LOVED ME LIKE CAIN LOVED ABLE! THAT'S THE KIND OF BROTHER YOU WERE! YOU SENT ME THE FORECLOSURE PAPERS, AND MONTE SENT ME THE DIVORCE PAPERS. ALL ON THE SAME DAY! WHAT A BROTHER! WHAT A WIFE! THANKS CAIN! THANKS A LOT! THANKS, JEZEBEL! THANKS A LOT! JESUS! THANKS FOR NOTHING!

Malcolm [Bowing his head, he then speaks with pleading hands.]: Look, Nick, I'm sorry. The company was in the delinquent loan department. The company owed the bank one and one-half million dollars. What could I do?

Nick [not paying attention to Malcolm]: Jacob, have you ever been to the delinquent loan department of a big bank?

Jacob [quietly]: No.

Nick [fiercely]: Well, it's not a very cheery place; I'll tell you that. Usually it's in another building – one apart from the big high-rise. In the big high-rise they're always happy to take your money with their slack-jawed bankers' smiles. But the delinquent loan department is in a little building, with a small set of offices, and there is a small room. There are no pictures, and there are no windows. It's like a morgue. In fact, it is a morgue . . . a morgue for dead companies. There they question you. They say, "Where is the money?" When you say, "There is none"; they say, "We're sorry." And then the nightmare really begins. The liquidation of business assets. The liquidation of jobs! The liquidation of homes!!! [Outraged, Nick stops and is quiet for a few seconds. slowly] Yes, now you know why banks are so liquid. They know how to liquidate! But when you tell your workers at Christmas time that they no longer have their jobs . . . well . . . that is something else again . . . something different . . . [Nick grins viciously at Malcolm.] Isn't that right, Malcolm? [There is a silence.]

Malcolm [fidgeting helplessly]: What can I say, Nick? Business is business. It's "THE INVISIBLE HAND," the unchartable process of commerce, the incomprehensible movement of the market which stretches its fingers over and through our lives . . .

Nick [furious]: Is that what it is? Ah, to hell with "THE INVISIBLE HAND"! I spit on "THE INVISIBLE HAND"! [raging] "THE INVISIBLE HAND" stabs you in the back: that's what "THE INVISIBLE HAND" does! Screw "THE INVISIBLE HAND"! [There is a silence. Malcolm stares at the floor. Jacob begins laughing.]

Jacob: I know what you mean.

Nick [viciously]: Yes, Jacob, you certainly do. [to Malcolm] Malcolm, Jacob escaped Hitler and his slave culture. Maybe the Gestapo had its "INVISIBLE HAND," too! [There is a silence, Nick begins laughing, and then takes a sip from his drink.] Hell, what am I saying? I haven't been through anything. Besides I had some good friends. I remember talking to Jim McClain when the bank would not extend the loan on the wheel company. McClain had a buyer, too. But, the buyer backed out of the deal when the bank would not give him another six months to turn the company around. Who can blame the bank? We were already a year behind in payments.

Malcolm [self-righteously raising his head]: Exactly.

Nick [staring at Malcolm with absolute wrath]: Exactly. But don't become too self-righteous over there, Malcolm! [Malcolm frowns, mutters to himself and bows his head. Nick seems satisfied with Malcolm's discomfiture.] I was about to lose everything, and I was in despair. I told McClain that I still had a life insurance policy for $500,000. I related to him that often times during this ordeal when I was driving home, I had the impulse to cause an accident, to turn the wheel into the on-coming traffic, to kill myself and to get it over with. McClain reminded me that I still had a wife and a daughter. [smiling] I told him that I still had a daughter, but that Monte was on the way out. He told me I was worth more alive than dead. [laughing] I don't think the bank thought so. Anyway, I got to thinking about being dead, and Monte having $500,000, and all. It occurred to me that she would probably spend the money on a weekend shopping spree! And I began to laugh. You see, at that time I was glad I had once studied the humanities. I remembered the story of Lord Byron. When he was about thirty-five, Byron thought of killing himself. He had his pistol on the table along with a bottle of wine. Byron was depressed. [Nick muses to himself] He probably had known too many women. They said he went through 800 women before he was thirty-five. No doubt poetic excess or some other kind of excess . . . Well, anyway, Lord Byron was contemplating suicide. He was weighing the pros and cons of such an act. Finally he said to himself "But if I kill myself it will make my mother-in-law happy." No doubt a man who had gone through 800 women would not be the ideal husband or son-in-law! Apparently his mother-in-law despised him. But Byron despised his mother-in-law! His final reasoning was, "If I kill myself it will make my mother-in-law happy, but I refuse to see her happy, so I will live!" That was reason enough for him to continue living! [There is a pause. Nick speaks cheerfully.] In like manner, I could not envision myself under the ground and Monte in the shopping mall! So I decided to live. A great thing, literature . . . [Nick grins blissfully and sips his drink.] Yes, literature is a great thing; you just have to know how to use it at the right time! [There is a long silence.]

Malcolm [totally confused and finding the silence unbearable]: Well, I'm sorry about this whole thing, Nick, I really am. It's just the way things are. That's all.

Nick [furiously]: Well, Malcolm, I'll tell you the way things are! I'll tell you, you son-of-a-bitch, you money-changing snake in the grass! I'll tell you everything; I will! Goddamn you and your kind! I hope you, your children, and your children's children have warts. I hope you all rot in hell! I do, you son-of-a-bitch! I'll tell you what I think! I carry this poem with me. I carry it next to my heart! And I want you to hear it, you son-of-a-bitch! I wrote it the night before I had to move out of my house on the next morning. It was a nice house, too. An acre in the Berkeley Hills! A subway ride to the financial district and the banks of Satan! Everything was peaceful there. [reflecting] . . . well, anyway, Monte – the bitch – had moved out. She had taken everything but my desk, a chair, my books and a sleeping bag. Monte was a real taker, a real winner . . . the bitch! So, I sat there contemplating my life and how it had all come to nothing. Everything I had ever lived for or believed in had come to nothing! [He laughs sardonically] Everything is nothing! Nothing! So I wrote this poem. Surely you know the melody. [Nick reaches into the left side of his coat with his right hand and pulls out a piece of paper.] The title of my poem is "The Bankers Cheateth Thee!" [In a rich baritone Nick begins singing to the melody of "My Country 'Tis of Thee"]

The bankers cheateth Thee
with interest's larceny –
Of this I sing.

Land of polluted skies,
Land where the poor one dies.
From every tall high-rise . . .
Let the bankers sing!

The bankers cheateth Thee
with cheap security –
Of this I sing.

Land of the corporate trust,
Land of the money-lust,
Amidst all the moths and rust . . .
Let the bankers sing!

The bankers cheateth Thee
with constant treachery . . .
Of this I sing.

Land where the small farm died,
Land of the money-pride.
From every COFFIN-SIDE . . .
Let the bankers sing!

[Nick leans back into his chair and takes a sip of his drink. He smiles at the audience and laughs good-naturedly. A brief silence ensues.]

Jacob [laughing and then speaking somberly]: That's quite a poem. I once felt that way. It's an old feeling, but a good feeling. You see, when I first came to this country, I got a job in a slaughter house. Have you ever read the book by a great American author, Upton Sinclair? He wrote the book called THE JUNGLE. What a book! He wrote about life in a slaughter house. They say the book changed the meat-packing industry. For once manufacturers had to be responsible for what they put on peoples' tables. A great book! We are what we eat . . . and we must eat . . . Well, I worked in the slaughter house, and I made good money. But then one of my Jewish friends got me a job selling men's suits coast to coast. I got a base salary, expenses, plus a commission on whatever I sold. No more slaughter house. [laughing] We Jews, especially the immigrants, call fine men's clothes "Jewish hardware"! Well, I dealt in Jewish hardware, and I was making a lot of money. [somberly] But the war was still going on against Hitler, and I was still classified as a German citizen. Since I was a German citizen, I was declared an undesirable alien. I was not allowed to go out at night. It was almost like being under Hitler again. Almost, but not quite. Actually not like being under Hitler at all. So, I had to give up my job. I was in America, but certain opportunities were denied me. [laughing] Anyway, I borrowed some money and started my butcher shops. I owned four of them before I bought the uniform company. [laughing] Always did want to stay close to food and clothing. Keep your life simple, and you won't lose your way. I made enough money for a happy life. That's all I really wanted . . . [reflecting] This country has its faults, but it's a lot better than life under Hitler. It really is. I know that the country's imperfect, but then there is no machine gun at your head.

Nick [glaring into his drink]: I think you're right, Jacob. [Nick reflects for a few moments.] McClain and I used to sell businesses. McClain was a tough Calvinist who believed in the work ethic. I was the son of a criminal lawyer. Now and then we'd talk about these things. In fact both of us decided to ask our clients if it was better in The United States of America than it was from whence they came. [Nick laughs.] We must have asked the question seven hundred times. Everybody said it was better here. [There is a silence. Nick speaks cheerfully.] Chinese, Vietnamese, Germans, Poles, Irishmen, Italians, Englishman [Nick sneers at Malcolm.] . . . every goddamn son-of-a-bitch we'd listen to, said it was better here. [There is a silence.] Well, you might go belly up like a whale in American business, but you're right that it's better than having a machine gun placed at your head! It is! [Again there is a silence. Nick reflects for a moment, and then becomes furious.] But we still have slums, gentlemen! We still have slums! Lincoln, Abraham Lincoln was a great American, the truly great American. A man that made himself . . . a man who was more than himself! He believed in free enterprise, but he also believed that we should not have slaves . . . wage slaves, corporate slaves, money slaves, slum slaves . . . any type of slave . . . But what do we have today? We have all types of slavery and what is worse, we still have slums and a horrible social indifference to everything that isn't "cute" or "fun" or "stupid." We are the wealthiest country in the world, but we still have slums! Our idiocy cries to heaven! It does!

Malcolm [Malcolm speaks sternly and self-righteously. His self-righteousness derives more from the fact that he has been ignored by the Italian and the Jew than by the fact that he, Malcolm, has nothing to say.]: Look, both of you are getting carried away. This is getting too emotional and irrational. It just is. Now, if there are slums, it is no doubt the fault of the people who live in them. Why just last week in church, I heard an excellent sermon based of the Biblical text that says, "Those who do not work, let them not eat." Now that is the way we have to look at the whole thing, and let's be sensible about it. [Nick looks at Jacob, and Jacob looks at Nick. Both Nick and Jacob shake their heads in disgust.]

Nick [furiously]: Well, that's a hell of a thing to say! Who is this goddamn preacher you go to listen to on Sunday morning?

Malcolm [self-righteously]: He's a Ph.D. in theology; that's what he is! And he knows what he is talking about! How can other people blame us for the world's problems? We do our work. We take care of our families. That's all we can do.

Nick [viciously]: Is that right?

Malcolm [just as viciously]: That's right!

Nick [sarcastically]: What does your "preacher" make a year?

Malcolm [taken aback]: How the hell should I know? I guess he does pretty well. I mean he has a parish in Green Meadows. [laughing good-naturedly in his "teddy bear" way] You know, people in Green Meadows aren't poor.

Nick [with dark sternness]: You haven't answered my question. What does the bastard make a year?

Malcolm [yawning]: Oh. I don't know . . . probably about ninety thousand. Yes, about that. Not a lot of money, but then he's also paid to take those who want to go to "The Holy Land" once a year. A few years ago I went with him. It was a very spiritual experience. It really was.

Nick [sardonically]: And what did you do in "The Holy Land"?

Malcolm [indignantly]: Why, we walked where Jesus walked, and we saw the sights. That's what we did!

Jacob [laughing]: It must have been great walking around all that Jewish real estate.

Malcolm [puzzled and reflecting]: Well, I don't know about that. I just remember that Bambi was interested in theology, and so I took her there. It was great for us both.

Nick [grinning]: And where did you stay?

Malcolm [pompously]: Why in the Jerusalem Hilton, where else? [Nick and Jacob laugh uproariously. Malcolm is confused.]

Nick [smirking]: It doesn't sound as though you really traversed the way of sorrows to the cross! [Nick lights a cigarette and reflects a moment.] Was there a good bar in the Jerusalem Hilton?

Malcolm [becoming annoyed]: Look, you're baiting me to make fun of me. If I need some spiritual solace, what is it to you?

Nick [furious and in a threatening manner]: Oh, go to the devil, or go make a loan you no good son-of-a-bitch! Or go to "The Holy Land." Who gives a damn? My God, the holy land is in the slums. That is what has to be redeemed! Don't you give a damn? Isn't there something down there that calls out to be corrected? Can't you hear God's voice in this for our own time on earth? Oh, go to "The Holy Land" or go to hell! Who gives a damn? [Nick picks up his drink and drains it.] Waiter, waiter! [The waiter appears.] Give me a double cognac . . . Courvoisier! [The waiter bows, and looks at both Malcolm and Jacob.] Gentlemen, help yourselves . . . I mean, to more liquor.

Jacob [smiling]: I'll have a cognac, too.

Malcolm [exhausted and upset]: No, nothing for me. I've had enough. I really have. [There is a silence, then quietly] Okay, I'll have one, too.

Nick [merrily]: Oh, c'mon, gentlemen, have a double. [He winks at Jacob and then he speaks to the waiter.] Three doubles. [The waiter bows and exits.] Now, where were we? [reflecting] Oh, yes . . . we still have slums. That's what we have, goddamn slums. Gentlemen, we all agree! Economically, and with all our great liberties, this is the promised land . . . but we still have slums! That's what we have! Slums! Goddamn slums! And we made them, so, we can destroy them! It's not like a child dying of cancer, or anyone dying of an incurable disease. It's something we made, so, it's something we can remedy! There's a lot of things you can't change, but we could change the slums, but we don't. No, we don't!

[There is a silence. Nick is grinning. So is Jacob. Malcolm is bewildered. The waiter returns with the drinks and places them on the table. The waiter exits.]

Malcolm [in an exasperated voice]: Well, what is anyone going to do about it? What are you going to do, Nick? What can be done? What is the bottom line? Besides, the kingdom of Christ is "a spiritual kingdom." That's what it is. A spiritual kingdom! Some are elected, and some are not. As our minister said, "Those who have very little, even the little they have will be taken away." That's from the Bible and the Bible can't be wrong. So it's fated, and that's it!!!! THAT'S IT, I TELL YOU!!! [vehemently] We can't do anything about it. It's predestined, so leave it at that. [Malcolm drinks with a type of fury.]

Jacob [Bowing his head then lifting it, he speaks with simple dignity.]: This is all wrong. It is absolutely wrong! You know nothing of true religion. You know nothing of it! True religion is described in THE BOOK OF AMOS. Amos was a shepherd. His book is a very short one. Amos came to town to sell his sheep. He heard all the so-called learned men of his day discussing religion. Amos grew disgusted with all the debates. Finally, Amos said, "True religion is to defend the orphan and the widow! True religion is to defend the oppressed!" And then Amos left town! That's what he did! He went back to taking care of his sheep. But if Amos were alive today, he would attack the slums! He would find a way to wipe them off the face of the earth! That's what he would do!

[There is a silence. Both Malcolm and Nick stare at Jacob. Then all three men take heavy drinks from their respective glasses. There is silence.]

Malcolm [very unsure of himself]: Ah . . . er, I mean I can

understand what you are saying, but let's be realistic. The world is what it is. I mean, there is wealth . . . and . . . and there is poverty. And, yes there are slums. But you must understand that Christianity is different from Judaism. Christianity, according to our minister, is a religion of spirituality – a religion of the soul and of the hereafter. Now, some are going to go to heaven and some . . . well . . . we don't know. We can't say. But God gives money to some and not to others. And that is the way it is. It's preordained, and all of history proves it. Some have it. Some don't. That's all. That's really all. [Malcolm bows his head and takes another sip from his drink.] Besides, it's all too complicated. [A silence ensues.]

Nick [sarcastically to Malcolm]: Well, I don't know how you read THE NEW TESTAMENT or what you and Bambi saw in "The Holy Land," but Jesus did feed the multitudes, and his great model was the The Good Samaritan. The Good Samaritan took care of a broken man in the ditch after the "priest" walked by and forgot him. [wearily] Perhaps there is a lesson in all of this, I don't know. I only know that we should bring Johnny home. This is what we should do! We should bring Johnny home! [Nick finishes his drink.]

Malcolm [staring at Nick]: What are you saying?

Nick [reflecting in a serious manner]: I was just thinking about my father and a lot of things. When my father was released from prison, we lived in a big house... twenty-one rooms, eleven bedrooms . . . As I have said before, when his friends got out of prison, he would try and help them get money and work. They had a place to stay. But the best evening was when Johnny Amalfi got out of jail. Johnny was very young when his father died. His mother, Flora, ran a pizzeria south of Market Street. Johnny was a good kid before he joined a street gang. Then he started taking drugs and breaking the law. Johnny was caught one night trying to rob a liquor store when he was nineteen. He had used a gun in the robbery. His sentence was twelve years in the penitentiary. My father met him there. Once my father was released, he did all he could to get Johnny's sentence reduced. Fortunately Johnny was out in seven years. [Nick stares into space.] Johnny later became a probation officer and a good one. But what I remember most was the night Johnny came home. His mother, Flora, was at our house. I remember her seeing her son, and then her weeping and kissing my father's hand for getting Johnny out of jail without his having to serve the whole twelve year sentence . . . So my father saved a man five years of his life. The woman was sobbing and kissing my father's hand . . . [Nick snarls at Malcolm.] Neither my father nor Johnny had "good blood" in them. My father had something different. He had a social conscience! That's what he had! I don't give a damn about what else he had or did . . . but he had that – a social conscience. He knew what a prison was, and he did something to get people out of prison and keep them out of prison. Johnny's mother through her tears said to my father, "You brought Johnny home!" And she would not stop crying. That was a great evening. I have never been so proud of any man! Especially because he was my father. [There is a brief silence.]

Jacob [smiling]: Why, that's beautiful. That's really beautiful. That's what we should all do. We should bring Johnny home! [raging] Is Johnny in prison? Bring him home! Is Johnny in slavery before a Hitler? Find him a home! Is Johnny in the slums? Get rid of the slums! Bring Johnny home! That's the way it should be! [reflecting] In my religion we have the story of Moses and our people. Moses freed our people from their slavery in Egypt. [He stands up with his drink and looks at the top of The Transamerica Pyramid Building.] There were pyramids in Egypt just like there is a pyramid in the city of San Francisco. And our Bible, THE OLD TESTAMENT to the Christians, says that out of Egypt God called his people Israel to a new land. [smiling at Nick] In a certain sense, God brought Johnny home. That is what we all should do. [reflecting] I just hope that we are not in another Egypt. [There is a silence.]

Malcolm [indignantly]: Oh, c'mon, this is a democracy! This is the greatest country in the world! There has never been such a country. [There is a long silence.]

Nick [wearily]: Yes . . . but we still have slums.

THE AUCTION

CHARACTERS

NICK CAVALCANTI
ANGELINA CAVALCANTI
JIM McCLAIN
A WAITRESS

[The same bar/restaurant, "The Singles," as in THE AGONY OF SHOPPING. It is now November, 1986. Nick Cavalcanti, Angelina Cavalcanti, and Jim McClain are seated at a table in such a way that all three can be seen by the audience. Jim and Nick have on sport shirts and slacks. Angelina is in a tennis outfit. Jim McClain is forty years old with gray hair. All three are drinking cocktails.]

Nick: Jim, it's great that you could join us. You remember Angelina, don't you?

Jim [cordially]: Oh, sure. It's been quite a while. How have you been?

Angelina [quietly]: I've been fine despite Monte's dying. [She takes a sip from her drink.]

Jim: Monte?

Angelina: Monte was my mother. Nick's wife.

Jim [quietly]: Oh, I'm sorry to hear that. How did it happen?

Angelina [softly]: Drinking. Alcohol. She couldn't shake her drinking. It destroyed her liver. She gained a lot of weight, and she died. It was horrible at the end. The whining, the crying, the drinking! I guess she never grew up.

Nick [sardonically, as he takes a sip of his drink]: No, she never grew up, but she blew up like a balloon, blew up like a balloon and popped! That's what she did!

Angelina [irritated]: Nick, don't talk that way. It's disrespectful. You know it is. She had a hard time of it at the end. She really did. [speaking to Nick, as she takes a sip from her drink] Nick, you must feel some sorrow, just a little sorrow. I know what she did to you, but you must feel some sorrow.

Nick [laughing caustically]: The only people I feel sorry for are the booze retailers of America and the bar owners and liquor store owners of Palm Springs and Beverly Hills! Especially for those noble Americans in the last two cities of industry! In fact, I feel sorry for the entire liquor industry throughout the world! It'll be a bad year for them without Monte around!!! [Nick continues to laugh caustically. Jim looks at Angelina. Both stare at Nick. Nick frowns.] Okay . . . okay. I do feel something . . . something more than relief. She was so beautiful once. Maybe I should have gone to the funeral. I sort of feel bad that I didn't. Tell me about the funeral, Angelina.

Angelina [soberly]: Well, it's best you didn't go to the funeral. It was really ghastly. Before she died she wrote her funeral instructions. Tom West, her husband, I, and two of her friends did what she wanted. We set sail on Tom's yacht with her ashes. We sailed out of San Pedro Harbor up the coast. She had recorded her own singing of "I Did It My Way." She wanted us to play the song as we placed her ashes into the sea. Well, we stopped somewhere on the coastline. We didn't know it, but there was a sewage plant nearby. Monte wanted us all to be drinking martinis and listening to her recorded voice as we let the ashes go over the side of the yacht. We did what she wanted. Just after we poured the ashes into the ocean we continued drinking and listening to her sing. But then a great gust of foul smelling wind arose and blew the ashes back on board and into our martini glasses. God! It was awful!!

Nick [howling with laughter]: Well, that's Monte, all right. She couldn't keep away from the booze even when she was dead!! [Nick continues laughing. Angelina and Jim look at each other. Jim doesn't know what to do. Angelina tries to repress her laughing but cannot.]

Angelina [laughing]: You're terrible, Nick . . . [She continues laughing.] You're just terrible.

Nick [good-naturedly]: Oh, c'mon. We should let her rest in peace . . . or in gin . . . [sarcastically] Who gives a damn, anyway? [He takes another sip from his drink.] We'd best go on with this catastrophe called life. [There is a brief silence. Nick changes the subject. He addresses Jim McClain.] So Malcolm Huntington sued you, eh, Jim?

Jim [relieved at least for the change in the topic of conversation]: Yes, he did.

Nick: For how much?

Jim: For five hundred thousand dollars.

Angelina [also relieved for the change in subject]: For what?

Jim [smirking]: Oh, the usual. For fraud and misrepresentation, although I did nothing wrong. I made sure that he was represented by his own attorney and accountant before I would begin negotiations. [yawning] I've been through all this before. Malcolm, like so many others bought a small business for tax purposes. In this case it was a fine wine store in Palm Springs. A huge food chain, Breakaway, started setting up fine wine stores all over the country. Breakaway could of course undercut the retail prices of any independent store. Malcolm went broke, and I got sued. [sarcastically] It must be the business broker's fault if anyone who buys a business does not become a millionaire. So I'm sued! [laughing] Big deal!

Angelina [concerned]: I specialize in bankruptcy law, but maybe I could refer you to a good business attorney.

Jim [smiling]: Thanks, Angelina, but one of the investors in my corporation specializes in these matters and is an attorney. I'm really not worried. I just feel bad that the wine store was not a success. That's all. Malcolm got very upset about the whole thing. He had really become overweight from too much drinking. Did both of you know that he died of a heart attack six months ago?

Nick [surprised]: No, really? No, I didn't know that.

Angelina: I'm sorry to hear that.

Jim [frowning]: Well, he died. His wife became hysterical and blamed his dying on his buying the wine store. She, or I should say his estate, has sued me. [shrugging his shoulders] The woman's hysterical and seeking vengeance. Really she's just having a difficult time dealing with death, and the fact that the foundations of her upper-middle-class world are being shaken. Something was taken away from her basis of security. It must be someone's fault. We all know that it's no one's fault, but certain people must always blame someone. Few people can stand the irrationality and the viciousness of this world. Even fewer can really stand up to death. So blame your misfortune on someone else! Sue the bastard! It's the national battle cry! [He takes a sip of his drink. There is a silence.]

Nick [thoughtfully]: Do you think that there are any real legal grounds for such a suit?

Jim [yawning]: No. But you never know what a jury will do. Besides, long ago, during another one of these nuisance suits, I put everything into my wife's name.

Angelina: That was a smart thing to do.

Nick [aghast]: A what? A smart thing to do? Are you crazy?

Angelina [authoritatively]: Sure, Nick. If Jim gets a judgment against his corporation, and it can be shown that certain assets were his wife's sole and separate property . . . well, Jim will probably be judgment-proof, and he will not have to pay anything.

Jim [grinning]: Yep, it's her sole and separate property, all right. I saw to that. And I'm Jim who's judgment-proof . . . [yawning] It's a nice feeling.

Nick [anxiously]: But what if your wife runs off with your money? What if she meets another man?

Jim [laughing]: If she runs off with my money, she won't be able to run very far. And, if she meets another man and takes off with him . . . Well, that only means that she has common sense. [Angelina giggles.] Besides. I'm forty, and I'm too old to worry about such things. [laughing] I have to worry about my twilight years, about senility, about the time when my boat begins to slip away from the dock . . . [drinking and smiling and looking at his watch] Yes, indeed, in just a few years they will be changing my diapers again. From diapers to diapers – thus is life on earth! [Angelina giggles. Nick laughs.]

Nick [after a few moments]: So Malcolm took the ten count, eh?

Jim [lighting a cigarette]: He sure did. What a guy! He had a home in San Francisco, another in Santa Barbara, and another in Palm Springs. He collected art and antiques. He played tennis, golf and polo. He traveled a lot. Yes, indeed, and he kept his lawns mowed! Yes, he did! [reflecting] Perhaps that is what will be said of this generation of Americans. It was a nation that kept its lawns mowed! What a nation! [There is a silence. Jim reflects in a beaming manner. He takes a drag on his cigarette.] Well, anyway, the inheritance tax people came to town and evaluated his estate at ten million dollars. His art had appreciated; his homes had appreciated; his lawns had appreciated. The family is now contesting a huge inheritance tax assessment. It's a real mess. They'll probably have to sell a lot of things to pay the state. In fact, they're arranging for an auction right now.

Nick [startled]: An auction?

Jim [serenely]: Sure, ashes to ashes, dust to dust. A life of earning for a life of spending . . . and then the auction . . . [laughing quietly] Yes, it's a sweet life.

Angelina [perplexed]: You seem very bitter, Jim.

Jim [yawning]: No, not bitter. Just realistic. It's the usual. People spend their lives accumulating wealth, only to be buried. Malcolm can't accumulate anymore. He's dead. He kept his lawn mowed, but he's dead. [Jim laughs.]

Angelina [annoyed]: What's wrong with you anyway?

Jim [also annoyed]: What do you mean?

Angelina [becoming furious]: You're just so sarcastic. What's wrong with the way Malcolm lived? What's wrong with that?

Jim [also furious]: What do you say you did for a living?

Angelina [indignantly]: I'm an attorney, a bankruptcy attorney.

Jim [laughing]: Oh. I see . . . [He continues laughing.] I know about bankruptcy attorneys. What is your "up-front fee"? Maybe I can send you some business.

Angelina [In the hope of doing some "business," she mollifies her rage.]: Why... well . . . usually $5,000 to begin with.

Jim [laughing uproariously]: I see. Well, that's pretty high.

Angelina [in a great fury and shouting]: Who do you think you are, anyway?

Jim [yawning]: Oh, lower your voice. It's the same as always. Take your cut on the misery of mankind! The lawyer, the doctor, the broker, the professor, the dentist, the priest, the rabbi, the minister . . . We all take our cut. It's what we're good for. We take our cut, and then we worship ourselves for our so-called "hard work." We don't work that hard. Maybe a coal miner works hard, but we don't. We just whine, call life good, and die. We whine, and we lie a lot. That's all we do!

Angelina [furiously taking a sip from her drink]: What a pessimist! God, I pity you!

Jim [sarcastically]: Don't pity me. Pity the human race! At times I think the whole thing is a regrettable mistake. People earning, spending, and dying. A regrettable mistake. [He yawns, and takes a sip from his drink. There is a silence.]

Nick [laughing]: You haven't changed a bit, Jim. You're just as rotten as ever. I think you studied too much theology once. Angelina, Jim studied a lot of theology once.

Angelina [bored and furious]: Oh, maybe that is why he is so weird.

Jim [laughing]: Yes, maybe that is why I am so weird. [reflecting] Say, Nick, do you still read philosophy and on religious topics? We used to have some great conversations. I read some theology now and then . . . But theology or no theology, I can't stop thinking.

Nick [laughing]: At times I read a little philosophy. But I've decided to leave religion alone. My motto is: "Leave God alone, and He'll return the favor!" [All laugh. There is a silence.]

Angelina [good-naturedly]: Are you sure that God is a "He"? Maybe God is a woman. A lot of women think God is a woman.

Nick [laughing]: Well, given the screwed up nature of this world, maybe God is a woman! [Nick and Jim laugh. Angelina frowns. There is a silence.]

Angelina [turning on Jim McClain]: Well, I think Mr. McClain is far too pessimistic.

Jim [laughing]: Just call me Jim.

Angelina [ignoring him]: My God, Nick, how could you ever work with someone like Jim McClain?

Nick [laughing]: Oh, stop it, Angelina. Jim and I had a great time together. [addressing Jim] Didn't we, Jim?

Jim [laughing]: We did.

Nick [smiling]: And we made a lot of money.

Jim [smiling]: We did.

Nick [laughing good-naturedly]: And we got sued a lot!

Jim (laughing]: We did . . . But we beat them all in court, didn't we?

Nick [laughing]: We did! [There is a silence.]

Jim [snarling at Angelina]: That's why I hate most lawyers. Many times we could have settled our business disputes with a minimum of difficulties. But the lawyers kept milking the cash cow until she went dry.

Angelina [furious]: Not all lawyers are like that.

Jim [sarcastically]: Okay, Angelina. You're a real saint. Give me a break, would you please. [He takes a sip of his drink.]

Angelina [outraged]: My God, what do you expect out of life anyway? You're just degrading everything and making life look very small.

Jim [laughing]: I'm not degrading anything. Look, let's put it this way. Nick and I both admire Lincoln. Abraham Lincoln once said that we are an "almost chosen" people and nation. And that's what we are . . . <u>ALMOST</u> chosen! A big word "ALMOST"! So, we've got a long way to go! We are in what theologians would call "a wilderness state."

Angelina [furiously]: Well. I wouldn't want to be in the wilderness with you!

Jim [sarcastically]: I don't blame you. Besides, there aren't many bankruptcies in the wilderness. You'd starve to death!

Being with you in the wilderness would be like being with a rattlesnake! Regardless, we are in a wilderness state.

Nick [interested]: What are you saying, Jim?

Angelina [very annoyed]: Yes, what are you saying? My God, I've never heard so many words. Can't you be more definitive? God, I'm thirsty . . . Waitress . . . Waitress! [The waitress in very short shorts and a tennis outfit appears. She is extremely attractive with beautiful legs. Both Jim and Nick stare at her. Nick looks at Jim. Jim begins laughing. Angelina is furious and fires her order at the waitress.] Another gin and tonic, please!

Nick: Another Gin Mary.

Jim: White Label and soda with a twist.

[The waitress smiles and leaves.]

Jim [staring at the waitress as she leaves]: Boy, is she good-looking.

Nick [laughing]: Jim, remember, you're a theologian.

Jim [also laughing]: To hell with that. That's pretty much what happens to theology in the end. It goes to hell. . . . Some minister or priest talking about sex when he doesn't know anything about it. Religion is the mouse breath of the world! To hell with religion! [reflecting] Where was I?

Angelina [bored]: Who cares?

Jim [smiling]: You're right, Angelina. . . . Who cares?

Angelina [groaning]: God, why didn't I play an extra set of tennis instead of listening to this!!!

Jim [sarcastically]: Why don't you go play that extra set of tennis? It'll be good for you. It will continue to numb your social conscience.

Angelina [smoldering in rage]: God, what an arrogant bastard you are!

Jim [smiling serenely]: We have a lot in common! Maybe we should get to know each other better. [Angelina frowns. The waitress appears, serves the drinks, and leaves. Jim stares at her as she leaves. All take a sip of their drinks. Jim and Angelina glare at each other. Nick is somewhat uncomfortable.]

Nick: Ah, Jim, c'mon tell us about the "wilderness state." What is "the wilderness state"?

Jim [affably]: Oh, it's very simple. It's as old as Moses. You know, Moses has freed his people from their slavery to Pharaoh. "Go down, Moses. . . . Let my people go." . . . and all of that. [addressing Angelina and baiting her] I'm sure you sing that hymn in church, Angelina.

Angelina [annoyed]: I don't go to church. Just get to the point.

Jim [needling]: Maybe we should play tennis some time.

Angelina [furious]: Just get to the point!

Jim [laughing]: Okay. It goes this way. Moses has freed his people. Moses and the people are out in the wilderness. Moses goes to the top of Mount Sinai trying to find out what to do with his people now that they are free. And what happens? Moses comes down from the mountain and the people are worshiping a calf of gold and having an orgy! That's what we're doing today! That's where we are today! We're in the wilderness! That's where we are!

Nick [laughing]: That's about it.

Angelina [furious]: That's terrible! You're terrible! Both of you! I have never heard such cynicism.

Nick [good-naturedly]: Oh, c'mon Angelina. You know Jim is

right. You know he is.

Angelina [raging]: He's not right. He's not right at all! Look at the rights and privileges people enjoy in this country! Look at our freedom!

Nick [with quiet irritation]: The rights, privileges and freedom that SOME of those with money have in this country. Yes . . . but we still have slums . . .

Angelina [annoyed]: Why do you say such depressing things?

Nick [quietly]: Because they're true.

Jim [intensely]: That's just the point. We fought a war with England to be free of a Pharaoh's tyranny. Then we became Pharaohs! We killed the Indians! We enslaved the Africans! We spilled blood all over the land in our Civil War to try to become free again. But where are we today? We're in the wilderness worshiping money and sex! That's all we're doing! We're worshiping money and sex and wandering aimlessly across the wasteland of time. And we'll continue to wander until some higher, spiritual purpose is made our own!!! [There is a long silence. Jim takes a sip from his drink.]

Angelina [uneasily]: Well, I think this is a great country, nonetheless. Look at "We Are the World" concert and "Hands Across America" for the homeless! We are a caring people!

Jim [vehemently]: It's not what the country is: it's what the country could become! Certainly it is one of the richest countries in the world, but what is the purpose of our wealth? As Christ says, "To whom much is given, much is required!" More is required than a rock concert for the great evils that confront us! More is required than a guilt-ridden people holding hands in some paltry token gesture! More is required, and more will always be required! There must be a higher purpose for us all!!!

Angelina [perplexed]: Must there always be a purpose for everything?

Jim [quietly]: You know there must be. Otherwise this world is absolutely senseless. Look at Monte! Look at Malcolm! Is that all there is? My, God, if that's all there is, then we are nothing more than animals gratifying ourselves until the undertaker comes. It just can't be that way! It just can't be!

Nick [quietly]: It is an affront to our dignity.

Jim [vehemently]: It is!

Angelina [quietly]: But what is to be done?

Jim [vehemently]: The principles of the United States Constitution are founded upon enlightened reason. Yet how "enlightened" are we today? We place our natural gifts and intellectual talents in the ground. We build hydrogen weapons and bury them! We bury our talents in the ground!!! That's what we do!!! We have enough resources to blow up the world or feed the world, but what do we do? We grin and make our money as if nothing was happening. [There is a silence.]

Angelina [sighing]: This is all getting too heavy.

Jim [indifferently]: Whether it be heavy or light, the truth remains. This nation was founded upon a revolution. Part of that revolution pertained to taxation and representation. The Boston Tea Party was a gesture against the English policy of taking money from the American people and giving them nothing in return. Think of your life! How much do you pay in taxes each year?

Angelina: I don't know. About thirty-three percent per year.

Jim: So, thirty-three percent of your working time on earth goes to the government.

Angelina: Yes.

Jim: Let us say that someone works forty-five years. Fifteen years of your life goes to the government. For what? For hydrogen weapons? For a fourth-rate medical system? For fear and trembling about what will become of you when you are too old to work? For a country that ranks thirteenth in the world for how it treats it senior citizens – thirteenth when it has the resources to be first! For homeless souls? For poverty? For slums? No! It's all wrong! Where are the long-lasting state and federal programs to overcome such evils? Where is the spirit of The Boston Tea Party? What happened to it? [raging] LET THE AMERICAN REVOLUTION CONTINUE! IT IS OUR ONLY HOPE! LET THE REVOLUTION CONTINUE! IT IS NOT OVER YET! [There is a long silence.]

Nick [smiling]: Indeed, let it continue.

Jim [wildly]: How are the people of the slums to be represented if big business buys the congress and the presidency? How are the poor to have a voice if money buys power? Do you realize that Abe Lincoln's entire campaign fund for election to the U.S. Senate was only $500! Today, to run for the U.S. Senate, you should have $20 million! How is there to be any social progress if the taxpayer does not demand that his or her tax dollars are there to create a better world? My God, we're wandering in a desert of human stupidity and greed!

Angelina [quietly]: Are you saying that we need another Moses?

Jim [sternly]: No. I am saying that we need the God of Moses to cleanse ourselves of our selfishness. That's what I am saying. We need the vision of a higher kingdom than any kingdom on earth to drive us to the full and charitable use of our talents. We need to remember the story of Dives.

Angelina: Dives?

Jim [smiling]: Sure, Dives. Nick, you'll like this. They once asked John Calvin why evil people prosper financially. Calvin was not the normal Bible-belter trying to make a big buck with TV evangelism. Calvin was a humanist scholar and a lawyer before he became a theologian. His reforms in Geneva made it more or less the banking capital it is today. Anyway, when they asked Calvin why evil people prospered and the poor were broken, his answer was quite simple. He said, "God is fattening the evil ones for the kill." [Jim takes a sip of his drink.] That's my opinion. Fatten them, and then kill them.

Angelina [Aghast, she stands up.]: I can't take anymore of this! I simply can't! Mr. McClain, you are the most depressing, the most offensive, the most arrogant, and the most vicious man that I have ever met! I don't know how your wife can be married to you. I don't know, and since it's none of my business, I don't care. But I'll have you know that this is the greatest country in the world! This is the land of opportunity! This is the land where you can be anything you want! Do you hear me! You can be anything you want! I'll not sit here and have you degrade this country! Good-bye, Mr. McClain. Good-bye, Nick. Please call me when you're back in San Francisco. [She grabs her purse and hurriedly exits before either Jim or Nick can say anything. Nick looks at Jim. Jim raises his eyebrows and frowns.]

Nick [smiling]: Don't mind her too much. She's still in her YUPPIE stage. Monte used to tell me the same things about "the land of opportunity" and "You can be whatever you want" when I was going bankrupt. [laughing] Somehow there were certain flaws in her argument. It's amazing that Angelina runs to the same argument.

Jim [frowning]: The argument of "the land of opportunity" and "You can be whatever you want" is just a drug to keep us from facing our real social problems. I dare say that someone born in the slums will have a different set of opportunities than someone born in Beverly Hills. [calling offstage] Waitress . . . [The waitress appears] Another round for Nick and me. [She exits. Jim lights a cigarette.] Well, Nick. I guess it's like the Bible says, "Only a remnant will remain." I guess that's us, Nick. We're the remnant. Not much of a remnant, but a remnant nonetheless. [laughing] "Many are called, but few are chosen!" [sarcastically] I guess when we talk about a social conscience in modern America we would have to say,

"Many are cold, but most are frozen!" [Nick and Jim laugh. The drinks are brought. The waitress exits.] Well, anyway, Calvin was quite a guy. Part of his stipend was two-hundred gallons of wine when he taught in Geneva. It's funny that the prohibitionists tried to claim Calvin as one of their allies. Anyway, a toast to John Calvin! [They clink glasses and take a sip.] Well, Nick, the truth of the matter is that we're all too precious. Everyone's earning money, raising their precious little cute-ems, buying houses, and dying. "All the rivers run into the sea, but the sea is not yet full." [Jim takes a sip from his drink and yawns.] Yep, it's a real mess. Well, anyway, I hope Angelina has a good tennis game and gets some sun. She seems like a nice woman, spoiled but nice. I bet she's good in the courtroom. Maybe I'll take her to lunch when I get back to San Francisco. [laughing] I'll tell her the whole story about Dives.

Nick [good-naturedly]: My God, you're as fearless as ever! It would probably be best if you left her alone. I really don't see the arrows of desire striking your and her hearts.

Jim [laughing and drinking]: You've got that right. Anyway, where was I?

Nick [interested]: You were talking about the Dives and Calvin. When I was in college everyone made a great deal of fun of Calvinism. You know, the sexual revolution was starting up and everyone loved to attack Puritanism. You know.

Jim [good-naturedly]: Sure, I know. Free'em all and let them worship money and sex. That's a mighty poor revolution. Anyway, Dives had his money. Dives ate like a pig. Lazarus, a beggar, asked for something to eat, but Lazarus was scorned and laughed at by Dives. Dives further taunted Lazarus by throwing food to the dogs. Dives was sort of like a slum lord or a country which does not take care of its poor. Lazarus went to heaven and peace. Dives went to hell with all its torments. I'm sure you have heard the story.

Nick [thoughtfully]: Yes. I've heard it. It is one of Christ's parables.

Jim: Yes, indeed. Jesus ends the parable with Dives asking that someone from the dead come and speak to those still living about the torments of hell. Dives hoped that someone from the dead might make people change their evil ways. Jesus says that the living have Moses and the prophets. If the living will not pay attention to Moses and the prophets, bringing someone back from the dead will do no good at all.

Nick [quietly]: Jim, do you believe that there is a hell?

Jim [sternly]: Whether there is a hell or not, I do not know. But from what I have seen of human indifference to human suffering, there ought to be a hell.

[Both men look at each other and lower their eyes as the lights fall.]

THOMAS THE SKEPTIC

CHARACTERS

THE BEAST-MAN
THOMAS

[The time is the evening on which Jesus Christ reportedly first appeared to ten of the remaining apostles after His resurrection. According to The Gospel of John (20:19-29), Thomas was absent from this occurrence. When the other apostles told him of Jesus' appearing to them, Thomas doubted their words.
The place is a tavern owned by a man once called "The Beast-Man of the Caves." Regardless of the overall shabbiness of the setting, the owner has made every effort to improve the place. Torn but bright colored tapestries hang on the walls. Bottles of varied colors, shapes, and sizes can be seen on the shelves in the background. Each of the two tables has a candle burning on it. As the conversation begins, Thomas is seen sitting at the center table staring at a glass of wine.]

The Beast-Man: The wine is not very good. Especially for someone who has climbed the hill to this lonely place. I paid too much for the whole cask. It will be vinegar in another week. Maybe you would like to try something else.

Thomas [in a monotone voice, like a man talking to himself in a dream]: No . . . I mean yes. Yes it will turn to vinegar soon, like everything else. [He gulps down the whole glass.]

The Beast-Man: Actually some good stuff came in from the north country. Here, try this. [He refills Thomas's glass.]

Thomas [draining the second glass in a single gulp]: Not bad. I'll buy the whole bottle. [As soon as the bottle is set on the table Thomas pours another glass and drinks it immediately. He then covers his mouth and runs offstage. Sounds of retching can be heard. After a few seconds, Thomas returns.] I made a mess of things out there. Let me pay you something for your trouble.

The Beast-Man: That's all right. There's some water in the back. I'll . . .

Thomas: I'll take care of it. [He exits immediately. A few seconds pass and he returns.] It's been taken care of. I'm really sorry.

The Beast-Man [laughing]: That's all right. At least you left the room in the first place. The Roman soldiers just vomit right on the table. When they get drunk and arrogant, they wouldn't move to please Caesar himself.

Thomas: Well, I don't want to have anything in common with Roman soldiers.

The Beast-Man [smiling]: I wouldn't give a glass of vinegar for a whole legion myself.

Thomas [wild-eyed]: Do you know what those bastards did last week?

The Beast-Man: You mean the crucifixion of Jesus of Nazareth.

Thomas: Yes, that's what I mean.

The Beast-Man [somberly]: That was not the first crucifixion that I have witnessed. They did the same thing long ago to my father. I do not see how anyone bears the torture.

Thomas: What had your father done?

The Beast-Man: My father was a madman, at least that's how I remember him. He used to import wood from the north country for wine casks. One day he made a deal with the Romans. They told him they wanted to export Judean wine to Rome for Caesar's throat. They paid him well. I think at first my father was just a simple man who had to make money like anyone else. He sold them the wood. The next day he watched the Romans crucify five men on the same wood. Something happened to him after that day. He began drinking all the time and wouldn't work. He sat at home and used to stare into his wine glass the way you were doing a little while ago. He vomited a lot too.

Thomas: How old were you then?

The Beast-Man: I must have been five or six. I can't really remember. I only remember my mother crying a lot and fearing for our lives. You see, my father would get so drunk that he would wander out into the streets at night and scream about Caesar's throat. Then he would mumble something about red wine and Caesar's blood and the blood on the wood of those five crucified men. It was always confusing and horrible. At first the townspeople tried to quiet him down. Finally, they grew afraid to be seen with him. Then the soldiers came and took him away. He was in prison for a while. They said he turned into an animal in prison. He would sit in the corner and hiss at the guards and throw his food at them. In the end, they crucified him.

Thomas [intently]: And your mother, what happened to your mother?

The Beast-Man: She went to see him on his cross. Two days after his death, she hanged herself. I became a slave of the Romans trained to serve my father's executioners and those who indirectly caused my mother's suicide. At the Roman military school designed for the patrician sons of the elite. I was forced to bring meat and drink to the young aristocrats. Whenever I had time, I watched the young boys use the sword and the shield in their training for death. Death – that was the thing – whether on the cross, at the end of a rope, or on the battlefield – that was the thing.

Thomas [returning to his own thoughts]: Yes, that is THE THING.

The Beast-Man: Times change but THE THING was always there. When I was about twelve years old, the Romans transferred me to view THE THING anew. I became a grave digger for those who had been crucified. Mangled body after mangled body was laid to rest with these hands. I worked with an old man who saw his task as just one more insult in the darkness. He too raged at the Romans, but he raged quietly and inwardly. He also raged about THE THING ITSELF saying that he and I knew something which all turn away from yet something finally true – that there is only darkness and nothing more.

Thomas: I once believed there was something else, but He was crucified and buried also.

The Beast-Man: You mean Jesus of Nazareth.

Thomas [pouring another glass of wine]: Yes, that is who I mean.

The Beast-Man: He is someone death will not conquer.

Thomas: I once believed that, but He is dead. You've been a gravedigger for the crucified ones. You know what the Romans can do to a human body. They did it to Him.

The Beast-Man [staring at Thomas]: I know I've seen you before.

Thomas [staring at his untouched glass of wine]: I probably remind you of your father.

The Beast-Man: No, you are one of the twelve, are you not?

Thomas: I <u>was</u> one of the twelve. I think there are ten left. Judas who betrayed Him, hanged himself. I left. [staring at the glass of wine.] Yes, without me there are ten left.

The Beast-Man: What are the other ten doing now?

Thomas [nervously]: They are either going mad or are already mad. The last time, this evening in fact, I met with them. They say Jesus has appeared to them. They are like hysterical, superstitious women who see a ghost in every darkened corner. [He takes a gulp of wine.]

The Beast-Man [watching him intently]: Perhaps you had best eat something. Here, I'll get . . .

Thomas: Don't bother, please. My stomach couldn't take it. I am not used to drinking, and food on top of everything else would only make me more sick.

The Beast-Man: All right, but let me tell you where I first saw you. There is great risk in my telling you, yet you should know, you must know.

Thomas [half-interested]: Why is that?

The Beast-Man: Because it concerns Jesus of Nazareth.

Thomas: Then please go on.

The Beast-Man: I was telling you that I was a gravedigger.

Thomas: Yes.

The Beast-Man: One day a Roman soldier came to the cemetery looking for an assistant.

Thomas: An assistant?

The Beast-Man: Yes . . . someone to assist at the crucifixions. Someone to "help" in the torture rooms, nailing the hands to the crosses, and placing the crosses in the ground. He promised me more money and all sorts of things.

Thomas: And what did you say?

The Beast-Man: Nothing.

Thomas: Nothing?

The Beast-Man: Yes, I said nothing. But I grabbed a pick and drove the sharp end through the left side of his forehead. At first the pick stayed stuck in his head and blood began to spray in every direction. He gave a horrible cry and fell to the ground. As he fell, the pick was dislodged. Blood poured out like a river all over his face and body. I saw what I had done, let out with a cry more horrible than his, and then I began to run. I ran it seemed for days though it was probably a few hours, and then I collapsed.

Thomas [staring intently at him]: You killed a Roman soldier, and yet you're alive . . . that's impossible.

The Beast-Man: Let us say that I wished I was dead when I awakened. Fear drove me to the high country near the region of the Gerasenes.*

Thomas [surprised]: The Gerasenes . . . no, it couldn't be. You couldn't have been there. Did you know "The Beast-Man" . . . Yes, that's what they called him – "The Beast-Man of the Caves"?

The Beast-Man: I was he.

Thomas [staring intently at his face]: No . . . it is not possible. I was with Jesus the day the Beast-Man was brought back to his right mind. He didn't look like you.

The Beast-Man [quietly]: I was the Beast-Man of the caves. Neither my hair nor my beard had been cut since the pick was driven into that Roman soldier's forehead. It was ten years' time between my killing that torturer and my meeting Jesus of Nazareth. Ten years in which I lived with the real torturer: myself.

Thomas: But you don't look that old.

The Beast-Man: Remember I killed the killer when I was fifteen. I am now twenty-seven. Two years have passed since my meeting your Master and mine.

Thomas: I am afraid that He is our dead Master.

---

* Mark 5:3. Luke 8:26.

The Beast-Man [vehemently]: It cannot be!

Thomas [sadly]: It is.

The Beast-Man: It is not. I believe He lives. I will tell you why. For ten years I hid and wandered alone in the caves of the Gerasenes. After a short time, no one would or could come near me. At the beginning, the swineherders thought I was just another holy man seeking solitude. [laughing mildly] Me! Holy! What a misunderstanding! In truth, I was at first so afraid of the Romans and their crucifying me that I was fearful of seeing anyone. [looking at Thomas] Have you ever faced your own possible tortured death alone?

Thomas: Only once, when Jesus said He was going to Jerusalem to be crucified and die. I knew what the religious authorities would do if He went to Jerusalem. Oh, I was brave then. The other apostles were confused and afraid, but I said to them, "Let us also go, that we may die with him."* I said this before I saw the mob's torches, swords, and spears in the garden at Gethsemane.** Then I ran away with all the others. [He drinks in a single gulp his glass of wine.]

The Beast-Man: Well, then perhaps you understand. I also ran, but where or to whom or to what was I to run?

Thomas [pouring another glass of wine]: I feel the same at this very moment.

The Beast-Man: I will tell you what I did. I ran from myself, and yet I ran up against myself. A ten year running to and from myself, that's what it was! I ran from my fear of death, but death was in me. Wherever men were, there was also certain death. The caves -- that is the place for hiding. The caves of the Gerasenes are winding and inviting much like the inward imaginings of all of us. A person can hide there just as a person in the world can hide from the fact of his own

---

* John 11:16
** John 18:1. Matthew 26:36.

certain death.

Thomas [vengefully]: The world – that is something worth hiding from! The world, the religious authorities, the Romans, the indignant and hostile mob which screams: "GIVE US BARABBAS!"* The world which honors the bandit and strives to destroy the good. Why, the world will always say "GIVE US BARABBAS THE BANDIT!" And the world will devour those who strive for The Light which is true, bright, and humane. The world did it last week: it did it to the prophets and wise men, and it will do it again.** If the world could only be buried we could write on its tombstone: "GIVE US BARABBAS THE BANDIT!" That alone would say enough for the earth's wretched lands, skies, seas, and hordes of murderers!

The Beast-Man [smiling]: You sound like a man who knows the caves of the Gerasenes.

Thomas [drinking another glass of wine]: All that I know is that this world is not worth tolerating much longer.

The Beast-Man: Then you are a man of the caves. You've come to understand the absurdity of being born simply to feed and to breed and then, like some over-bloated slug, to die.

Thomas [irritated]: I understood that long ago. Why do you think I wandered like a vagabond all over the countryside with Jesus of Nazareth? That man was The Truth: He was from God; He was . . .

The Beast-Man [also becoming irritated]: He was, according to you, just another man who died.

Thomas [still irritated]: I didn't say He was just another man who died. I said He was dead and that's that.

The Beast-Man [becoming irate]: Well, if he died and that's that, then He's just another man as far as I'm concerned.

---

* Matthew 27:15-23.
** Matthew 23:29-36.

Thomas [also becoming irate]: Look, He was not just another man [Thomas reaches for the wine bottle, holds it up to the light and sees that it is empty.] The wine's gone. Bring me another bottle.

The Beast-Man [smiling sarcastically]: Are you sure you're up to it?

Thomas [sullenly]: Just bring me another bottle. [The Beast-Man brings a bottle with another glass. He sits down. The angle should be such that he can see Thomas, and the audience can see both of them.]

The Beast-Man [filling Thomas's glass]: Here, this is a gift from "The Beast-Man of the Caves."

Thomas [very irritated]: Look, I'll pay for it.

The Beast-Man [sternly]: I said it's on me. [smiling] Besides, I intended to drink some myself.

Thomas [indifferently]: Whatever you want. [The Beast-Man fills his own glass to the brim. Thomas drinks half of the glass previously poured for him and then sets it down. Thomas speaks matter of factly.] Now, where were we?

The Beast-Man [indifferently]: I don't know, and I don't care. [after a few sips of wine] I was telling you about the caves.

Thomas [indifferently]: Yes, go on.

The Beast-Man: In a sense I really liked the caves of the Gerasenes.

Thomas: You what?

The Beast-Man: Well, think about what you just said about the world and the world's viciousness. The world tears down, maims, and crucifies whomever and whatever it can. The brighter the light, the more the darkness of the world tries to overcome it.

Thomas [sadly]: True, very true.

The Beast-Man: And the caves, well the caves were a type of freedom from the world. No demands, no worries, no authorities to obey, no annoying humans with their paltry problems . . . just one's self screaming wild words and the silence after the caves stopped echoing the screams. Although I screamed and howled alone for ten years, it was not always unpleasant.

Thomas [drinking]: I'm starting to howl and scream inwardly myself and . . . for me, it is anything but pleasant.

The Beast-Man: You are new to your inward caves. Wait a while. At first I was so frightened and terrified that I was sure I would destroy myself simply to get some type of relief from my fear and terror. But gradually, after months of my mind racing backward and forward from thought to thought and from alternative to alternative, a new image of myself came to me. Was I at fault for my father's going mad, being crucified and my mother hanging herself? NO! Did I do wrong when I was solicited by a professional Roman torturer and murderer to kill him? NO! There was no forethought in the matter. Impulsively I had simply killed one of my father's murderers. Further, I had killed part of the slave-driving monster known as the Roman army. Perhaps I had done a just deed. Perhaps a noble deed. At least these hands would not add to the history of human torture. If I had disobeyed the Roman soldier and refused his offer, certainly he would have tortured and crucified me. Yes, eventually a new image of my self was presented – an image of which I was proud. With this pride came a new sort of strength, a strength which was not completely good and not completely evil. I began to feel that I was above the human race. I did not need other humans. I ate very little. There were enough fresh springs for water in the hill country I could find honey and wild grain to eat. But when I say that I did not need other humans, I should also say that I secretly still feared the Romans and what they would do to me. I resolved not to cut my hair and beard. Then no one would know who I was. This fear coupled with the pride of my own self image kept me away from everyone for ten years.

Thomas: To hear you tell it, you really had no need of Jesus in the first place. I remember you quite differently. I remember you as a man-beast howling at the entrance of your cave. No one could approach you, give you anything, or in any way help. If you were so pleased with your self image, why did you display such an outward show of madness? You would throw offered food at the giver. You even threw food, sticks, and rocks at Jesus Himself. Why didn't you simply hide in the cave when we were in the region of the Gerasenes?

The Beast-Man: I will tell you why. I grew arrogantly proud of my ability to live apart from the world. I had convinced myself that I could live without the wretched creature comforts which most people burn up their lives to acquire. I didn't need the animal warmth of the herd which flocks together like cattle waiting for the slaughterer's axe. I had seen death. I had buried the dead. I would howl at the entrance of my cave. "Kill me if you dare!" No one came near me! Once I was so wild that I manacled my own hands with two bracelets and a chain I had found in the hill country. Standing before my caves, I shouted at the swine herders passing by. "Look what I do to the bondage of this world!" I then smashed and smashed the chain with a rock until it broke. I saw my hands filled with blood and gore, but it seemed to make little difference to the pig keepers. They knew I was mad. They simply waited until the chain broke. Some shrugged. Some felt sorry for me. Some laughed.

    It was at that time that a horrible conflict came forth in me. I watched the herdsmen walk away. I said to myself, "Where can they be going?" and I knew all too well. They were going home to their wives, their children, their suppers, and I was going back to my caves. At first I laughed hysterically. I was justified to myself I had overcome this world. They would slop hogs in the morning. I would rejoice in my pride in the morning. I was superior, and that was all. Yet that evening, alone in the darkness, I gazed out at the star-strewn sky, and for once I thought of the future. I would have my self-image, my caves, and nothing else. I also thought of the herdsmen before the fire with their wives, children, and hot food.

Now the real conflict began. I could not give up my thoughts of so many years which had in a sense justified me. I had become superior. I had really overcome the world. But what was left? Every normal human need had been rooted out of me, or so I thought. But human needs appeared again and again. Hermits call such needs "temptations." I can only call them human needs. Yet this need to be justified for being born without my consent, for seeing my mother and father destroyed, for being forced to dig graves, for living ten years as a beast – that need of justification was always there to mock any normal and accepted human needs.

I had once heard that when armies are in a long and vicious war, both sides are almost destroyed, and every battlefield is a scene in hell. My inward conflict was like such a war. The superhuman need of justification battling the genuine normal human needs were the armies at war. I was the battlefield or hell itself. Each combatant in the war also became horribly distorted. When isolation and loneliness began to succeed, I told myself I was a "god" capable of bearing any suffering. When my image of myself as a justified god began to succeed, I would ask myself what good that was since I was an isolated god unable to change anything in the world. I would then envy the lives of the pigs themselves. They were at least unconscious of such conflicts. So I was a "god" envying swine. That's how confused I became. The conflict went on with horrible distortions, images, howlings, and ravings all in solitary, self-imposed isolation.

Finally Jesus of Nazareth came to the caves. By then I did not want to hear another word or see another human face. I was sure I would scream myself to death for being human and wanting to be God.

Thomas [sadly]: Perhaps what you are saying first attracted me to Jesus of Nazareth. Perhaps in your caves you have discovered what is in all of us. So many crowds followed that man. He was able to bring to light the deepest human desires. He was able to overcome this world, to overcome death's fear, and He was still able to do so much good for His time on earth. You mentioned your overpowering desire for justification: justification for being born without one's consent. While He lived, I believed that somehow in the end He would justify our lives and make all things possible. Now that He is dead, everything seems hopeless and impossible.

The Beast-Man: Then you believed in Him for only as long as you could actually see Him. That is quite unfair.

Thomas [annoyed]: What is unfair about it?

The Beast-Man: What is unfair about it is that you wish to disregard the generations which will come. The generations which will also seek justification! Sure, you live in Galilee for a period of years. You meet a person like no other. One who can work miracles, draw crowds to Himself, overcome established legalistic religious traditions by Himself. One who could even draw a skeptic like yourself to follow Him. Well, what can I say, is it only you? You who happened to be "fortunate" enough to be in a particular place at a particular time. You say that the man was from God. What does that mean? Is God "fate" or "fortune" or something else that smiles on you for a while until the dice are thrown again, and then you are in misery? What do you mean when you say Jesus of Nazareth was from God?

Thomas [drinking]: I don't know what I mean. I suppose what I mean is that whatever was high, true, good, right and powerful was in Jesus of Nazareth including the justification for our being born without our consent.

The Beast-Man: So then fate or fortune or chance is not your God.

Thomas: Fortune is either good or bad. Fate justifies no one. Chance gives nothing of itself. Fortune does not sacrifice itself. No, neither fortune nor fate nor chance is God. I suppose fortune or fate or chance is just another human imagining which gives an untrustworthy and indefinite hope to desperate human beings.

The Beast-Man: Yet you imply that you were "fortunate"

enough to meet Jesus of Nazareth, feel justified for a time, and now that Jesus has been "unfortunate" enough to die, you are in despair. Think of what you are saying. If you say that He was from God then you yourself have defined God. You say that God justifies human life: you say that God gives of Himself: you say that God will sacrifice Himself for desperate human beings. In short, you say that God is like Jesus of Nazareth.

Thomas [quietly]: Yes. God is like Him.

The Beast-Man: And luck or fate or fortune is not God.

Thomas: No.

The Beast-Man: Then do you not somehow feel that Jesus had some purpose in asking you to be His apostle? We agree that it was not a chance occurrence that happened to pick you.

Thomas: He instructed me and the other eleven to aid Him in bringing forth God's kingdom. We all thought we knew what that meant. Now I'm not so sure.

The Beast-Man: Well, I know what it means. It means that a powerful Light has come into this world. A Light that has and will overcome the darkness of confusion, conflict, and death. Perhaps I believe more in this Light than you because I was so long in the caves.

Thomas [listening intently]: Perhaps.

The Beast-Man: Do you remember the evening you landed the boat on the beach near the region of the Gerasenes?

Thomas: I vaguely remember it.

The Beast-Man: I looked down upon your group and laughed. I yelled down at Jesus from my high country, "It's the prince of fools with his band of clowns!" I don't know why I said it. I just wanted to challenge anyone who lived beyond my caves. I hated everyone and loved to sneer at the world. Then I watched Jesus talk to some swineherders about me. I could see them shake their heads and point at me. Then Jesus began to climb the rocky path to the caves. One of the pig watchers tried to hold Him back with warnings. Jesus simply smiled at him and kept climbing the rocky path.

Thomas: I remember now. We were all afraid for His life. When He got to your cave we saw rocks, sticks, and pieces of food come careening down the face of the cliffs. At the same time we heard your insane and bestial howling echo in the caves. The howling lasted a short time, and then there was an unbearable silence.

The Beast-Man: What happened was that He let me throw things at Him and howl until I was exhausted. In fact, I could barely lift my arms. My voice after a short time could only make a hoarse rasping sound. It's amazing what noises humans can make for a short time. But then their energy is spent and there is a type of peaceful exhaustion. He let me yell until I could yell no more, then I broke down and started crying. Why that was I do not know. Perhaps I was only glad to have a human being visit me. Perhaps it was total emotional exhaustion. I do not know. He waited until the crying stopped. He then asked me if I wanted Him to leave. Again, why He asked me such a question I don't know. Perhaps it was to give me back my dignity; perhaps it was just His way. I said nothing, and He stayed.

Thomas: It was His way. I mean He usually let someone respond before He acted. I believe He greatly loved the freedom of everyone. Many people told Him to leave and He did so. But sometimes He stayed regardless of what they said.

The Beast-Man [not listening but remembering]: Something in me told Him to go, and yet I fought that response in myself. I told Him to go and then immediately I told him to stay. At this time He said to me, "I know that you are a man split in two. All that you have is the type of freedom of a madman: a wild, uncompromising assertion of the sufferings you have had to bear. For this, I have compassion for you. What you are is not unknown to me or to the One who sent Me. But I have chosen you and your suffering to manifest real freedom to this world, a freedom quite contrary to that of a madman." To this I wanted to respond, "And who sent you, and who are you?" but something stopped me . . . I seemed to inwardly know Who sent Him and Who He was. He continued to speak, "I said you are a man split in two. You love your life in the cave because it secures for yourself your image of yourself. You see yourself as one who is 'god.' No one can attack you or your image here. You are safe in the wondrous image of yourself. Yet at the same time you hate this cave. Your very nature cries out against it. The reason is you love freedom too much to see your own share of freedom wasted year after year. You know that if you remain here you will never change another human being's life. You will do no good for another. Your place in the world will be no different than the huge proud rocks which surround your cave."

At this point I began to rage. "If you are the Son of God, and that is Who I think you are, what would you have me do? Would you have me go back down amongst wretched and murderous humans who would kill me? I am not like you. People seek my death! Romans seek my death!"

Hearing this, He quietly and mournfully said, "Soon they will seek my life also. And although I am afraid like you are, I know there is a higher and truer Power than the powers of this world. It is faith in that Power which will give me courage when my time has come."

If He had not said this I would have not listened to Him any longer. I then said, "Tell me of this power." He responded, "If I told you, you would not believe. But do this: come down from this cave with me and I will show you throughout your life Who that Power is. Believe in me and you will know Who the Power is, and, very soon, you will fear no more." To this I said. "And what if I die?"

He said, "Follow me. I am to die for you and for everyone. After it is proven through me that the Power of God cannot die, you will not fear anything. You will know that you cannot die."

Puzzled, confused, doubting but trying to understand Him, I said, "I will try to come down the mountain with you. I am afraid, but I am horribly tired of life among the caves. But please have pity on me as we descend. I do not want to leave here, but I must." Saying nothing, He walked outside the cave. I tried to look back at my darkened home but could not. We walked to the ridge in front of the caves and a dense fog had covered the mountain. I said, "Perhaps we should wait until morning."

He responded, "No. Follow me. Have courage." We descended the mountain. Earth and rocks fell out from under our feet. When I doubted, although I said nothing, He would say, "Believe! Have courage!" Several times I thought I would slide down the mountain and be mangled, but always the words resounded. "Believe! Have courage!" In the dense fog it took us a long time to descend the mountain. I never thought we would make it. At the bottom, I was exhausted. The swineherders and you with the other disciples were waiting for us. I sat down ever so quietly. All of you thought I was in my right mind. I think I was, but I was also so extremely confused, tired and at peace.

[A few seconds of silence pass. Thomas, not knowing what to do, looks at the Beast-Man cautiously.]

Thomas: Do you have any more wine?

The Beast-Man [as though waking from a dream]: Of course. [He goes into the back, and Thomas stares at his own glass.] Here we are. The best I have in memory of the best thing that ever happened to me. [The Beast-Man pours Thomas's glass full until it overflows. The Beast-Man laughs.] Sorry, but that's what happens with good memories. Good memories overflow whenever you have them.

Thomas [For the first time, he laughs.]: I know. He was the Good!

The Beast-Man [filling his own glass until it overflows]: He certainly was!

[They both drink a full glass. The glasses are refilled and remain on the table.]

Thomas: What did you do after that?

The Beast-Man: After an evening's rest, a rest and peace which was like nothing I had known before, I asked Him if I could follow Him as the other disciples did. His response was, "These men have much to learn. They must learn things you yourself know. You will follow me long after I have gone to my Father, because I will be with you. Go now and tell others what I have done for you. You do not need my physical presence as these men now do. From your sufferings, you have learned faith. You know that can and will be with you always!" I believe He understood that I again wanted to be among people. Immediately that day I spoke to many of the swineherders. At first they were afraid of me, but soon, from a distance, they listened. As you will remember, they asked Him to depart from their lands. He did as they asked. But I was left to talk to them about Him. From there I went to the neighboring towns and spoke of Jesus, The Son and Light of God. Although some laughed at me, although some threatened me, and although some ignored me: a few listened. Now and then I meet those who listened and we rejoice in the Good that God has given us. [Pushing his wine glass away.] I had heard that they have crucified Him, but I do not believe that they have killed Him.

Thomas: Oh, that I were you!!!!

The Beast-Man: Your doubt and suffering has brought you to the inward caves. If I were you, I would go back and seek the few who listened.

Thomas [rising]: I had best go. Morning grows near and the fog has set in. It is a difficult way down the hill.

The Beast-Man [blowing out one of the two candles]: I will go part way with you. [Now only one candle is burning on the center table. The Beast-Man smiles gently.] As has been said to me, "Believe . . . have courage . . . " [The final candle is extinguished by the Beast-Man.]

SOREN KIERKEGAARD

CHARACTERS

PROFESSOR
CONSTANTINE CONSTANTIUS
SOREN KIERKEGAARD'S FATHER
SOREN KIERKEGAARD
MANASSEH
SIMON
SEA CAPTAIN
GENTLEMAN
MARGARET
SONJA
ERIK
NEBUCHADNEZZAR
2 SERVANTS

PROLOGUE

[A churchyard located somewhere in the reflective imagination. The entire background of the stage is presented in black and grays. The tombstones are at all angles. The cemetery is unkempt and in a very deteriorated condition. A professor, approximately 55 years old, is seen walking about and attempting to read the tombstones. He is not able to find what he seeks and becomes frustrated. Constantine Constantius* enters with a book under his arm. Unseen by the professor, Constantine, approximately 25 years old, watches him until the professor sees him.]

Professor: The cemetery seems unused.

Constantine Constantius [ironically]: Look again.

Professor: I mean it doesn't seem as if anyone is maintaining the graves.

Constantine Constantius: One of the few signs of wisdom of those still living.

Professor: That's rather disrespectful.

Constantine Constantius: I'm sure the inhabitants will forgive us. [brief pause]

Professor: You wouldn't be able to show me the grave of Soren Kierkegaard would you?

---

* One of Kierkegaard's pseudonyms. Soren Kirekegaard, <u>Repetition</u>, trans. with intro. and notes by Walter Lowrie, Harper and Row, 1941.

Constantine Constantius: You merely have to go to a library. I suggest you look under "K" and forget about the commentaries, anthologies, and all the rest.

Professor: No, what I meant was the actual place where his body was buried.

Constantine Constantius: But that isn't Soren Kierkegaard.

Professor: You know what I mean.

Constantine Constantius: I'm sorry, but we are not speaking about the same person. [brief silence. The professor becomes impatient.]

Professor: Look, I have only a short time. After this I must go to Germany and visit the grave of Nietzsche, and then to Rome to visit the grave of Shelley, and then . . .

Constantine Constantius [interrupting him]: You're something of a demoniac, aren't you?

Professor: I resent that . . . [He is not sure that he has been insulted.] . . . What do you mean?

Constantine Constantius: You seem to be gnashing your thoughts about the graves of the illustrious dead.

Professor [with dignity]: Young man, I'll have you know that I am not a demoniac at all. . . . Why, I'm a professor of systematic, dogmatic, historical, philosophical, and Biblical theology.

Constantine Constantius: Who romps around tombstones.

Professor [pontificating]: I resent that. I really do. I am simply taking my vacation between my professorship and my . . . **ahem** . . . other duties.

Constantine Constantius: What are your . . . **ahem** . . . other duties?

Professor [pompously]: When I am not teaching, I am an official gamewarden for The United States Department of Parks and Recreation.

Constantine Constantius [cautiously]: You mean whether you teach or whether you don't teach, you keep others from catching the fish.

Professor [infuriated]: If you are referring to Our Blessed Lord and my dutiful service in catching men . . . if you dare to insinuate in your guttersnipe way that I am not a responsible teacher bound to His Holy Service . . . Why, I'll . . . I'll . . .

Constantine Constantius [blandly interested]: You'll what?

Professor [gulping and then piously]: I'll . . . well . . . I'll excuse your lack of manners and overlook the offense this time.

Constantine Constantius [impishly]: . . . and still stop the catching of the fish.

Professor [becoming irate]: Now listen . . .

Constantine Constantius: Okay . . . okay. But this simply brings us to your problem of finding Kierkegaard's grave.

Professor: How so?

Constantine Constantius: Every time his name is mentioned there should be a violent conflict over what it means to be a Christian. His life is a complete reflection of his striving to become a Christian. Yet you want to give a pious nod over a few feet of earth and go home raving about "The Grave of Kierkegaard," but you don't want to crawl in after him.

Professor: And how will I do that since I am still alive?

Constantine Constantius: Yes you're alive in the sense that you "live" in your official and objective capacities. You cannot find Kierkegaard that way.

Professor [annoyed]: All right . . . I've read his books....How do I "crawl in after him" as you say?

Constantine Constantius: That's up to you.

Professor: Look, you stand here as some kind of pinnacle of wisdom . . . what you have to say -- say. After all, everything can be communicated.

Constantine Constantius [austerely]: Everything?

Professor [self-righteously]: EVERYTHING!!

Constantine Constantius: How much time do you have?

Professor: I have enough time to listen to a rational statement.

Constantine Constantius: That is only partial time.

Professor: Look, say what you have to say. I'll listen.

Constantine Constantius [opening his book]:
Gethsemane has cried out for blood
and found its violent call fulfilled.
The mob itself has called for death
and still is not contented.
Nature, man –
man – nature . . .
Both pull, drive, denounce . . .
head down – spirit crushed.
Both crack, break, split . . .
soul down – spirit crushed –

Ah, to will – Ah, the drive
inward through it all:
Through desires' flames
and laws' constrictions . . .
Through to <u>WILL</u>: the pulling together of self
and then to strike out
against it all.

To will – yes.
To will one's self in The Power of God Himself.

To despair and then to despair of despairing.

Into God –
Into God.

spirit/will
WILLING SPIRIT.
The lonely, solitary decision
 for the Power
 in the Power –
Christ, Christ Himself.

Through beauty's dreams,
Through decisions' screams,
Through "religious" speculation,
Through the world's ensnaring . . .
 . . . spirit willing . . .
WILLING SPIRIT
 through life's stages
to Christ, to Christ Himself.

[The professor's face becomes filled with anxiety. He looks at Constantine who appears to be quite serene.]

ACT ONE

[This act is based on the fragment "The Quiet Despair" in Kierkegaard's <u>Stages on Life's Way</u>, translated by Walter Lowrie, 1940, Schocken Books, p. 191 ff. The scene is an upper-class living room in a Danish home. The year is 1826. It is early morning. A young frail boy of thirteen is sitting idly watching his father.]

Father [His age should be about 65.]: Soren, would you like to go outside and play?

Soren: No, thank you.

Father: Would you rather we went for a ride in the carriage?

Soren: No, thank you, father.

Father: All my business affairs have been completed and there is time for a free day. What shall we do?

Soren: May we do the same as always?

Father: Yes . . . yes, of course. Let's go to Spain and see the king's court.

Soren [enthusiastically]: Yes . . . yes. The king's castles and the knights.

Father [smiling]: And the ladies.

Soren: Yes, the beautiful Spanish ladies.

Father: The king has declared war. The knights on horseback have assembled.

Soren: And the knights are riding from all sides of the regiments to give the notice "All ready!" to their lords.

Father: And alone, a knight cries in sorrow.

Soren: For he has left his love and may meet his God.

Father [sorrowfully]: We must all meet our God, Soren.

Soren [more intent on his describing what he sees]: In armor shining in the Spanish sun, he sits upon his horse. No one can see his tears for his face is hidden behind his helmet's visor. Only the red scarf of his lady's colors can be seen around his neck. How bright and courageous and immaculate he looks to his page and squire! How devotedly his lieutenants fear and admire him! And no one sees him cry. No . . . not one.

Father: The battle must start, Soren. The battle must start!

Soren: Father, why must there always be battle?

Father: Because there is always struggle: struggle against sin and loss and death.

Soren: And so the knight must weep.

Father: And must do battle, Soren. He must do battle.

Soren: With sin, father?

Father: With sin and man. With both at once.

Soren: And now the knight and his legions ride forth. The cannons explode. The bullets fly. The knight falls wounded.

Father: But he gets up, Soren, as Our Lord did when He bore His cross. He fell, but He got up. We must all do the same.

Soren [concentrating]: And he gets up.

Father: And he gets up, and . . .

Soren [holding his ears with both of his palms]: And he curses man, and he curses God, and he curses sin, and he curses the devil. He curses. He screams, "Why have you made me?" . . . And there is no reply.

Father: I once cursed God and everything. I had nothing. I was hungry. It was on the barren heath of Jutland. I am no longer hungry, but I hunger to be at peace with the God I cursed.*

Soren [concentrating]: But father, the enemy is thrown back! The enemies' lines are broken, father! Look! See! He conquers – the enemy retreats!

Father: Look hard, Soren – does he still weep?

Soren [disturbed]: Yes, but why, father? Why?

Father: Look once more.

Soren: The knight is very weak now; his armor weighs him down. He tries to get up again but falls. He has lost all his strength.

Father: Where are his men?

Soren: They have left him to pursue the enemy.

Father: Is he still alive?

Soren: Yes, but he is dying, father. He is dying and clutching his red scarf.

Father: And there is no one there?

Soren: No. No one.
[A servant enters the room.]

---

* See Walter Lowrie's Kierkegaard New York: Harper and Brothers, 1962, vol. 1, p. 22.

Servant [addressing the father]: Sir, the parson is here.

Father [in a trance]: Send him away. He is dying. [to himself] What good is a parson?

Servant: But, sir . . .

Father [irate]: GET OUT! And don't disturb us for the rest of the day.

Servant: Yes, sir. [The servant exits.]

Father [resuming the conversation as one in a trance]: Soren, does he remember the lady of the red scarf?

Soren: Yes, father, he dreams of her for a moment and then ...

Father [delirious]: And then . . .

Soren: He is no more.

Father [shaken]: No more?

Soren: He is dead. [a few seconds of silence.]

Father: And he did not have time to repent for his sin?

Soren: He could not repent, father. All was too sudden.

Father: Then it is over.

Soren [frightened]: Or it has just begun.

Father [filled with anxiety]: Stop it, Soren. Stop it.

Soren: But where is he, father?

Father [shuddering]: He is before the living God.
[Both look down in a melancholic and desperate way as the lights fall.]

ACT TWO

[The scene is a cemetery in Jerusalem during the first century C.E. It should appear more barren than the cemetery in The Prologue. This act is based on "A Leper's Soliloquy" in Kierkegaard's Stages of Life's Way, same edition as stated in Act One, pp. 220-222. Simon the leper is seen standing surrounded by tombstones. His right forearm has withered away. He is dressed in rags and bandages. His entire face is contorted by immense sores and swellings. What can be seen of his body through the rags shows brown patches where the blood has coagulated in scabs amidst his reddened sores and swellings. Manasseh, another leper, is with him. Manasseh's leprosy is only in its initial stage. Only a few small sores can be seen on his face, his arms, and his hands. His rags are not as tattered as Simon's.]

Manasseh: How long, Oh God? How long?

Simon: We've just begun.

Manasseh: I feel the disease crawling like lice under my skin. The marrow of my bones is alive with disease. The crawling, the eternal crawling of insects devouring my flesh. . . . Is there no cure? Is there none?

Simon: It is not eternal. We only suffer once although it be seventy years.*

Manasseh: Seventy years?

---

* See Kierkegaard's Christian Discourses. "The Joy of It-That We Suffer Only Once, But Triumph Eternally." London: Oxford University Press, 1940, pp. 101-110.

Simon [radiant]: The joy of it! That you only suffer once . . . and then eternity.

Manasseh: But time . . . this torture.

Simon: Once! Only once! And then eternity!

Manasseh: There must be some salve, some ointment for this bodily torment.

Simon: There is an ointment, but it drives the leprosy into the soul and then the soul becomes infected. It is better that the body be sick and not the soul.

Manasseh: Quick! The ointment! Where is it?

Simon: It is only for the moment, this torture. Should we not endure it?

Manasseh: The ointment! I must have the ointment.

Simon: If I tell you of the ointment, you will never be cured.

Manasseh: Will I find relief?

Simon: Only for this life, but then . . .

Manasseh: But then . . . Who knows about "then"? Give me the ointment!

Simon: I cannot give it to you. Go to the towns and be humanly meek, look dejected; go to the temple and cry out in pain. You will have a temporal, false cure. But the inward, eternal cry will rend you. It will destroy you.

Manasseh: So then there is relief.

Simon: Yes, but such a poor relief which costs the wealthy priests nothing and salves <u>their</u> consciences. It heals the priest as much as the priest's victim, yet both live in inward despair. It costs the priest nothing, and thus the sufferer receives nothing.

Manasseh: I must know its name.

Simon: Oh, you will know it. Go and cry out. Scream in their ears. They will give it to you and try to hide their own internal leprosy.

Manasseh: I . . . I do not know what to do. I am held here with the dead, yet I want to go to the town . . . to life . . .

Simon: Would you call the city life? Go to the city! Find out for yourself! [Simon lies down on one of the graves. He appears to have fallen asleep. Manasseh walks back and forth among the graves. He looks closely into Simon's face. He shudders. He looks at his own sores and in anguish leaves the stage. Simon slumbers for a few moments more and then awakes. He attempts to scratch his face with his right withered arm. His right arm is too short to reach his face. He stops and then scratches his face with his left hand. In a tortured, mad voice he cries out as he stands up.]

Simon: Who is there? Who is speaking? Is it I? "It is you." Who is speaking to me? "It is yourself." Is it not the dead, my companions? "No, far worse, it is yourself among the dead." It is I. It is I, the one led to the graves of burning sand. The one drawn here awaiting a saving lotion. [He stops speaking for a few moments.] Where is Manasseh? He has not left! Oh, no! Oh, no! He has gone to the temple. He has gone to receive what not even the dogs who once licked Lazarus' sores would accept. The dogs could at least snap at those who would pretend to be their masters. He has gone to receive "priestly" compassion – a compassion changing with the winds – a compassion which relieves the giver of his guilt – a compassion like the rancid food which the rich man once threw to stray dogs. The compassion which costs nothing and is worth less. Oh, God, I once used such an ointment. When one suffers, one seeks any relief. But you have led me away from the living dead to the dead who live with Thee. Abraham, Isaac, Jacob – through suffering they came to know

Thy Compassion which I seek, seek upon the graves. Oh God, help Manasseh! Lead him away from illusory peace! Do not let him fall a lost victim to the world's grunting, emotive solace, and cheap contentment. If need be, drive him back to the graves so that he will know death's truth and seek Thy Compassion. Manasseh is no different from the simple and downtrodden, the lame, the insane, and the persecuted. He is like all of these who truly need Thy Compassion. Help them all and help me. Help me to believe in the place where a table is set and Abraham and Isaac and Jacob await the leper's entrance to fulfill their joy.

[Simon becomes silent. He turns his back to the audience and sits down behind a gravestone so that the gravestone is between himself and the audience. The lights fall.]

[There should be an intermission with silence and darkness for a few seconds. When the lights come up the cemetery scene of The Prologue is again in view. The professor is becoming irritated and begins to scold Constantine Constantius.]

Professor: Now wait just a minute. Just a minute. I am failing to grasp what you are trying to say. This entire treatment is both undisciplined and defies the prescribed canons of truly religious and truly human art.

Constantine Constantius: You mean that the "treatment" of the theme does not meet your systematic standards of philosophical-theological investigation. Further, the form lacks the essential criteria of modern drama stemming from what is currently accepted.

Professor [pompously]: Precisely.

Constantine Constantius: Precisely. We have just at this moment said "precisely" nothing to each other.

Professor [pedantically]: Precisely . . . ah, I mean . . . I mean . . .

Constantine Constantius: Precisely!

Professor [becoming frustrated]: No, that isn't what I mean.

Constantine Constantius: What do you mean?

Professor: It does seem that we can have a rational, systematic, disciplined interpretation of Soren Kierkegaard. You are presenting something else.

Constantine Constantius: Perhaps you would like a commentary on Kierkegaard or a biographical drama.

Professor: Precisely. A biographical drama would be in order. I have already written two commentaries on modern theology and Kierkegaard's basic theses have been covered.

Constantine Constantius: Then it's true.

Professor: What is true?

Constantine Constantius: What Kierkegaard said about his work being used by parasitical priests and professors to gain worldly reputation.[*]

Professor [not used to such comments]: You're rather ill-tempered and bellicose, do you know that? However, that is not the point. What the point is . . .

Constantine Constantius: Is that you are a professor because Someone was crucified.[**]

Professor: Now I resent that. Do you here me? I resent that.

Constantine Constantius: I thought we were discussing Kierkegaard and not your resentments. I was simply

---

[*] Soren Kierkegaard, The Last Years, translated by R. G. Smith. New York: Harper & Row, 1965, p. 310.
[**] Walter Lowrie, Kierkegaard, vol. 2, p. 507.

presenting Kierkegaard's attitude towards resentful or unresentful professors.

Professor: Well, yes, but . . . after all . . .

Constantine Constantius: But after all . . . nothing! We are discussing Kierkegaard, aren't we?

Professor: Yes . . . but . . .

Constantine Constantius: But you want some edifying thoughts about the man, some edifying prattle to discuss with your wife and students over coffee and crumpets.

Professor [trying to be cute]: Actually, I prefer tea.

Constantine Constantius [becoming irritated]: Fine. Anyway you don't want Who Kierkegaard wanted – Christ Himself!

Professor: Now just a minute. That is a philosophical-theological problem subsumed under the categories of biblical, historical, and systematic theology.

Constantine Constantius: But what about yourself?

Professor [confused]: What? About whom? Look! I don't have to be insulted.

Constantine Constantius [bored]: I know . . . you're a professor.

Professor [irate]: Look, you're supposed to be presenting a play. What does all this nonsense about an old man and a boy and a leper have to do with the matter at hand?

Constantine Constantius: Just that Kierkegaard drew religious reflection from himself. What transpires in this work are the most secret and enigmatic statements he recorded about himself during the varied stages of his coming to his goal. This goal was to become contemporaneous with Jesus Christ.

Professor: But there is no viable statement about the Christian community in all of this.

Constantine Constantius: Soren Kierkegaard was only interested in one thing – realizing that God is love. That someone says that God is love or that everyone says that God is love, and <u>you do not know</u> that God is love demands that you yourself decide whether some men or all men are liars.

Professor: Yes, of course . . . I know, but . . .

Constantine Constantius: Well, either God is love or He is not. What is transpiring is the struggle to uncover the nature of such love and what is required of the individual to make the statement to herself or himself, "I know God is love."

Professor: All right . . . okay . . . existentialism . . . I know . . .

Constantine Constantius: No, not existentialism, I know; but God is love, that I <u>inwardly</u> know.

Professor [mumbling]: Yes . . . yes, the strangeness of our being, our doubt, our . . .

Constantine Constantius: No, let's not make it all that complicated. Let's remain with the questions: "Is God Love?"

Professor [mumbling again]: Well, the anxiety of estrangement could symbolically point to the need for redemption and . . .

Constantine Constantius: Oh nonsense. The anxiety of estrangement could symbolically point to the statement "God is Evil." Regardless, one must <u>struggle</u> for light; one must find whatever light there is in one's self and seek The Source of that light everyday.

Professor [becoming confused]: But our finitude . . . and the historical process . . . and the historical Jesus . . . and ecumenism, . . . and, I . . . and the relation of all this to form criticism . . . and neo-orthodoxy . . . and . . .

Constantine Constantius: May I continue?

Professor [as the personification of The Tower of Babel]: . . . and secularism in a world come of age . . . and oh, yes, . . . and the social gospel in the age of pluralism . . . and the god is dead movement . . . and the Dead Sea Scrolls in relation to Vatican II . . .

Constantine Constantius: Say, are you all right?

Professor [starting to recover]: Yes, it is very easy to lose one's self in theology. There is so much to examine scholarly, that I think I have forgotten to examine my own self.*

Constantine Constantius: I cannot see how it will profit anyone to lose her or his soul in the idol palace of theological slogans. I think Kierkegaard's major thesis has always been neglected: each individual should at all times struggle to become a believer, and by believing, become contemporaneous with Jesus Christ Himself!

Professor: Can we leave it at that?

Constantine Constantius: No!

Professor: Why not?

Constantine Constantius: Because of what one must endure in order to believe!

---

* See Kierkegaard's For Self-Examination, trans. by Walter Lowrie, Princeton University Press, 1941.

ACT THREE

[The same Danish living room as Act One. This act is based on "Solomon's Dream" in Kierkegaard's <u>Stages on Life's Way</u>, same edition as cited in Act One, p. 236.]

Soren: Father . . .

Father: Yes, Soren?

Soren: Father, shall we never be happy?

Father [sadly]: It is not our place to be happy in this life.

Soren: Can no one be happy? Surely wisdom must lead to happiness. Surely wisdom and wealth must lead to happiness. Was not Solomon happy? Surely Solomon must have been happy and at peace.

Father: How do you see Solomon?

Soren: I see Solomon sitting amidst his scrolls, finding pleasure and peace in knowledge and wisdom. I see him gathered amongst his colorful thoughts which are all bright red and green and purple – beautiful and edifying thoughts.

Father [smiling]: But amongst these thoughts does he not think now and then of his father?

Soren [delighted that his father, is engaged seriously in the same thoughts]: Oh yes! The mighty King David! How proud Solomon is! His father has conquered all their enemies and rules the land. David is also the elect of God. To have David as a father! No one could have a better father! Solomon and

David – wisdom and strength! David and Solomon – kingship and knowledge! They <u>must</u> have been happy!

Father [sadly]: Yes, but Solomon must rest from his happiness and his many colored thoughts, must he not?

Soren [startled]: Yes, he must.

Father: And so he goes to his chambers one evening and, being the king's son, his chambers adjoin his father's.

Soren: Of course, yes, of course, father.

Father [darkly]: And he begins to doze and to sleep and he is not sure whether he is sleeping or awake. . . . He hears moans and cries from his father's room. . . .

Soren: Moans and cries?

Father: Yes, Soren. His father is kneeling and weeping. His father is repenting, Soren. He is repenting that he has cursed God by disobeying the prophet Nathan – that he has killed a good man to have that good man's wife. He has disobeyed God, Soren, and he despairs.

Soren: Despairs, father?

Father: His soul is shaken and broken and he cries out in torture to God. He cries out for forgiveness, for some hope. And David is alone, Soren, he is dreadfully alone.

Soren [quietly]: Alone.

Father: Yes, all alone. And Solomon who has always seen David as the most powerful of men, now sees him as a wretched cripple. He sees David as one beneath a crushing burden, the burden of his guilt before God; and for once Solomon does not understand.

Soren: But he is wise, father.

Father: Yes, he is wise after the fashion of our professors and our pastors. He is wise in that way. Indeed, Solomon shines in a worldly glory. But he is not in the darkness of God. He has not come to know sin and its wretched power which inwardly corrupts the soul. He has not despaired of himself and become strong through the inward knowledge of his own weakness and God's strength.

Soren: I do not understand.

Father: You cannot understand everything at once, Soren. You, too, must live and be broken.

Soren: . . . and be broken . . .

Father: Yes.

Soren [anxiously]: Can no one escape this breaking?

Father: Yes, some do. Perhaps Solomon did. Solomon continued in his worldly wisdom, but he did not know God's foolishness. And Solomon always had a place of honor in the temple, but he did not become a man of prayer. And Solomon was praised by men but oh, what trouble there was within him, for he could really only value the praise which came from David. But David was broken and divided and only upheld by the living God. And so Solomon walked in his brightly colored realm of beauty, exquisite thoughts, and desires. What is more, Solomon inherited his father's earthly kingdom, but Solomon was troubled, Soren, so infinitely troubled for he never approached that <u>other kingdom</u> where David only wished to be a slave!

Soren [anxiously]: And what happens, father? How then does Solomon live and die?

Father [sadly]: In vexation of spirit because his colored thoughts give him no rest, he returns to his harem. To escape his troubles with pleasure he cries out to all the women, "Strike the tambourines, dance before me!" But his inward restlessness permits him no lasting consolation, and drifting in this realm of desire upon desire, he awaits his end in disquiet dreams. Finally the Queen of Sheba visited him in her magnificence with her false gods. She sought his worldly wisdom, and Solomon, for diversion's sake, spoke of exotic earthly ecstasy. Thus the queen and the spending of great fortunes amused Solomon until his death.

Soren [terrified]: And how did he die, father?

Father: He died with his final prayer being a confused intermingling of his own worldly wisdom and the strange prayer of David.

[Both look at each other as though recognizing a mysterious truth from their conversation. Then both stare at the floor.]

ACT FOUR

[This act is based on Kierkegaard's fragment "A Possibility" in Stages on Life's Way, pp. 258-268. The stage is set in such a manner as to place the entrance of a longbridge to the left of the stage as the audience sees the set. In the center of the stage is a small garden with chairs and a bench. The entire sky is black and dreary. A man with white hair, age 40, is sitting in such a way as to expose his hunched back. He is dressed in the fashionable attire of Danish gentlemen of the 1840's. A robust, heavily bearded sea captain in uniform enters.]

Sea Captain: My friend, how is it that you are not pacing? [jovially] After all, this is your sacred hour for the march, is it not? [He takes out a watch from his vest pocket.] Yes, ten-thirty. This is not like you. No, not like you at all.

Gentleman [somewhat startled]: Yes . . . I mean no, it is not like me. [recovering himself] Heinrich! Have you just arrived? Where have you come from?

Sea Captain: We just docked yesterday evening. Came in from The West Indies. What a storm! One man overboard in the middle of the Atlantic. I had to fight both God and the devil to turn our tub around and rescue him. But we got him back. By God, we got him back.

Gentleman [smiling]: And how long will you be staying?

Sea Captain: Until the weather improves or until I get sick of the rum in Copenhagen. But, you, why is it that you are not pacing? I knew I could find you here with your restless thoughts, marching back and forth, just like I've found you for the past twenty years pacing and fretting before the longbridge . . . I'm glad I found you . . . But this isn't quite like you. Are you well?

Gentleman: I'm marvelously well. Yes, I feel better than I have felt in a long time.

Sea Captain: Well what happened, man? I never seen you resting in dry dock at this hour.

Gentleman: A certainty that was uncertain became certain.

Sea Captain [perplexed]: Well, that's too much for me. The only thing that is certain is a last voyage. It's there. Someday I will take it, and it will be the last. But that's a long way off . . . I hope.

Gentleman [musing to himself]: Yes, the last voyage, that is certain. Say, how would you like some rum?

Sea Captain: Well, it's for certain that I would. [Both laugh.] But first tell me, before we talk about anything else, do you have any of your drawings left?

Gentleman: Drawings?

Sea Captain: You know, those fine things you do in your spare time. The children's faces.

Gentleman: You mean the drawings I have displayed in my rooms.

Sea Captain: Yes, those drawings. I'd like to have one of them. The face of the little girl with the big eyes and the wide mouth. Do you remember?

Gentleman [recollecting]: No, I don't remember. There are so many drawings. I . . . [He begins to pace absentmindedly.] I had almost forgotten the drawings. [He recollects something and then sits down. There is a brief pause.] The drawings . . . yes, you can have whichever one you want.

Sea Captain: Are you sure you're feeling well?

Gentleman: Oh yes. Yes. Is there any reason you want that particular one?

Sea Captain: The little girl reminds me of my sister's daughter who died of consumption while I was at sea. The resemblance is quite remarkable. I thought I would give it to my sister to try and console her. [A ragged beggar woman with two children, a boy age ten and a girl age eight, appears at the side of the stage. The little girl wishes to rush to the gentleman, but the mother constrains her.]

Girl [Her name is Sonja.]: But mother . . .

Mother [Her name is Margaret.]: Sonja. Be still!

[The Sea Captain and the Gentleman turn to discover the source of the noise. They both go and greet their visitors.]

Gentleman: Margaret, how are you? Sonja, my little princess . . . and who is this?

Sonja: This is Eric.

Gentleman: Eric, well, well. Sonja, is Eric a new friend?

Sonja: Of course he is, but he has trouble saying things.

Eric [Eric is partially retarded]: I . . . I . . . I . . . aaam glaaaaad . . . to . . . to . . . [He strikes his head with his fists and begins crying.]

Margaret [going to Eric]: Now that's all right, Eric. That's okay. You're with a kind and good man – a very kind and good man. [to the Gentleman and Sea Captain] Eric finds it hard to talk to strangers. It took Sonja and me two days before he would trust us. We found him four days ago at dawn walking about the streets and crying.

Sonja [to the Gentleman]: Do you remember the dawn four days ago?

Gentleman [attempting to reflect but gives up the attempt]: No, I seem to have forgotten it.

Sonja: Oh, you must remember it! You must! The sun came up and everything was like gold. All the streets glowed in a quiet splendor, and the morning light made Copenhagen look like a dream – a white-gold dream. Yes, a peaceful, quiet, beautiful dream. [sadly] And there was Eric in the midst of it . . . and there was Eric in the midst of the white-gold dream reminding mother and me that we were awake.

Gentleman: So Eric has no home.

Sonja: Oh yes he does . . . with mother and me. [Shyly, for the first time, she looks at the Sea Captain.] Who is the man with the beard and the beautiful uniform?

Gentleman [smiling]: He is a great wanderer – a sea captain who visits enchanted lands and fights dragons and pirates and knows more stories than anyone else.

Sonja: Will he tell Eric and me a story? [The gentleman looks at the Sea Captain.]

Sea Captain [drying his eyes]: Of course . . . of course. But no captain can remember well or speak with his mates without first putting in for supplies, so to speak . . . [Since the Captain is used to speaking in a tavern, he becomes a little confused.] . . . at a bakery and a candy store. [He looks relieved especially after seeing Margaret's look of approval.] Will you be my mates and come with me? [Still hesitating, he turns to Margaret.] Is that all right, ma'am?

Margaret: Oh, of course it is.

Gentleman: Heinrich, you take Sonja and Eric for a . . . how did you put it? . . . a "putting in for supplies" [with good-natured mockery to the Sea Captain] . . . yes, that was it . . .

"a putting in for supplies"... not bad, Heinrich, not bad at all ... and Margaret and I will see you soon. [Sonja takes Eric by the hand and they both skip off together before the Sea Captain to the right of stage as the audience sees the set.]

Gentleman: Margaret, please sit down.

Margaret: Why, thank you, sir. Thank you.

Gentleman [sitting down next to her]: And what brings you to see me on such a miserable day?

Margaret: More misery, unfortunately. I had almost figured out how to support Sonja and myself by taking in laundry and occasional cleaning jobs. But then we found Eric in the streets. Neither Sonja nor I could turn away from him and so ...

[The Gentleman expressionlessly and almost mechanically reaches for his wallet in his coat pocket. Without looking at the bills, he hands all his money to her.]

Margaret [her eyes widening]: No, sir! No! This is too much! You won't have anything for yourself or for the other people.

Gentleman [laughing]: Oh, please take it. [looking at the longbridge] I won't need it where I will be going and ... yes, and for the others I must make some arrangements ... for them, and for you and Sonja and Eric ...

Margaret: Sir ... [troubled and embarrassed, not knowing what to say] Sir, I did not see you pacing today. ... Was it because the Sea Captain is here?

Gentleman: No. Despite Heinrich's arrival I was not pacing at all today. It's funny Heinrich also asked me why I wasn't pacing. I must have a reputation like that of a caged animal which paces incessantly back and forth over its limited space and time. [sensing Margaret's embarrassment] But this is all too complicated. The truth is simple. Today, you see, I discovered that I must take a long and awesome journey across a dreadful bridge, yes . . . a very long and dreadful bridge . . . [attempting with difficulty to clarify his own statements] You see, you see in my youth when I was working very hard to succeed in my business, I lived alone. I had few friends and I had no wife. [staring at the longbridge] One evening . . . one evening long ago in my youth I had dinner with a few of my business acquaintances . . . and drinking too much and filled with youth's fire, we visited one of the houses down the street from here. I only remember in my drunkenness being lifted through the threshold into the house, and the unhappy women who were forced to work there with false smiles on their bizarrely painted faces. That is all that I remember. What I never forgot was the next morning. That next morning it occurred to me that it was now possible that someone in this world could be carrying my child. I was too ashamed to go back to the house even if I could have found it. I was so drunk I doubt that I could have found it. Besides, the women would have only thought I was crazy. Still, the possibility that I might be a father, that I might be responsible for someone besides myself began to grow and feed itself within me. The thought overcame me. I became obsessed with trying to fulfill my potential responsibility and be done with it . . . but it was not that easy. I did not know where to begin. Then I thought of scientifically attempting to solve my problem by studying the faces of children and comparing their faces to my own.

Margaret: So that is why all these years you've studied the faces of the poor children hereabouts.

Gentleman: Yes . . . that is so. One can never be sure – no, never. My doubts and worries increased. I studied books on physiology and anatomy. I made drawings in my leisure time. I did all of this in the hope of being certain – of somehow deriving a system by which I could be certain what my child would look like. All of this only to know for certain and then pay for my evil and be free . . . I never reached such certainty.

Margaret: And your pacing?

Gentleman: Yes, each day I would pace back and forth. My problem took everything from me. From, ten to eleven each morning I would walk back and forth hoping to discover certainty. For twenty-five years I searched for certainty and now . . .

Margaret: Now . . .

Gentleman: Now. Today, I have discovered that I have no more than a short time to live, and my search for certainty has fallen away to another certainty which all the pacing in the world will not resolve. [a brief silence.] I will be crossing over a long and dreadful bridge from this world to the next. [again, a silence]

Margaret [She begins to speak slowly and deliberately.]: Sir, I . . . I am not very smart and I do not understand everything you have said. . . . But I know this for certain: within a short time you will not cross the longbridge alone. Perhaps your worries have blinded you to one thing – the most important thing to God. All the poor women and children you have taken care of for all these years have never stopped worrying and praying for you. We have watched you from a distance and we did not understand, but we watched and prayed. And so, sir, it is impossible for you to cross that longbridge alone. The prayers of the poor outrun you. They are before God right now. And when you die the poor will meet you and you will be carried across that bridge; you will be carried! We could not have survived without your kindness; and God, well, He can forget sin, but He cannot forget goodness. And so we go with you, sir, we go with you. [There is a brief silence.]

Gentleman [quietly]: Then you believe that I am not alone.

Margaret [smiling]: No, sir; you can't be. I and the other woman and children won't permit it. And God, well, He always listens to the poor, I know He does. So you're surrounded and might as well accept defeat.

Gentleman [smiling]: But such a defeat! [Both laugh.]

[Off stage the Sea Captain can be heard speaking.]

Margaret [anxiously]: Does your friend, the captain, know about . . .

Gentleman: No, not yet, and please don't mention it. I will tell him later. We shouldn't spoil the day for the children.

Margaret: The day, sir?

Gentleman: Yes, the day. We're going to the amusement park in Copenhagen.

Margaret: But do you feel well enough?

Gentleman: I feel wonderful and, thanks to you, I feel like having some fun . . . [reflecting to himself] a word I almost forgot, yes, an excellent word "fun."

Margaret: Oh, Sonja and Eric will love this!

Gentleman [laughing]: But you will have to loan us some money! [Both laugh. The Sea Captain enters with Sonja and Eric.]

Sea Captain [continuing his story]: So there I was off the southwest coast of Africa, and a pirate with a beard reaching to his belt, boards our ship! It was him or me! I grabbed him by his beard. [to a wide-eyed Sonja and Eric] You should have heard him scream! He sounded like a pinched Gypsy dancer! [He notices Margaret and he becomes embarrassed.] Pardon me, ma'am. Anyway, so I threw the pirate overboard. But his smell was so bad that not even the sharks would touch him. So I fished him out, gave him a shave, and made him my first mate. And then . . .

Gentleman [laughing]: I don't want to interrupt such a story, but we have an appointment.

Sea Captain [confused]: A what?

Gentleman: An appointment at the amusement park.

Sonja: Hooray!!

Eric: At the what?

Sonja: Eric's speaking like everyone else. I think it's because he likes the Sea Captain and the captain's uniform. I know he likes cookies and candy. [All laugh except for Eric who is a little puzzled.]

Margaret: We'll show you what an amusement park is, Eric.

Gentleman: We certainly will! Let's cross the longbridge!

[Eric and Sonja skip across the longbridge. Margaret follows them. The Sea Captain places his arm around the Gentleman's shoulders, and they walk across the longbridge after Margaret. However, as the Gentleman and the Sea Captain cross the bridge, the Sea Captain continues his story.]

Sea Captain: You should have seen that pirate's beard. Thick as a whale's head and twice as strong . . . [The Gentleman listens and is thoroughly amused.]

[There should again be a few seconds of darkness. There is the same scene as The Prologue.]

Professor: Okay . . . okay. Realized eschatology and all of that. . . . God "here and now" and the rest of it. We've all seen the development of Kierkegaard's thought through Twentieth Century existentialism. The "infinite qualitative difference between God and man" has been scholarly investigated, as well as the "leap of faith" and Kierkegaard's relation to Hegel. I think the scholars have done a fine job . . . I just wish I could find his grave and get out of here.

Constantine Constantius [smiling]: Well, if you must know, Kierkegaard is buried next to his father. On the day he was buried a quarrel began between the students and the professors,* a quarrel, I might add, which I intend to perpetuate.

Professor: Well, you certainly are adept at quarreling. Now, where is Kierkegaard's father's grave?

Constantine Constantius: I don't know.

Professor: What?

Constantine Constantius: It would be superfluous knowledge and not the knowledge of "faith." Since Kierkegaard's entire life's work is simply an attempt to come to faith, a noble and lonely attempt, I don't think he should be thought of as a rotting carcass occupying six feet of turf. As I said before, if you want to know where Kierkegaard is, go to a library. If you want any more information ask the gravedigger; there are plenty of them in this world.

Professor [confused]: Well, yes. [regaining professorial control] I want to thank you for the ah . . . stuff you were reading to me. However, I don't think that's the way to approach the writing of a scholarly work. After all, the Kierkegaard corpus, [laughing to himself] I don't mean his physical body, is being analyzed by a legion of Danish, German, English, and American scholars. They will no doubt give us all the truth we need to know about Kierkegaard's thought, style, language, and life. [He looks at his watch.] Now I must be going. I still have to find the gravedigger, and then I have a luncheon appointment. Thank you for your time and your . . .

Constantine Constantius: My "stuff."

Professor: Yes, your reading of your writings.

Constantine Constantius: Yes, good-bye.

---

* See Walter Lowrie's Kierkegaard, vol. 2, pp. 586-588.

[The professor leaves. Constantine Constantius looks at the graves surrounding him. He opens his book and continues reading.]

ACT FIVE

[This act is based on "A School Exercise: Periander" in <u>Stages on Life's Way</u>, pp. 298-302. The scene is Kierkegaard's father's bedroom. The father is sitting in bed supported by pillows. Soren, now age 25, is sitting in a chair next to him. Soren is extremely well dressed having almost the appearance of a dandy. He gives every impression of being a sophisticated man of the world.]

Soren: Father, do you feel as weak as you did yesterday?

Father: No. I think some of my strength is returning. I think I have the strength . . . yes, I do . . . if you are willing.

Soren: Strength to do what, father?

Father: When you were younger do you remember how we would walk all about the world by imagining things.

Soren: Yes, father.

Father: If you do not feel that you are too old, perhaps we could do that today.

Soren: No, I am not too old, father. Where shall we go? That is, if you feel well enough.

Father: I am well enough. First, I wanted to tell you before I . . . became any weaker, the reasons for our past visits to different places in history and in the world.

Soren: Yes, father.

Father: I only wanted you to come to properly believe in Jesus Christ. That is what the individual must do in this life.

Soren [stricken with anxiety]: That is a heavy task, father.

Father: Our Lord says that although we must bear our cross, yet His burden is light. I have never completely understood that, but perhaps you will.

Soren: Father, you know I have lost interest in such matters.

Father [becoming annoyed]: Soren, you are still quite young. Frivolous interest in artistic reveries and chasing the ladies will not save anyone. Now I am sorry that I will probably not have the time to speak more about this with you. [He begins coughing again. Soren stands up to look for assistance.] Sit down! Sit down! I am fine. Please listen to what I have to say and see if in any way it does not remind you of many of the stories which we used to tell each another. Perhaps you've read about Periander, the tyrant of Corinth.

Soren: Why, yes. Not long ago I read something about him in Diogenes Laertius.

Father: Fine. What did you learn from Diogenes' account?

Soren [melancholically]: Only that he spoke like a wise man and acted like a madman.

Father: Yes, he was a man totally split in half. That is to say, he was a monster. His reign was characterized by equitable leniency and a consuming passion. However, these two characteristics were never drawn together, solidified, and purified within the man. He would pay homage to the gods, defend the poor, and conduct himself with wisdom among men of understanding. Yet the same man had sexual relations with his mother, kicked his wife to death, and tried to murder his own sons. His madness ended in an elaborate plot of suicide in which seven other men were killed as well as himself.

Soren: Yes, father, the story comes back to me now.

Father: Have you discovered in your experiences or in your studies a way in which to reconcile the conflicts of an individual like Periander?

Soren [anxiously recognizing himself as another Periander]: What do you mean?

Father [begins coughing]: I only mean. [coughing] Learn to love and serve Jesus Christ; He is the Way . . . [The coughing continues. Soren Kierkegaard leaves the room in order to get a servant.]

ACT SIX

[This is based on "Nebuchadnezzar" in Kierkegaard's <u>Stages on Life's Way</u>, pp. 330-333. The scene is Nebuchadnezzar's bed chamber in his palace at Babel. He is seated in bed. Around him are strewn rolled and unrolled scrolls. His servant is apprehensively watching him.]

Nebuchadnezzar [impatiently]: Daniel . . . where is Daniel?

Servant: My lord, I will get him.

Nebuchadnezzar [raging]: I am not your lord!! Call Daniel. No, wait. Perhaps Daniel will not speak to me. Here, quickly, find something on which to write. Quickly, quickly. [The servant nervously rushes out about the room in confusion.] Here, take this. [He hands him an unraveled scroll.] Write on this.

Servant: But, my lord.

Nebuchadnezzar [excitedly]: I said don't call me that. Write! I, Nebuchadnezzar, once king of Babel, proud and sure in conquest and defiant in rage, placed all hope in my glory and majesty. My kingdom reached to all the ends of the earth; my power and wrath caused all mortals to tremble.
And then THE WORD came to me.

THE WORD shrouded itself in darkness and gave me a secret dream that I would be like a beast which eats grass until seven seasons passed.

I then jumped to my feet, girded on my sword, and assembled my legions. I told them to warn me when the enemy approached. My general said, "No army can attack proud

Babel and survive!" My captain said, "He who even entertains evil thoughts against Nebuchadnezzar will breathe no more." My servant said, "My lord, I would strike my son dead if he offended thee!" Then my general, my captain, and my servant led me to a high mountain and showed me that the earth was mine. In secured comfort, I mocked my fears and smirked before the dream.

But THE WORD!

THE WORD came in a voice and, more quickly than does a woman change her thoughts, I was transformed! Grass was my food, its dew added to my tears, and no one knew me for whom I was.

But I knew Babel, and was I not Babel's king? On all fours I cried out, "I am king of Babel; more so, I am king of the universe!" But no one listened and everything that I said sounded like the grunting and the bellowing of a beast.

My thoughts terrified me. Like an implacable legion they assembled against me and reminded me of my great arrogance. They cried out against me; they howled like victims near death; the thoughts were against me and my own voice was silenced. Like a muzzled dog who is burned alive, so was I to myself.

Amongst the legions of thoughts and my silent screams
I wondered and finally said to myself. "Who really is
The Mighty One? The Lord, The True Lord whose wisdom
brings itself to the deepest, secret and darkest dream.
Who aids Him in the interpretation of my dream, and who
will force Him to allow interpretation if He does not
so wish?
Where is my general? Where is my captain? Where is
my servant?
How am I to ride into The Lord's kingdom?
Where is such a chariot?
Who makes the spear with which to strike against Him?
Who can even guide me to the place of surrender?
What need does He have of human power?

What need does He have of spies to watch His realm?
The Lord cannot be found, nor harnessed, nor put off.
He does not wait for tomorrow but perpetually He says, "Today!"
In His own inward counsels He says do it, and it is done.
He says now and it is not later.
He says seven years an animal, an animal will be the
king of Babel, and for seven years I ate grass!"

At the end of the seven years I again became Nebuchadnezzar. I called together my wise men who were not wise in The Wisdom of the Lord. I asked them to explain the why and the how of That Power by which I became a beast of the field. Surrounded by their scrolls, they laughed and smirked and said, "Great Nebuchadnezzar, this is but an evil dream, an imagination. Who could do that to thee?"

And my wrath was kindled against these "wise" men. My blood ran hot, hotter than the flames which devoured the muzzled dog. My blood called out for theirs and I saw their blood run like the overflow from a cask of wine split by an axe. For The Lord possesses all might, wisdom and truth. He needs not such "wise men." Nor does He need the city of Babel and its king.

Henceforth I decree that every seventh year a feast will be held in Babel. It will be called "The Feast of the Transformation." On that day the lepers, the poor, the orphans, the widows, and all those spiritually and physically crippled are to be praised as God's beloved. The transformation of Nebuchadnezzar is to be recited; all are to be told how Nebuchadnezzar became a beast and was no longer king. They are to be told how he spent his last years thanking The True God for having made him a beast and for having known The True God's might.

And, if during The Feast of the Transformation, a false "wise" man is found, he is to be led through the streets clad like a beast. He is to carry his writings with him. His writings, however, are to be torn to shreds and bound like a torch of hay. As he is pushed through the streets, let everyone cry,

"The Lord, The Lord is the Mighty one. His actions are swift and powerful. His secrets no man knows, no, not one."

And now I will wait for soon <u>The Fashioner of Kings and Beasts</u> will again transform me. I do not know if this mere trifle of a testimony to His power will find favor in His eyes. I only know that there is in the distance an invisible land where The Almighty One's favor and peace turn nightmare into joy.

Thus have I, I – Nebuchadnezzar made known to all people the power of The True God. Great Babel is humbled. It has One True Lord and should seek no other.

RUNNING FOX

CHARACTERS

PIONEER I
PIONEER II
RUNNING FOX
RABBIT EARS
LIEUTENANT LANDMARK
DR. BEN GOODWILL
GOVERNOR EVANS OF THE COLORADO TERRITORY
COLONEL CHIVINOTON
MAJOR WYNKOOP
BLACK KETTLE
WHITE ANTELOPE
MAJOR ANTHONY
INDIAN WOMEN AND CHILDREN
ARMY OFFICERS AND SOLDIERS

Unfortunately, the historical events portrayed in this drama are true.

ACT ONE

[A barren desert near Denver, Colorado. It is early September of 1864. Two covered wagons are seen. The one on stage left has in large letters "PIKES PEAK OR BUST." The wagon on stage right has in large letters "BUSTED." Pioneer II is leaning against his wagon which says "PIKE'S PEAK OR BUST." Pioneer I is leaning against his wagon entitled "BUSTED." Although both pioneers appear to be exhausted, Pioneer I seems to radiate despair and Pioneer II optimism. Both pioneers are in their late thirties.]

Pioneer I [gazing at Pioneer II's wagon]: "Pike's Peak or Bust" . . . well, I hope you find more than I did.

Pioneer II [staring at the wagon marked "BUSTED"]: The newspaper said, "Go West, young man!" I'm not that young. But I'm going West. Gold is out there . . . and land.

Pioneer I [thoughtfully]: And Indians, and death, and despair. I'm going East.

Pioneer II: What? There are no opportunities left in the East. Half of Europe is pouring into that part of the world. Too many people. Too much cheap labor. The cost of land is too high. A man my age has to find something to call his own.

Pioneer I [bitterly]: Well, make sure you don't find an early grave to call your own. Six feet of dirt are what many people are finding out West. You can find that kind of real estate East or West.

Pioneer II [gazing at the "BUSTED" wagon]: I don't care what happens. Anything's better than being caught up in our Civil War. I would do anything to avoid it. Did you know that if you don't have $300, they can draft you? The rich pay others . . . the poor are taking the $300 and fighting to defend the rich man and the rich man's property. I'm no fool. I took my money, and I put it into this wagon. I am no fool. I got the hell out of Ohio. The war between the states could last forever. To hell with it. I'm going to find my own piece of land, maybe buy some cattle . . . I'm going to have something of my own.

Pioneer I: Well, be careful. Make sure you don't get an arrow from an Indian or a bullet from a white man claim jumper. Watch out for the mining companies, too. They're buying up everything. [Pioneer I notices something on stage left.] Hey, look, here comes an Indian with a white man. That's unusual. Maybe they've got some news from Denver. That's where I'm headed. I'm going East. I'm busted.

[Running Fox enters with his partner, Rabbit Ears. Running Fox is a young man in his mid-twenties. He is approximately 5'8" and very slender. He has black hair of an Indian, but he also has fair skin and blue eyes. He is attired in a buckskin shirt and buckskin trousers. He has a knife and a revolver on his cartridge belt around his waist. Rabbit Ears is an immense, muscular Indian over 6'4". Rabbit Ears has a huge scar running across the right side of his nose down to the right side of his neck. His face is pock-marked and surrounded by long, black hair. His ears are enormous. His demeanor is very stern. He is dressed in a used U.S. Army coat. Across his chest are crisscrossed rifle cartridge belts. He is in his early thirties. Both men wear riding boots.]

Running Fox [looking at the two wagons and laughing]: Gentlemen, it seems we have a difference of opinions. I couldn't help overhearing your conversation. The wind blows where it will, and the wind can hear men's words. One of you seems full of hope and the other, well, the other is probably a little disappointed. But, anyway, let me introduce myself. I'm Running Fox, Indian scout, Indian language interpreter, trail blazer, furs-for-beads negotiator, and general adviser to anyone who can pay me and my partner $10.00 per day. The $10.00 includes both my partner and myself. My partner and friend is Rabbit Ears, former Crow warrior, who has decided that humanity as we know it today is something of a miserable failure. Right Rabbit Ears? [Rabbit Ears nods his assent, and grunts in an affable enough way.] Yes, sir, Rabbit Ears doesn't say much, but he can listen! Boy, can he listen! Right, Rabbit Ears? [Rabbit Ears nods his assent again and grunts affably.] That's about all you can get from Rabbit Ears until we get our ten bucks up front. Rabbit Ears and I work together. He doesn't believe in credit. He believes that credit is just another one of the white man's tricks. For him credit is the same as the white man's smallpox, the white man's whiskey, the white man's religion, the white man's lust for land, and the white man's insane craving for gold. Rabbit Ears knows a lot about all these things, but he won't say anything until we're paid up front.

Pioneer I [furiously]: Well, I only have fifty dollars left, and I've got to get to Denver somehow in this broken down wagon. I'm not going to pay some goddamn Indian and his big-mouthed, half-breed friend a nickel. [Rabbit Ears takes a menacing step towards Pioneer I. Running Fox gently puts his hand on Rabbit Ear's shoulder to calm him.]

Running Fox [seriously]: Now, that's really not the way to approach Rabbit Ears. He can be very mean when he's not respected. Besides, we've got work in Denver. The governor of the Colorado Territory has hired us as interpreters. So, keep your money. With your attitude, you'll need it. We'll be on our way. [Running Fox and Rabbit Ears start to leave.]

Pioneer II [anxiously reaching in to his pocket]: Wait! Wait! Just wait! Don't judge all white men by just one white man! I want to know more. I've just gotten here. I'll pay. Here take this. [He hands Running Fox a ten dollar gold piece. Running Fox takes the coin, looks at it closely, and turns it over in his hands a couple of times.]

Running Fox [addressing Rabbit Ears and handing him the coin]: It looks okay to me. But Rabbit Ears, you had better check it out. [Rabbit Ears studies the coin, sniffs it, and then bites it. Rabbit Ears then grunts his assent and places the coin in his pocket.]

Pioneer I [furiously]: You're crazy to be giving them money. You should have given it to me. What could they possibly know that's worth a ten dollar gold piece.

Pioneer II [scornfully]: Why should I pay you? What could YOU possibly know? You're busted! You're leaving! I don't want to wind up like you. I want to make something of what's left of my life, and I'll pay a fair price to anyone who can help me.

Pioneer I [indifferently]: Do what you want, you will anyway. [shrugging his shoulders] Besides, it's your money.

Pioneer II [self-righteously]: Yes, it's my money, and I'll do what I want. And I want to know. Now tell me Running Ears, I mean . . .

Running Fox [laughing]: My name is Running Fox. My partner is named Rabbit Ears.

Pioneer II [also laughing]: Okay . . . excuse me, Running Fox. I want you and Rabbit Ears to tell me the quickest and surest way to a long and happy life out here.

Rabbit Ears [smiling]: Go East, young man!

Running Fox [laughing] Now, now, Rabbit Ears, the man has paid good money and we must give him good advice.

Rabbit Ears [sternly]: But I just gave him good advice.

Running Fox [laughing]: But it is not the advice he wants to hear. [devoting his full attention to Pioneer II] Let me tell you a little about myself and Rabbit Ears and then you will know more. My father, like yourself, was a white man. He came out West some thirty years ago from your big city, New York. He was tired of all those people in one place. He started a trading post many miles north of here. There he met my mother, a Sioux Indian. In those years there was peace between the Indian and the white man. Buffalo robes were traded for the white man's things. [reflecting] A buffalo robe could bring good white man's things like coffee and sugar. [in a somber tone] The same robe could also bring bad white man's things such as whiskey.

Rabbit Ears [furiously]: The white man brought death. Look at my face. Smallpox – red berry marks for life. [sternly] At least I am still alive. Whole villages of my people, the Crow Indian, were destroyed by smallpox, the white man's disease.

Running Fox [quietly]: The white man brought good and bad.

Pioneer II [to Rabbit Ears]: Did the white man cut your face like that?

Rabbit Ears [fiercely]: No. the Sioux Indians did that. In battle I was wounded and captured by the Sioux. That is how they count coup on their enemies.

Pioneer II: Count coup?

Running Fox: Counting coup means leaving a mark on the enemy. It is what some Indian warriors do to their enemies.

Rabbit Ears: Some had it worse. Sometimes the whole nose is cut off.

Pioneer II [shuddering]: Oh.

Pioneer I [sarcastically]: It looks like you are getting your money's worth.

Pioneer I [frowning]: Oh, shut up! This is horrible. [to Rabbit Ears] Your own people, Indians, did that to you.

Rabbit Ears [proudly]: The Sioux are not my people. The Crows are my people. The Crows had the land and the buffalo until the Sioux came. The Crows fought the Sioux. But the Sioux were many. They had the white man's fire stick, the rifle. [Reflecting for a moment and then waving his own rifle] But the Crows now have rifles, too. The Sioux still fight us, and we fight them. We fight. Many of us have joined the white man to fight the Sioux.

Pioneer II: Yet you are partners with Running Fox who is part Sioux.

Rabbit Ears: Running Fox is also part white. Running Fox and I must live. We must eat. We have known each other for many moons. We have our own tribe between ourselves. It is called friendship. It is older than the coming of the Sioux or the coming of the white man. The Great Spirit would like us all to be of the tribe of friendship, but few listen to The Great Spirit.

Pioneer II: You speak a strange wisdom, but you speak the white man's language well.

Rabbit Ears: That is because of Running Fox.

Running Fox: Like I said. Rabbit Ears hears a lot. He's done more talking than he usually does. But I'll make it very simple for you. My father was a white man and my mother was a Sioux Indian. I learned the white man's language from my father. I also learned that my father preferred the Indian ways to those of the white man. He married my mother and was very happy in Indian country until he died a quiet and peaceful death. [There is a brief silence. Running Fox speaks respectfully to Pioneer I.] You are right in calling me a half-breed because that is what I am. I like being called a half-breed. I don't have to be an Indian, and I don't have to be a white man. There is a lot of freedom in that.

Pioneer I [bored]: You probably make more money sitting on the fence. You half-breeds are no good.

Running Fox [scowling]: You probably wanted to make a lot of money going West. Now you're "busted." You want to take it out on someone. You want to blame someone. Don't blame me. As far as I'm concerned, the white man should learn to appreciate the Indian's property rights as much as his own. He should . . .

Pioneer I [furiously]: We shouldn't have to listen to you. Why, you little half-breed, I ought to . . . [Pioneer I grabs Running Fox by the shirt. Immediately Rabbit Ears grabs Pioneer I by the throat. Pioneer I releases Running Fox and is thrown up against his "BUSTED" wagon by Rabbit Ears.]

Rabbit Ears [Holding Pioneer I up against his "BUSTED" wagon with one hand on Pioneer I's throat.]: Ought to what? Hurt Running Fox? No one hurts Running Fox!!! [Rabbit Ears with his free hand smashes Pioneer I in the stomach. Pioneer I groans and collapses.] Wake up, wake up, white man! [Rabbit Ears slaps Pioneer I in the face a few times and then spits into his face.] Wake up! Wake up, white man, or I'll hit you again.

Pioneer I [groggy and trying to regain consciousness]: Okay, okay . . . Okay. [Rabbit Ears continues to hold Pioneer I against the "BUSTED" wagon during this whole ordeal.]

Running Fox: Put him down, Rabbit Ears! That's enough! Put him down.

Rabbit Ears [still holding Pioneer I by the throat.]: He grabbed you, Running Fox, so I grabbed him. He'll leave you alone now. [He releases a choking Pioneer I. Rabbit Ears then trips Pioneer I, grabs him again, and throws him to the ground. Rabbit Ears then sits on Pioneer I's stomach. Rabbit Ears is grinning as he speaks.] You can always trust the white man when you sit on him. Then you know where he is.

Running Fox [bending over to speak to Pioneer I]: You shouldn't upset Rabbit Ears. He has what the white man calls "a short fuse." He has trouble understanding the white man's ways.

Pioneer I [groaning]: Apparently. Would you tell him to get off me?

Rabbit Ears [sneering at Pioneer I]: The white man speaks with forked tongue. I'll cut out his tongue. [Rabbit Ears pulls out a hunting knife from his boot. He holds the knife directly before the eyes of Pioneer I.] I will cut out his tongue.

Pioneer I [horrified and groaning]: Oh. God! Oh. God! Somebody stop him! Somebody stop him!

Running Fox [grinning]: Rabbit Ears, don't cut out his tongue.

Rabbit Ears [also grinning]: Why not?

Running Fox [laughing]: Because it would be too messy. Just sit on him for a while. It will do him good.

Pioneer I [moaning]: Oh. God!

Rabbit Ears [frowning]: The white man speaks with forked tongue. He should have his tongue cut out. [Sullenly he puts his knife back into his boot and stands up. He stares at Pioneer I who is moaning on the ground. Rabbit Ears shakes his head in a negative manner and spits on the ground. He then goes to the side of the stage and leans against "THE BUSTED" wagon. Pioneer I continues to moan and cough on the ground.]

Running Fox [to Pioneer II]: Rabbit Ears is hard to understand. We've been together for five years in the white man's time. We take care of each other. Many white men cannot understand this. Most white men want everything for themselves. They do not understand us. They do not understand our Indian ways.

Pioneer II: But what are the Indian ways?

Running Fox: In an Indian village . . . after a buffalo hunt, the first meat from the hunt is given to the old, the poor, and the sick. Only then will the hunters themselves eat. The old, the poor, and the sick eat first. This is very different from your people. Each white man wants to take care of himself first. He cares little or nothing for the old, the poor, and the sick. The Indian cannot understand why a strong white man will not protect those of his own tribe who are weak. The white man cannot understand why the strong Indians take care of others first.

Pioneer II: But that is not true! The white man wants to take care of his family, his wife, his children. That is why so many men are coming West. To have something! To have some land! To have a future! To get there first! To build a life!

Running Fox: But does the white man really care for anyone beyond his own family? Will he go through a village and make sure that all are eating before he eats? The white man grabs for himself and his family first! He cannot even think his own village's problems much less solve them. I know! I was taught this by my father, a white man. He once lived in your great city of New York. But he left it. He left it because he could not stand seeing so many hungry children and so many rich people who cared nothing for those hungry children. As a trader he learned the Indian ways. Later he married my mother. He preferred the Indian ways. He liked the idea that in an Indian village all go hungry or none go hungry. The white people considered him a dreamer. A dreamer? He was no dreamer! In his heart he was a Sioux warrior! That is what a Sioux warrior is! One who takes care of the weak, and the poor, before he takes care of himself. [There is a brief silence. Running Fox speaks in a more subdued tone.] Tell me, tell me this . . . why do you come into Indian territory? If life is so good in the white man's land, why does the white man come West?

Pioneer II: I don't know why each white man comes West, but I am here because the white man in the North fights the white man in the South.

Running Fox [laughing]: So you have tribes too, don't you? Just as the Sioux fights the Crow, the Union Army fights the Confederate Army. I am a half-breed, part Sioux and part white, but I can read the white paper with the black marks. I can read your newspapers. My father taught me that.

Rabbit Ears [laughing and sneering at Pioneer I who is still groggy and holding his stomach]: The white man speaks with a forked tongue. Let the Indian cut out the tongue! Kill the white man!

Pioneer II [speaking as though his words were common knowledge and as though they should be accepted without question.]: The white man believes that the western lands of our country should be developed. We have "a manifest destiny" to spread Christian civilization and progress to the Pacific Coast. We have . . .

Running Fox [laughing]: You have land lust! This is what you have! Land lust! You cannot live with each other and with your land lust in the East, so you will spread it West! You cannot even keep North and South together in your own world. Why bring your killing out here? What are these words "Christian Civilization?" I have read your book called The New Testament. The book which has the acts and the words of the holy man, Jesus. Did Jesus grab land from others? Did he send out blue coat soldiers to make a few men rich? Did Jesus tell you to use rifles against women and children? No. Jesus did none of those things, but you do! You use your God in a cowardly way to make yourselves rich! I don't believe the God of Jesus has anything to do with you. Jesus told you to love one another. Do you love one another? Do the Northerners love the Southerners? Do the Southerners love the Northerners? No!!! Now you have your troubles for having enslaved the black people. You will get more trouble if you try to enslave the Indian and take Indian land. My father warned me about you.

Rabbit Ears [laughing]: You who speak with forked tongue!

Running Fox: Yes, with very forked tongue.

Pioneer II [somberly]: Well, that's why I am here. To escape the white man's forked tongue. You see in America today, if you don't have $300 you must go to war or they will throw you in jail or execute you. You must have $300 to escape the white man's war. What they call The Civil War. If you have the $300 you can pay someone to take your place on the battlefield. The Great White Father, President Lincoln, has said that down through history the drafting of men is an accepted policy of government. I had begun to believe that our government was different than other governments. I guess I was wrong. What Lincoln is really saying is let someone else kill or be killed just so you pay three hundred bucks. Well, I thought I would save my money just like old Abe Lincoln will save his votes and remain in the White House. Lincoln can go to hell! He wants to free the black man now that it is politically expedient, but he also wants to enslave men into killing others. So, I took my money, and I came West before the drafting power could get their hands on me. [laughing] Yes, sir, this is the land of opportunity . . . if you can live long enough to find the opportunities.

Running Fox [thoughtfully]: So the white man can buy poor people to do his fighting just as he can make slaves of others to do his work. So that is why the white man loves money so much. He can buy others with it.

Pioneer II: Yes. When I was growing up I was told that all have an equal chance in life, but then I would see that black people and poor people had no chance at all. They were enslaved by their color or by their poverty. [reflecting] Maybe the Indian does have a better way to take care of the poor and the weak first. Maybe we will learn this once our "manifest destiny" is completed.

Running Fox: What is the white man's "manifest destiny"?

Pioneer II: Why to develop all the land, all the land from the Atlantic Ocean to the Pacific Ocean. There is all that land and all those white people. It is the command of history. It is in our holy book, the Bible. The Bible, "the Word of God," has told us to be fruitful and multiply, and to subdue the land. God wills it.

Running Fox [frowning]: Are you saying that The Great Spirit desires to give all the land to you? Again I tell you, I have read your Bible many times. My father taught me to read your book and try to understand it. I remember no words such as "manifest destiny" in that book.

Pioneer II [laughing]: Oh, no, you won't find the words "manifest destiny" in the Bible. President Polk used those words about twenty years ago. President Polk, one of The Great White Fathers to the Indian. The Great White Father Polk told us that we have a "manifest destiny."

Running Fox [shaking his head in a negative manner]: I do not like those words "Great White Father." It has been proven many times that such a man is neither great to the Indian nor a father to the Indian. Time after time "The Great White Father" and his sons have broken their word to the Indian. Treaty after treaty has been broken and more and more Indian land has been taken by the white man. "The Great White Father" is neither great nor a very good father. About all that can be said about him is that he is white.

[Rabbit Ears nods his head approvingly and then spits on the ground.]

Pioneer II [shrugging his shoulders]: Regardless, it is the white man's destiny under the Providence of God to develop the land.

Running Fox [again shaking his head negatively]: It seems that the white man tries to use The Great Spirit for the white man's own greed. <u>The white man</u> says that he has "a manifest destiny" and then <u>the white man</u> says that The Great Spirit wants <u>the white man</u> to own all the land. All this is very convenient for <u>the white man</u>. [laughing] Yes, very convenient for <u>the white man</u>. Most Indians feel that The Great Spirit gave life and land to all living creatures. There is no need to "own" land and enslave others. The white man, however, always wants to own land and enslave others. The white man now fights a great war in the North and in the South because of owned land and owned slaves. I do not think The Great Spirit is on the side of the white man. I think The Great Spirit is on the side of life and freedom.

Pioneer II [reflecting]: Much of what you say is true. That is why I have come West. The Civil War makes the Eastern states run red with blood. They estimate that over 500,000 men will die in that war before it is over.

Running Fox: 500,000 men! Why, there are not 25,000 men in the entire Sioux nation, and the Sioux are considered to be more numerous than the countless grains of sand to the Crow! 500,000 men to die in a war! That is impossible! Certainly The Great Spirit does not want that!

Pioneer II: In the last four years there has been a call for over 800,000 men to war in the North alone. Probably 400,000 have been called to war in the South. And as for killing, well, a few years ago, 24,000 men; 12,000 from each side died at Antietam in just one day! 24,000 men died in just one day!

Rabbit Ears [listening intensely and then speaking seriously]: In a Crow and Sioux battle if five warriors from both sides are killed, it is considered a horrible day of death, but 24,000 warriors in one day, that is hard to think of . . . it would be the end of both tribes. Maybe the white man is so many, he cannot respect life. The Indian has much to fear.

Pioneer II [frowning]: The white man has much to fear from the white man. If you do not go to war or pay someone to go in your place, you can be imprisoned, shot or hanged. The Northern politicians say they want to free the slaves in the South, yet the same politicians want to enslave other men to do the killing. The individual has no rights and no freedom during war time. He had best play the fox, or he'll be dead.

Running Fox: I am glad that I am part white and part Indian. This way I can choose my own life. Sioux warriors glory in battle. It is a disgrace for a Sioux warrior to live past the age of forty. He loves death in battle. His great war cry is "Hookay Hey!" "Hookay Hey!" "It's a great day to fight!" "It is a great day to die!" [There is a brief silence. Running Fox begins laughing.] Me . . . I'm Running Fox. For me, it is always a great day to live. So I became an interpreter. [to Pioneer I] Sure, I sit on the fence . . . sometimes the fence is made of barbed wire and it is very uncomfortable . . . but, well, sitting is part of living even if it's uncomfortable, and living is what I intend to do.

Pioneer II: So you live by being an interpreter?

Running Fox: That is the advantage of being part white and part Indian. I met Rabbit Ears when he was captured by my tribe. We have become great friends. Neither of us care much for the glories of war. Both the white man and the Indian use us . . . and we use them. We try to stay out of trouble, and usually trouble stays away from us. But a lot of trouble is on the way. And I think it is all because of the white man's "manifest destiny" . . . a destiny which has nothing to do with The Great Spirit. When the white man first took the land from the Sioux, he pushed the Sioux into Crow territory. Indians must have land to live. Buffalo live on the land, and the Indian lives on the buffalo. White men have taken the land and the buffalo. Indians will fight each other . . . for a while. But soon the Indian will understand that he must fight the white man, if the Indian is to survive. I can only see trouble in the future.

Pioneer II: Why cannot the Indian learn the white man's ways? Surely there is enough land for all of us.

Running Fox: Some Indians will learn the white man's ways, and some Indians will not. But, will the white man learn some of the Indian's ways? Will your strong protect your weak? Will the white man respect Indian land just as he respects another white man's land? Land lust . . . can the white man control his land lust? Can he see that there is One Spirit who wants us to live together in peace? Can the white man learn some of the Indian's ways?

Pioneer II [thoughtfully]: We will, no doubt, see what happens.

Running Fox [thoughtfully]: We certainly will [There is a long silence as the lights fall.]

ACT TWO

[A doctor's office in the city of Denver, Colorado. It is mid-September, 1864. Dr. Ben Goodwill is speaking with Lieutenant Landmark. Dr. Ben is in his early thirties and shows signs of going bald. He is about 5'10" and weighs close to two hundred pounds. He is very robust with large shoulders and a solid looking chest and stomach. Lieutenant Landmark is in his late twenties. He is dressed in a Union Army officer's uniform. He is about 5'7" and is quite slender. He is wearing spectacles. He is also holding a towel with red blood splotches on it to his cheek. The office has a door in the center of the stage background. There are three chairs and a table. Shelves and cabinets are in the background. The shelves and cabinets display books, towels, specimens, medical apparatus of the mid-19th century, and various bottles. A doctor's diploma hangs on the wall. As the act begins, a bottle of whiskey and a bottle of horse liniment are placed on the table along with a pitcher of water and a basin.]

Lt. Landmark [holding the towel to his own cheek]: Jesus, doctor, that hurts like hell.

Dr. Goodwill [frowning professionally]: It was a nasty impacted wisdom tooth. I'm sorry, but I had to cut around it. It was a real fight to dig it out. But it's out, and that is the important thing. About all that I have now is whiskey or horse liniment to ease the pain. Which do you prefer?

Lt. Landmark: Give me the whiskey to gargle with for the inside of my mouth. I'll probably need the horse liniment for the outside. Jesus, my whole mouth feels like it's been hit with a sledge hammer.

Dr Goodwill [pouring water into a basin and washing his

hands]: I'm sorry about the pain. I ordered pain killers from the East some time ago, but they haven't arrived. With the war going on and the Indian trouble, it is hard to get supplies into Denver. The best I can offer you is whiskey for gargling and the horse liniment for the soreness. You'll be fine in a day or so.

[Lt. Landmark puts down his towel, gargles the whiskey, and then looks around helplessly with the blood and whiskey still in his mouth.]

Dr. Goodwill [Watching the lieutenant's confusion, the doctor laughs and places the basin in front of the lieutenant.]: Here. just spit into this. [Gratefully, the lieutenant spits into the basin.]

Lt. Landmark: Thanks, Doc. [He again places the towel to his cheek. A few seconds pass. The lieutenant places a portion of the towel in his own mouth then removes the towel from his mouth and stares at it.] The bleeding seems to have stopped. [looking at the whiskey bottle] Do you mind if . . .

Dr. Goodwill [going to a shelf, getting a glass, and handing it to the lieutenant]: Go right ahead. Help yourself. It will be good for you. [The lieutenant pours a half glass of whiskey and drinks it.]

Lt. Landmark [sighing a few seconds]: Boy, that can knock out the pain. [reflecting] What do I owe you?

Dr. Goodwill: Two bucks. [smiling] No charge for the whiskey.

Lt. Landmark: That's cheap. The major told me you were the cheapest in town. He's usually right when it comes to money. He has to be.

Dr. Goodwill: Why is that?

Lt. Landmark: The major and I are both in the army's Quartermaster Corps. You know, we make sure that the government isn't being cheated by civilians trying to make a fast buck on the war. The major has just been called back East. Something is wrong with the cost of supplies now that the Union forces are fighting in the South. Too much money is changing hands too quickly. There is not the right amount of guns, ammunitions, and food for the money spent. He has to find out who is cheating the government. I am taking his place out here. It seems that certain people are also cheating the Indians.

Dr. Goodwill [staring at the lieutenant's uniform]: You're a lieutenant, aren't you?

Lt. Landmark: Yes, Lieutenant Landmark. Quartermaster Corps. And you are Doctor Ben Goodwill, the cheapest dentist and doctor in Denver.

Dr. Goodwill [laughing]: Actually I just wanted to be a veterinarian. I like being around horses, cattle, dogs, and cats. Most of the time I prefer them to humans. They don't have wisdom teeth, but they are wiser than most humans. Nothing personal, mind you, but I think animals are smarter than men. They leave each other alone most of the time.

Lt. Landmark: Well, let me pay you an extra dollar for some more of your whiskey. [He pours himself another half glass, then reaches into his pocket and gives the doctor three dollars.]

Dr. Goodwill [taking the money and shrugging his shoulders good-naturedly]: Be my guest. I might as well be a bartender, too. At my stage of the game I might as well be everything. [The doctor stands up, gets a glass, sits down at the table, and pours himself a shot. A few seconds pass. The doctor speaks as though he were alone in the room.] Quartermaster Corps. Government contracts. Guns, ammunition, blankets, food. [quietly] Everyone making a buck off human misery. [He pulls himself away from his reverie and speaks directly to the lieutenant.] I wish you luck in trying to figure out this Indian mess. I wish you major luck in figuring out the Civil War mess. I wonder what would happen if humans could ever spend as much money for peace as they can for war.

[somberly] But I don't think that is in the cards. Money and war. War and money. The two great curses of the human race. [taking a sip from his glass and laughing] You can see why I wanted to be a veterinarian.

Lt. Landmark [looking around at the office]: You seem to be doing okay for yourself. You've probably got a nice little practice out here. Been here long?

Dr. Goodwill: Oh, about a year. It's been pretty good. [sighing] Anything would be better than being a doctor back East. I was at the battle of Antietam. [shaking his head in a negative manner] You're in the Quartermaster Corps, but have you seen combat?

Lt. Landmark: No. I just watch out for government fraud behind the lines. I try to keep our men armed and fed. It is not always easy.

Dr. Goodwill [somberly]: No. I'm sure it isn't, but it's worse in a field hospital with men screaming and trying to hold their guts together after cannon shot has blown their stomachs open. It's worse when you have to amputate an arm or leg with nothing to knock out the pain and you have to place a leather strap between a soldier's teeth to stop him from breaking those teeth because of the pain. It's worse when you see all those mangled bodies amidst a sky full of gray gun powder, and the sickening smell of blood and burned flesh. Screams, and pain, and leather and gun powder and blood and burned flesh . . . [shaking his head negatively] I couldn't have taken much more of it. When my time in hell was over, that is, when I had served my time in the U.S. Army, I left for Denver. [taking a sip of his drink] I came West to be a veterinarian and find some mental peace. But it isn't working. It isn't working at all. No, there are too many humans . . . far too many humans. [He pours himself another drink.]

Lt. Landmark [critically]: Oh, come on, now. The Colorado Territory will soon become a state. The citizens turned down statehood during the last election, but it's inevitable that Colorado will join the Union. It's destiny. A man can better himself out here. Why, right now I'm scouting land investments for The United States Land and Cattle Company in my spare time. [beaming] Think of the future that stands before us with the railroads coming West, the mining companies, and the . . .

Dr. Goodwill [quietly]: And the Indians.

Lt. Landmark [self-righteously]: The Indians. Yes, that is what I am here to correct, the injustice done to the Indians. Many people in the East know that the Indians have not been treated fairly. Government contractors have made dishonest fortunes supplying the Indians with rotten flour, diseased cattle, and . . .

Dr. Goodwill [cynically]: And grabbing their land. [somberly] Lieutenant Landmark, you are in a very strange position. On the one hand you are trying to make sure that the Indians will get a fair shake because of the U.S. treaties which demand that the Indians be provided for. On the other hand, you want to be on the side of land developers and work for a cattle company. Don't you understand that the Indian depends on the buffalo for his subsistence, and the buffalo requires land for grazing? The Indian tribes are perpetually pushed West, and more and more land is grabbed by either the government or private interests for big profits.

Lt. Landmark [self-righteously]: Now, wait just a minute, just a minute. You can't tell me that the Indians should own all the land from Colorado to the Pacific Ocean!

Dr. Goodwill [as though in a semi-dream state]: At first Indians attacked other Indians for buffalo grazing territories. But those days are coming to an end. More and more the Indian fights the white man because of broken treaties, bad food from the government or not enough of it, and the loss of the Indian way of life. Just a little while ago a farmer named Hungate and his family were found murdered and mutilated. They say that Indians did it . . . Indians who no doubt resented a white man fencing their land. [shaking his head negatively] And I thought I was just going to deal with animals and escape the horrors of war. But no, that is impossible now. Hungate's two children were found with their throats cut so that their heads were almost severed from their bodies. Mrs. Hungate was stabbed in several places and had been raped. Hungate himself was horribly mutilated with his scalp torn off. Their bodies were put on public display for the people of Denver. . . . The bodies were placed in a box, side by side, the two children between the parents. . . . After seeing the bodies, many people became so frightened that they barricaded approximately 500 women and children in the center of town for their protection. There aren't enough soldiers to protect every farm and ranch in the territory. But, well, the people couldn't stay barricaded forever. They had to go back to their farms and ranches. But you can imagine the fear and hysteria that is rampant throughout Denver. All sorts of stories are about. There is the story of a woman raped by twelve Indians. There is another report of a man found with his arms and legs cut off, and his testicles and penis jammed in his mouth. There is a war cry against the Indian in this town which is like nothing that has ever been heard before. Do you think that "The Quartermaster Corps'" worrying about government contracts and some barrels of rotten flour is going to stop the hysteria of a whole city? I don't think so. The government had better send plenty of seasoned and well disciplined troops to keep what peace is left or there will no end to the slaughter.

Lt. Landmark: The government is mounting a huge offensive against the Confederates right now. Every man who can be spared is fighting for the Union cause. Troops cannot be spared at this time. When the war is over then, well, maybe . .

Dr Goodwill [furiously]: Then . . . well . . . well . . . then there is going to be so much death and mutilation that no one will be able to stomach it. No one. [The door to the office is thrown open. A wild and furious Rabbit Ears enters. Running Fox is unconscious and is cradled in Rabbit Ears' arms. Both Rabbit Ears' and Running Fox's faces are covered with blood.]

Rabbit Ears [anxiously setting Running Fox in a chair]: Which one of you is the doctor? I need a doctor right away.

Running Fox and I were attacked by soldiers in the streets. We had been hired by the government as Interpreters and scouts, but we were attacked on the streets! Running Fox tried to explain who we were to the soldiers, but they just kept hitting us.

[Dr Goodwill takes a look at Running Fox. He also scrutinizes Rabbit Ears.]

Dr. Goodwill: I think I had better get a good look at both of you.

Rabbit Ears: Don't worry about me. I'm okay. Just take care of Running Fox. [Dr Goodwill goes to the shelves and gets some towels. He hands a towel to Rabbit Ears.]

Dr. Goodwill: Here, wipe your face with this. Let's see what they have done to your friend. [Rabbit Ears wipes his own face. Dr. Goodwill wipes the face of Running Fox. After both faces are wiped, cuts and bruises can be seen. Dr. Goodwill then puts some horse liniment on his towel and then touches the cuts and bruises on Running Fox's face. He takes Rabbit Ears' towel and also puts horse liniment on it.] Here, put some horse liniment on your own cuts and bruises. It will be good for the pain. [Rabbit Ears applies his towel with the liniment to his own bruises on his own face.]

Rabbit Ears [wincing from the sting]: I never should have left my rifle at the governor's office. I never should have left it. You cannot trust the white man. You cannot.

Lt. Landmark: What happened?

Rabbit Ears: We had been hired as scouts and interpreters by both Governor Evans and Colonel Chivington to speak with Chief Black Kettle of the Cheyenne Indians. Just an hour ago we were talking with the governor and the colonel. They advised us to leave our weapons with them rather than appear as armed Indians in the streets of Denver. And what happened? We were beaten up by soldiers! That's what happened. [raging] I have such a hot fire within me that I so want to go get my rifle and take care of those soldiers myself. . . . What did they do to Running Fox?

Dr Goodwill: He'll be okay. You call him Running Fox? Maybe someone should teach Running Fox how to duck. He's got some bruises and some bad cuts. It looks like they knocked the wind out of him. Let me try this. [He takes a whiskey glass and pours a shot into it. He places the glass under Running Fox's nose. Running Fox smells the liquor and pulls his head to one side. Dr. Goodwill again moves the whiskey glass so that it is under Running Fox's nose. Whenever the glass is under Running Fox's nose, Running Fox moves his head away from it. This goes on for a few moments. Finally, he revives, opens his eyes, looks at his new surroundings, and places his hand on the bruises on his face. He begins to speak slowly.]

Running Fox: What? What happened? [He notices Rabbit Ears.] What? . . . Where are we?

Rabbit Ears [fiercely]: It's okay, Running Fox. It's okay. They hit you pretty bad, but I busted up two of them pretty good. When I got my rifle back, I'll kill a few more.

Running Fox [as though he were in a dream]: No, don't do that. Don't do that. We've got to find Black Kettle of the Cheyenne and speak with him. There is the possibility of peace. If we can only find Black Kettle and get him to listen to reason.

Rabbit Ears [scowling and addressing Dr. Goodwill and Lt. Landmark]: Running Fox thinks you can reason with the white man. He thinks the Indian should listen to the white man. He thinks talk is going to make everything right.

Running Fox: If both sides don't talk, there will be war.

Rabbit Ears [furiously]: Then let there be war.

Lt. Landmark: You don't mean that.

Rabbit Ears [sternly]: I mean what I say.

Dr. Goodwill [to Rabbit Ears]: I think that you had better listen to your friend.

Rabbit Ears [scowling]: Look what you white men have done to my friend!

Dr. Goodwill [annoyed]: It seems what I have done for your friend is wipe the blood off his face and revive him. [Rabbit Ears listens to the doctor, grunts stoically, and begins to cool off.] It seems that both of you have met up with some of the Colorado Volunteers. The regular army has been called East for the big fight against the Confederates. Volunteers had to be called up because of the Indian troubles. These volunteers are rowdies. They are drunk most of the time. They have been waiting in bars and gambling houses for their chance to fight Indians. I have come to think that they are more trouble than the Indians.

Running Fox [reflecting]: So, that's it. Rabbit Ears and I were hired to help bring peace to the territory. We had just met with your officials . . . Governor . . . Governor Evans and Colonel . . . Colonel . . .

Dr. Goodwill [sighing]: Governor Evans and Colonel Chivington. You fellows just didn't hit town at the right time. This whole place is mad with fear. Indians massacred and mutilated a farmer and his family. The townspeople saw the bodies, and the smell of the blood vengeance is in the air.

Running Fox: Well, Rabbit Ears and I had nothing to do with that.

Dr Goodwill: When the smell of blood vengeance is in the air, when drunken volunteers wander the street without military discipline, when no one is safe either in town or on the plains; then the mob rules. You can't argue with the mob. No matter what your intentions, you can't reason with the mob. To make matters worse, Governor Evans has made an official statement that all hostile Indians are to be shot on sight. The

Indians' possessions can be kept by whoever kills them. [laughing sarcastically] Who knows a hostile Indian from a friendly Indian? What Governor Evans has done is give a license to kill to every outlaw, cardsharp, and murderer in the territory.

Rabbit Ears [scowling]: Listen to this white man, Running Fox. Listen to him. Feel the bruises and cuts on your face and listen to him. I'm for giving the governor and the colonel back their money and getting out of here. This is no place for an Indian.

Running Fox [sternly]: Rabbit Ears, we have been paid good money, and we will do a good job.

Dr. Goodwill: Just understand what you are getting into. I don't know if both of you understand the white man and what is most important to him.

Rabbit Ears [scowling]: Sure, that's easy to understand. The white man loves two things: gold and land. He will die for gold, and he will die for land. Every Indian knows that. The yellow metal drives the white man crazy. And land . . . to own land, to rent land, to sell land . . . from the land he can get more yellow metal. Indians care nothing for the yellow metal. . . . They care nothing for gold. Indians believe that the land was given for all. Owning land or gold makes no sense. But the white man will do anything for land or gold. Anything. There you have it all. The Great Spirit gave the land to everyone. The white man spits at the Great Spirit when the few enslave the many for land and gold.

Dr. Goodwill [smiling]: Your name is Rabbit Ears, isn't it?

Rabbit Ears: Yes.

Dr Goodwill: Rabbit Ears, you have certainly listened well and come to know the soul of many a white man. In fact Colonel Chivington with whom you met today, would agree with you. He was a Christian minister before he became a soldier. When he was younger he used to say that he thought the Christian God and the Great Spirit were pretty much the same. No doubt that would have shocked his bishop. The colonel, when he was a minister, was also against slavery. His congregation was pro-slavery, and the congregation threatened to tar and feather him if he gave a sermon defending the rights of black people. [laughing] On a Sunday morning Chivington placed the Bible and two pistols on top of the pulpit. His opening sentence of the sermon was: "By the grace of God and these two revolvers. I am going to preach today." Well, Chivington, as you know, is a mighty big man, over 6'6". The revolvers made him even bigger. He gave his sermon and no one tarred and feathered him. Some time later Chivington left the ministry to fight for the Union cause against the Confederates in New Mexico. He was victorious in his campaigns and won some important battles. He is now known as "The Fighting Parson" and is quite the hero for many people in the Colorado territory.

Running Fox: All of this is good to know. It sounds as though Colonel Chivington will be a great help at the peace meeting.

Dr. Goodwill [somberly]: I don't know if that is true.

Running Fox: Why isn't it true?

Dr. Goodwill: Because of what has happened in the last few months. Recently Colorado's bid for statehood was voted down. Many people thought if Colorado came into the Union now, war taxes would be levied against the people. The mining interests were especially against it as they would have had to pay the most. In addition, if Colorado were part of the United States, men could be drafted to fight in the Civil War. So, statehood was voted down. Governor Evans had hoped to become one of Colorado's first United States senators. Chivington wanted his place in the U.S. House of Representatives. Let us say that both of them saw their political stars fading. In addition, the Indian atrocities have made the people question the leadership of both Governor Evans and Colonel Chivington. Who knows what men will do to see their political stars shine again? Who knows.

Running Fox [perplexed]: What do you mean?

Dr. Goodwill [gravely shaking his head in a negative and ominous manner]: Who knows what men will do to see their stars shine again?
[This last line should be delivered less as a question as an ominous prophecy. Lt. Landmark, Running Fox and Rabbit Ears stare intensely and thoughtfully at Dr. Goodwill as the lights fall.]

ACT THREE

[A large meeting room at Camp Weld, September 28, 1864. A door is at the back of the stage. There are approximately ten chairs arranged in a semi-circle. Governor Evans of the Colorado Territory is speaking with Colonel Chivington of the Third Colorado Volunteers. Governor Evans is well dressed in mid-19th Century fashion. He wears a vested suit with a gold watch chain. Colonel Chivington is attired in a Union officer's uniform. Governor Evans is approximately 5'10" and weighs 180 pounds. Chivington is over 6'6", weighs nearly 300 pounds, and has a reddish colored beard and mustache. Both men are in their late forties/early fifties.]

Evans: Well, Chivington, we find ourselves in a very sorry state of affairs. A few weeks ago the people rejected statehood, yet the people want the government to protect them from the Indians. We don't have the manpower to give them that protection. The people don't seem to understand the magnitude of the problem.

Chivington: Governor Evans, there is nothing but unrest in Denver. At first the people were so frightened by the Hungate massacre, and seeing those bodies displayed in the city, that they wanted military protection. The regular army for the most part was called East to fight the Confederates. Yet the people still wanted protection. We both agreed that something had to be done, and I was able to form the regiment of The Third Colorado Volunteers. I told you in the beginning that they were to serve for one hundred days. It is now the end of September and fifty days of their service have passed and the people are complaining. They are complaining because the volunteers haven't done anything but sit in the saloons all day, get drunk, and boast about what they will do to the Indians. A lot of them have never seen a hostile Indian.

Unlike the regular soldiers, these ones are totally undisciplined and are harassing the citizens. I really don't know what to do. We need the volunteers to protect us from the Indians, but who will protect us from the volunteers?

Evans [sarcastically]: Well, Colonel, you are going to have to do something. Can't you assemble the men and go on an expedition to rid the territory of hostile Indians? Can't you do something to get public opinion on our side?

Chivington [furiously]: How can you fight the enemy if you don't know where the enemy is? It's not like my fighting the Confederates in New Mexico. The Confederates were white men who fought like white men. You met them on the open field and you killed them. But this . . . this fighting on the run, this chasing a few Indians here and a few Indians there, well, it's impossible. In addition, the volunteers are complaining that they haven't been paid.

Evans [thoughtfully]: It will be a lot easier to get the volunteers money once they have achieved a victory.

Chivington [scornfully]: Look, Governor, finding Indians out on a prairie is like finding a row boat in the middle of the ocean. I can't kill what I can't find. I'm good at winning battles, but I have to get to the battle. What do you expect me to do?

Evans [furious in his frustration]: I EXPECT YOU TO DO SOMETHING! YOU'RE THE COLONEL OVER THE VOLUNTEERS! DO SOMETHIING! My God, we can't let a whole territory be intimidated by a handful of savages.

[There is a knock at the door.]

Evans (furiously]: COME IN!

[Major Wynkoop, a young officer over 6' tall in his late twenties, enters. He is wearing a Union army officer's uniform, has dark hair and a mustache, and is quite handsome.]

Wynkoop [good-naturedly shaking hands with the governor and the colonel]: Governor, Colonel, good to see you both. I think I have great news for all of us. Chief Black Kettle and White Antelope of the Cheyenne tribe are on their way here to Camp Weld to talk peace! Think of it! Peace! Peace at last! I have sent the interpreter, Running Fox, and the Crow Indian scout, Rabbit Ears, to bring them here today. They should all be here within an hour. [exuberantly] Think of it! Peace!

Chivington: Who gave you the permission to arrange peace talks? I didn't order you to do that!

Wynkoop [brushing the remark aside]: No one said I could, and no one said I couldn't. What I have done makes good military sense. Most of our men are being ordered East to fight the Confederates. We don't have the soldiers to fight two enemies at once. That is, we cannot fight both the Confederates and the Indians at the same time. When the Confederates are defeated, there will be more men to defend the Colorado Territory. [cheerfully] But I don't think that will even be necessary. If we treat Black Kettle and his Cheyennes fairly, there will he no need for extra troops.

Evans [furiously]: WHAT DO YOU MEAN? WHAT DO YOU MEAN? I sent word to Black Kettle immediately after the massacre of the Hungate family. I told him to deliver the Indians responsible for the atrocities to me for trial. Nothing happened. NOTHING! Black Kettle said he would not come to talk . . . now you say he will come to talk. What is the meaning of this?

Wynkoop: I and 130 soldiers rode out to Black Kettle's camp and spoke to him. He explained to me that he could not turn over those responsible for the massacre to you because he did not know who committed the crimes. He didn't know if the warriors were of his particular tribe or of another. You can't hold him responsible for what other Indians have done.

Evans [exploding]: WELL, THE PEOPLE . . . THE CITIZENS WILL HOLD HIM RESPONSIBLE!!! Someone has to be responsible! There were Cheyenne arrows in those poor Hungate people, and the Cheyennes will pay for what they have done. It is that simple.

Chivington [breathing heavily in a warlike manner]: Yes, it is that simple.

Wynkoop [annoyed]: No, it is not that simple.

Evans [furiously]: Oh, yes, it is.

Wynkoop [vehemently]: Oh, no, it is not. Governor, you can't even keep the volunteers under control in the city of Denver. Most of them are drunk all day. They are firing firearms in the city. They are beating up civilians. The people are beginning to fear the volunteers more than the Indians.

Chivington: Yes, that's another problem we have. The volunteers were only commissioned for one hundred days' service. The citizens now call the volunteers: "The Bloodless Hundred Dazers!" Soon the volunteers' time will be up, and they haven't caught or killed a single Indian.

Wynkoop [frowning]: We don't have to catch or kill Indians. We have to learn to live with them. They are human beings just like we are. They have their hostile renegades. We have our drunken volunteers.

Evans [furiously]: But our volunteers don't mutilate women and children!

Wvnkoop [quietly]: I don't think that Black Kettle or his peaceful Cheyennes have done any such thing.

Evans [sneering]: Tell it to the people! Tell it to the people who want the federal government's military protection, but who don't want to pay their taxes and join the Union! Tell it to the people who want volunteers, but who don't want to pay the volunteers! Tell it to the people who want everything, but who don't want to pay for it! [A few seconds pass. Governor Evans sighs.] Tell it to the people.

Wvnkoop [conciliatory]: Look, Governor Evans. President Lincoln appointed you Governor of the Colorado Territory, didn't he.

Evans: Yes.

Wynkoop: How did Lincoln resolve the Sioux uprising in Minnesota two years ago? The authorities wanted over three hundred Indians hanged. 495 white men, women and children had been either killed, maimed or raped. Their farms and homes had been burned. The "people" . . . the white people wanted three hundred Indians hanged. Lincoln himself investigated the matter. He read the trial material, and then he decided that only thirty-three Indians were really guilty. Those thirty-three were hanged. [There is a silence.] I think that sets a pretty good precedent, Governor. Find out who are guilty, try them, and, if found guilty – punish them. But don't punish a whole tribe for what a few renegades have done.

Chivington [frowning]: It is not that simple.

Wynkoop [also frowning]: It is that simple.

Chivington: No it isn't. In Minnesota they had the Indians in their hands for the trials. We have no prisoners here. The citizens of Denver are hysterical in their demands for action... but we can give them no action.

Wynkoop: Well, give them action, but legal and correct action.

Evans: It is not that simple.

Wynkoop: What's complicated about it?

Evans: It is what the people want here, today, in Colorado. It is not what other people wanted somewhere else at some other time.

Wynkoop [very seriously]: You, as the governor, should make sure that the mob doesn't rule you.

Evans: That's easy for you to say.

Wynkoop [scowling]: Sure, it's easy for me to say. It's the truth, and I'm not a politician.

[There is a knock at the door.]

[Black Kettle and White Antelope appear in white, full-length buckskin robes. Both are in their early forties. Their black hair is parted in the middle and hangs in braids over their shoulders. Running Fox and Rabbit Ears both enter behind Black Kettle and White Antelope. All the Indians are unarmed. Running Fox and Rabbit Ears have bandages on their faces.]

Wynkoop: Governor Evans, Colonel Chivington, I want you to meet Chief Black Kettle. White Antelope, Running Fox, and Rabbit Ears. [With limited formality all bow slightly to one another. Black Kettle and White Antelope sit in the center of the semi-circle of chairs, Evans and Chivington to one side of them. Wynkoop, Running Fox and Rabbit Ears to the other side. Wynkoop should be sitting next to Black Kettle.]

Black Kettle [Placing his hand gently on Wynkoop's shoulder, he addresses Wynkoop as "Tall Chief"]: Tall Chief, I have told Running Fox what needs to be said. Let him speak for me and the Cheyenne people. Both of you know the white man's language and the white man's ways. But Running Fox also knows the Cheyenne tongue and the Cheyenne ways. Let Running Fox speak for me and my people.

Wvnkoop [pleased]: Fine, Running Fox, what has Black Kettle told you?

Running Fox: Major Wvnkoop, Black Kettle has told me that the Cheyenne people want peace. Black Kettle has also told me that he respects and admires you because you are brave and you have risked your life for peace. He trusts you because with only 130 bluecoat soldiers you rode into his camp. Over 500 of his warriors surrounded you. You and your men could have been killed. You went to Black Kettle's camp to try for peace. He and the Cheyenne people now call you "Tall Chief," because you are tall in spirit . . . because you are tall in courage.

Chivington [frowning]: Does Black Kettle know that Major Wynkoop had no such authority to do such a thing? [Black Kettle and White Antelope stare at Chivington apprehensively. Harsh looks appear on the faces of Black Kettle and White Antelope. Running Fox stares attentively at Black Kettle and White Antelope. Running Fox then addresses Chivington with carefully chosen words.]

Running Fox: Colonel Chivington, Major Wynkoop has the respect of Black Kettle, White Antelope, and the Cheyenne people. He is considered a great warrior, a warrior for peace between the white man and the Indian. Please try to understand that with this respect we can begin to talk about ending this terrible killing that is going on all around us.

Evans [irritated]: It is all well and good to talk about "respect" but who had respect for the Hungate family? Where was the "respect" for them? A father and a son scalped. The bodies of two women found mutilated after God knows what kind of degradation and torture. Black Kettle had best understand that those bodies were put on public display before the people of Denver, and the people of Denver are in a wild state of fear and panic. It is going to take more than "respect" to bring these people back to their right minds.

[Black Kettle and White Antelope listen attentively. They both then whisper to Running Fox. Running Fox then whispers to Rabbit Ears. There is a brief silence.]

Running Fox [with somber seriousness]: Governor Evans, the white man signed a treaty with Black Kettle and the Cheyenne people three years ago. Since that time white men seeking gold on Pike's Peak mountain have broken that treaty. But Black Kettle has not attacked them. But it is well known that one of Culonel Chivington's officers had given the command to "Burn villages and kill Cheyennes whenever and wherever found." This is precisely what the white man has done. Five months ago, last May in fact, Lean Bear, one of Black Kettle's own men, had recently returned from Washington after meeting with President Lincoln. Lean Bear actually had a letter signed by Lincoln himself saying that Lean Bear was a man of peace. On the Smoky River, Lean Bear, Black Kettle, and a peaceful Cheyenne village met with some of Colonel Chivington's soldiers. Lean Bear, waving papers of peace and friendship signed by President Lincoln, rode out to show the papers to the soldiers. What did the soldiers do? [Running Fox begins to rage furiously.] THE SOLDIERS SHOT HIM FROM HIS PONY, AND THEN OPENED UP WITH THEIR BIG KILLER GUNS ON THE REST OF THE INDIANS!!! [There is a silence. Evans and Chivington look at each other apprehensively.]

Wynkoop: Colonel, Governor, you know what Running Fox says is true. I would consider my actions very carefully henceforth. It is not good politics to harm Indians friendly to a president, much less kill them when they have letters from the President himself. Colonel, your men opened up with howitzers on peaceful Indians. I wonder what the Eastern newspapers would print about all of this.

Evans [irritated]: Oh damn the Eastern newspapers! A mistake happened. That's all. There is whole territory to be developed out here. There are bound to be a few mistakes.

Chivington: Sure, how was my officer supposed to know who the Indian was, or that he had papers from Lincoln?

Wynkoop [scowling]: Waving a few pieces of paper in the air is not the same thing as waving a rifle in the air, is it, Colonel? Your officer could have tried to find out who the Indian was and what were his intentions. But no, the soldiers had been ordered to "Burn villages and kill Cheyennes whenever and wherever found." Is that how we're supposed to "develop" the Colorado Territory, Governor Evans?

Chivington [Menacingly, he stands up.]: That's enough, Major! You're insubordinate! Right now, you're under my command, and I say you're insubordinate. [Rabbit Ears who has been silent and meditative also stands up. He is almost as tall as Colonel Chivington but leaner. Rabbit Ears has become quite menacing towards Chivington.]

Rabbit Ears [glaring at Chivington]: Watch out how you speak to Tall Chief! I am not afraid of you or any white man. Watch out how you speak to Tall Chief!

[Black Kettle pulls Rabbit Ears aside and whispers to him. Rabbit Ears wants to get into a fight. Rabbit Ears and Chivington continue to glare at each other. Black Kettle places his arm in a brotherly fashion on Rabbit Ears' shoulder and continues to whisper to him. Finally, through great effort, Rabbit Ears controls himself and sits down. Black Kettle also sits down.]

Rabbit Ears [He speaks quietly and is staring at the ground]: Watch how you speak to Tall Chief!

Wynkoop [attempting a mood of reconciliation]: I am sorry for my outburst, gentlemen. We are all here to discuss peace. I believe we all want peace. [He stares at the very stolid expressions on the faces of Governor Evans and Colonel Chivington.] At least, I hope we all want peace. If I was insubordinate, then I apologize. Perhaps it would be best if I let Running Fox continue. [The same stolid looks remain on the faces of Governor Evans and Colonel Chivington. There is a silence.]

Running Fox [very slowly]: When Lean Bear was shot from his horse . . . when the letter for peace from President Lincoln flew to the prairie winds . . . when the killer guns, the howitzers, began to roar . . . well, the Cheyennes fought back. What else could they do? [Addressing Governor Evans and Colonel Chivington.] What would you have done in their place? [Evans and Chivington look at each other uncomfortably. There is a silence. The silence is broken when White Antelope for the first time speaks.]

White Antelope [with great dignity]: I was at the Smoky Hill

River on that day. As soon as Lean Bear was shot by the soldiers, hot war blood began flowing in the spirits of the young warriors. Arrows and bullets from our warriors answered the shooting down of Lean Bear. I told them to stop, but they would not. It was not until Black Kettle rode up that the warriors would listen. Black Kettle told the warriors, "We must not fight with the white people." Because Black Kettle said this, the warriors stopped. Soon then, the soldiers rode away . . . but twenty-eight Indians lay dead.

[There is a silence. Governor Evans frowns. Colonel Chivington breathes heavily. Major Wynkoop speaks in a subdued tone.]

Wynkoop: So you see, gentlemen, even at the cost of losing prestige with his warriors. Black Kettle pleaded for peace. Governor, this is something for you to consider with what you are having to face with the people of Colorado. The majority of the white people want war just as Black Kettle's warriors wanted war. Black Kettle, in the heat of battle, said. "We must not fight with the white people." I think that the leader of the white people should now say, "We must not fight with the Indian people." It is the right thing to say. It is the right thing to do.

Evans [in a surly and scowling manner]: Major Wynkoop, I'll thank you to leave the political decisions pertaining to The Colorado Territory to me and to Colonel Chivington.

Wynkoop [affably]: I was just stating my opinion as a soldier and a citizen.

Chivington [growling]: We have heard your "opinion," Major Wynkoop. But it is unsatisfactory. We want the Indians responsible for the massacre of the Hungate family turned over to us at once. We will give them a fair trial. If they are innocent, we will release them. If they are guilty, we will punish them.

Running Fox [annoyed]: Fine, but are you willing to turn over the soldiers who killed Lean Bear? Are you willing to let the

Cheyenne Indians try the soldiers who killed the Indian friend of President Lincoln?

Evans: Don't be ridiculous! What sort of justice would the soldiers get from the Indians?

Running Fox [more annoyed]: And what sort of justice will Indians get from white men? Let me explain something. There are thousands of Cheyenne warriors. Not all of them are of Black Kettle's tribe. Black Kettle doesn't know which Indians attacked the Hungate family. If he did, he would tell you. Black Kettle is for peace. In addition to stopping the killing when Lean Bear was shot down, Black Kettle has turned over four white prisoners to Major Wynkoop when the Major asked for the prisoners. Black Kettle will do whatever you ask of him to attain peace. But you cannot expect him to do what he cannot do.

Chivington [exasperated]: My rule of fighting white men or Indians is to fight them until they lay down their arms and submit to military authority.

Wynkoop: But that is precisely what Black Kettle, White Antelope, and their Cheyenne people are willing to do. They are willing . . . in fact, they want to lay down their arms and move their village to Sand Creek.

Chivington [to Running Fox]: It appears that Black Kettle and his tribe respect Major Wynkoop. They are nearer to Major Wynkoop than anyone else, and they can go to him when they are ready to settle peacefully at Sand Creek.

Black Kettle: Then we wish to go to Sand Creek with Tall Chief now. We only want peace.

Wynkoop [leaping joyfully to his feet]: Wonderful Colonel Chivington, absolutely wonderful. [addressing Black Kettle and White Antelope] Colonel Chivington is saying that you and your people can move to Sand Creek under the government's protection.

Black Kettle: Thank you, Tall Chief. That is what I needed to tell my people. We will all move to Sand Creek.

Wynkoop [jubilantly]: Running Fox, Rabbit Ears, please stay with Black Kettle and White Antelope. Help them explain to their people what has happened here today. There is going to be peace!

[All stand, shake hands and bow in high spirits. Black Kettle affectionately embraces Wynkoop and Evans. Wvnkoop is beaming ecstatically and returns the embrace. Evans has a blank look on his face and is very wooden and motionless to Black Kettle's embrace of friendship. All leave except Evans and Chivington. Remaining alone, they stare at each other, and then sit down. There is a brief silence.]

Evans [with his head in his hands]: Colonel, I did not stop you, but do you know what you have just done? Over a month ago I received permission from the United States Congress to recruit your regiment, The Third Cavalry, to serve for one hundred days. Your regiment had but one purpose: to fight Indians. Fifty of the one hundred days have passed. You yourself have said that not one Indian has been killed, and that the people of The Colorado Territory refer to the regiment as "The Bloodless One Hundred Dazers." Two weeks ago we lost the election for statehood. With that, I lost my bid for the U.S. Senate and you lost a possible seat in The United States House of Representatives . . . and, now . . . and, now you are giving the Indians a peace treaty. Don't you understand that the people expect us to be fighting Indians, not making peace with them? The political consequences of your little peace promise are devastating. Our political futures are over.

Chivington [Expressionlessly, he pulls out a piece of paper from his pocket.]: Don't be so sure of that. Here, read this. It is an order I received from General Sam Curtis this morning.

Evans [Dumbfounded, he studies the sheet of paper.]: Why this says, "I want no peace till the Indians suffer more. No peace must be made without my directions." What is the meaning of this, Colonel?

Chivington [with a cold, expressionless manner]: It means my orders are to make the Indians suffer. I cannot make them suffer, if I cannot find them. But I will be able to find them at Sand Creek.

Evans [expressionlessly]: You have your orders, Colonel.

Chivington [with cold determination]: Yes. Governor, I have my orders.

[The two men stare at the piece of paper as the lights fall.]

ACT FOUR

[Sand Creek, Colorado Territory, November 28, 1864. Two-thirds of stage left is covered with Indian tepees. In the midst of these tepees an American flag is hoisted on a flagpole. The other one-third of stage right is in darkness. Black Kettle, White Antelope, Major Wynkoop and Major Anthony are speaking. Major Anthony is much shorter that Major Wynkoop, is cadaverously thin, and has a thick black beard.]

Black Kettle [anxiously to Major Wynkoop]: Tall Chief, what is that you are saying? You are going to leave us? But why is that? We have been at peace since the meeting with Governor Evans and Colonel Chivington not long ago. Is it something we have done? Is it something that I have done? I think you know that we have done nothing wrong. [pointing towards the American flag] Look, we have raised the red, white and blue colors of your people over our camp. What more must we do to prove our friendship with the white people?

Wynkoop: It is good that you have hoisted the flag to mark your camp as friendly. You have done nothing wrong. I have been told to report to General Samuel Curtis. Why, I really don't know for sure. He wants an explanation for why I have been feeding your people for the past two months. He says he wants it explained by me personally.

White Antelope [laughing]: Why don't you tell your chief that you have been feeding us because we are hungry.

Wynkoop [smiling]: That is precisely what I am going to tell him. The general needs to understand that peace is not just a word. The white man must supply food to maintain the peace. The white man must pay for the food. I have been issuing you army rations to keep your people alive. General Curtis must learn to understand this. In the meantime, Major Anthony will take my place.

Black Kettle [anxiously]: But I do not know Major Anthony. My people do not know Major Anthony. I and my people know you. Tall Chief, I mean nothing against Major Anthony, but I do not know him.

Anthony [marter-of-factly]: I suppose I will have to earn you trust just as Major Wynkoop did. However, please try to understand that the army cannot afford to continue feeding over 600 of your people every day. Major Wynkoop has fed you for over a month. I have done the same thing for ten days. Neither of us really had the authority to do this. . . . Black Kettle, you have to understand that the army needs the food for its own men. We no longer have the supplies to feed your people. However, I have seen to it that your weapons have been returned to you so that you can again hunt for game. See to it that your weapons are only used for hunting, and there should be no problem.

Wynkoop [cheerfully]: You see, Black Kettle and White Antelope, the government trusts you enough to return your weapons to you. Now, I am going to General Curtis, and I am going to explain to him the needs of your people. I am sure that he will listen. I will return as soon as I can. In the meantime, if you have any questions, please see and speak with Major Anthony.

Black Kettle [sadly]: Tall Chief, cannot you arrange it that Major Anthony go and speak to your chief, and you remain with us. You have been to the peace meeting with the other chiefs, Evans and Chivington. You have watched over our people. Why do they call you away now, now when all the warriors will be armed again? I can understand that the army has no more food. But I cannot understand why your chief calls you away from us.

Wynkoop [smiling]: Well, you see, Black Kettle, I did not have full authority to issue you the Army rations and neither did Major Anthony. Someone has to explain all of this. You are right in saying that I have been for peace and for your people from the beginning. So, should I not go and explain all of this to my chief?

White Antelope [to Black Kettle]: Black Kettle, Tall Chief is right. Let Tall Chief go and say that our Cheyenne people do not want to fight the white man. Let him say that we need food. Let him say that we are for peace.

Black Kettle [somberly]: You are right, White Antelope. Let Tall Chief go and say all those things. [turning to Major Anthony] Major Anthony, so that you know we are for peace, I will do this. [Black Kettle walks into the tepee next to him and immediately walks out with a spear on which is tied a large white flag. The flag is tied on the opposite end of the spear from the pointed spearhead. Black Kettle speaks solemnly.] So that all white people and all white soldiers will know that the Cheyennes under Black Kettle are for peace, I do this! [With great force he drives the head of the spear deep into the ground, so deep in fact that the spearhead itself almost disappears. A large white flag at the opposite end of the spearhead is seen implanted next to Black Kettle's tepee. Major Wynkoop, overjoyed, goes and embraces both Black Kettle and White Antelope who also embrace him. Major Anthony studies the three of them in a very non-committal way.]

Wynkoop [enthusiastically]: Black Kettle, you have done the right thing. Major Anthony will see to it that your people are left undisturbed until I can explain everything to General Curtis. Isn't that right, Major?

Anthony [quietly]: Yes, that is right.

[The lights fall slowly. There are a few seconds of darkness. The first light to be seen is a spotlight on the white flag and then on the U.S. flag. This is brought up to half-light. The half-light then spreads among the Indian tepees. Out from behind the flags slowly and silently appear three Indian women with four small children. Two of the Indian women also have babies in their arms. The women and children sit down and remain motionless. All is quiet, natural, and serene. This scene encompassing two-thirds of stage left in half-light remains in silence for about ten seconds. With this half-light of the motionless Indian village with women and children on two-thirds of stage left remaining in place, full light is brought up on the remaining one-third of stage right which discloses an Army barrack. In the barrack, Colonel Chivington, three officers, Running Fox and Rabbit Ears are seen. Rabbit Ears and Running Fox are unarmed. Colonel Chivington is listening to Rabbit Ears.]

Running Fox: Colonel Chivington, Major Anthony will be here soon. He has sent me in advance to tell you that the Cheyenne Indians under Black Kettle have hoisted a white flag of unconditional peace with the army. Because the government will not feed them any longer, their weapons have been returned to them to hunt game. They have promised to use their weapons only to hunt game. In every way these Indians wish to comply with the wishes of your army. Everything is as you would have it.

Chivington [scowling]: No, everything is NOT as I would have it. The atrocities continue throughout the territory. Remember, that not too long ago a woman was raped by more than twelve Indians. She was then dragged to death by horses and her body was hacked to pieces. We found another woman who hanged herself after she was captured by these red-skinned fiends. She would rather have been dead than violated by these monsters. [raging] AND NOT ONE INDIAN HAS YET PAID FOR THESE ATROCITIES! NOT ONE! BUT I TELL YOU THIS: MORE THAN ONE WILL PAY!!! MORE THAN ONE WILL PAY!!!

[There is a silence. Rabbit Ears studies Colonel Chivington closely. Rabbit Ears frowns and then speaks in a somber tone.]

Rabbit Ears: You cannot blame innocent Indians for what hostile Indians have done.

Chivington [snarling]: I believe it right and honorable to use any means under God's heaven to kill Indians who kill and torture women and children. ANY MEANS!!! Damn any man who is in sympathy with them.

[There is a silence. In a quiet manner, Running Fox studies Colonel Chivington. In a resolute voice, Running Fox speaks to the colonel.]

Running Fox: But at least make sure the Indians you attack <u>did in fact</u> kill women and children.

Chivington frowning]: I don't say kill all ages and sex, but I intend to remember our slaughtered women and children! [quietly] I think the two of you had better go. You have reported to me that Major Anthony is on his way here. The rest will depend on his report to me.

Running Fox: Then Rabbit Ears and I will go and stay with the Cheyennes at Sand Creek.

Chivington [quietly]: Do as you wish. [Running Fox and Rabbit Ears leave. Several seconds pass. Soon they are seen sitting noiselessly in the half-light with the women and children among the tepees. A few more seconds pass. Major Anthony enters the army barrack. Two soldiers are with him.]

Anthony: Colonel, the Cheyenne Indians, at least 600 of them, are assembled at Sand Creek.

Chivington [snarling]: I hope you told them that we are not going to feed them anymore. I hope that they understand that the U.S. Army is not going to fatten them so that they can torture, rape and slaughter our women.

Anthony: Colonel, you outrank me. I feel that the future of these Indians should be in your hands.

Chivington: And Major Wynkoop has left the Sand Creek area?

Anthony: Major Wynkoop is on his way to see General Curtis.

The general is busy fighting the Confederates in the East. It will probably be some time before we see or hear from Major Wynkoop again. At present, the Indians at Sand Creek appear to be peaceful. However, I have told them that we cannot continue to feed them. Their weapons have been given back to them for the sole purpose of hunting game. My problem is that there are over 600 Indians at Sand Creek. Some of them, no doubt, are hostiles and have committed atrocities. Many of them are peaceful. If the hostiles break loose and cause trouble, I will be blamed. If the peaceful Indians are attacked by any group of white men, I will also be blamed.

Chivington [gruffly]: Then it is quite simple. I have my orders from General Curtis.

Anthony: What are the orders, Colonel?

Chivington [snarling]: That the Indians are to suffer much more before there are to be any more peace talks. [There is a silence. Major Anthony makes no response to Chivington. Chivington now speaks coldly and deliberately.] We can be at Sand Creek before morning. [addressing one of his officers] How many men can we assemble at once?

First Officer: We have over 900 men. They are armed and ready for battle.

Second Officer: The volunteers' 100 days are almost over, Colonel, and we haven't killed one Indian.

Third Officer: The men are tired of being called: "The Bloodless Hundred Dazers" by the citizens.

Chivington [With cold, vicious determination, he addresses all the officers and soldiers present.]: Tomorrow morning we will be at Sand Creek. Tell each and every one of your men that they will henceforth neither be called "bloodless" nor "dazers." As we march tonight, tell each man to remember the murdered white women and white children. Remind them to dwell upon the mutilated bodies of the Hungate family. Place vividly before their minds the fate of the white woman raped twelve times by these savages . . . raped . . . and then dragged to death by horses . . . and then hacked to pieces. [fiercely] And then tell them to call up to their minds every atrocity, every scalping, and every torture that these red fiends from hell have committed! Tell them I want each and every soldier to brood on all these horrors during our night march. Then, there is to be absolute silence until the Indian camp is surrounded. When I give the cry: "Remember the murdered women and children!" they are to attack with full and mighty fury. The red devils from hell have shown us no mercy . . . [roaring] WE WILL SHOW THEM NO MERCY! [Chivington glares about the room like a madman. He quickly disciplines himself. The soldiers study him. There is a silence. Resolutely, Chivington speaks.] Are my orders clear, gentlemen?

Anthony [as one obeying orders]: Yes, Colonel, your orders are clear.

First Officer: Very clear, Colonel Chivington. [The other officers and soldiers nod their heads in agreement. All the army men remain frozen as the lights fall on their one-third of the stage. When the lights again come up on this one-third of the stage, the barracks have been removed. Instead, soldiers are entering from the former barracks' area which is now blended into becoming the natural area directly adjacent to the Indian camp. Silently and stealthily officers and soldiers surround the Indian camp. The lights continue to come up gradually to full light. Finally, when the village is completely surrounded, Colonel Chivington enters with Major Anthony. There is a brief silence until Chivington sees that all the officers and men are in place. The silence continues until the right moment of tension is reached.]

Chivington [Drawing his sword, he yells with absolute rage.]: REMEMBER THE MURDERED WOMEN AND CHILDREN! REMEMBER THE MURDERED WOMEN AND CHILDREN! REMEMBER THE MURDERED WOMEN AND CHILDREN!

[At once, rifle and howitzer fire explode. Bewildered women

are seen grabbing their children and attempting to run. They are stopped by soldiers Women are shot or knocked to the ground with rifle butts. Children are bayoneted. Complete panic ensues amidst frenzied screams. Black Kettle, White Antelope, Running Fox, and Rabbit Ears appear from near the tepee closest to the white flag. The four men are startled by the confusion White Antelope at first waves his arm to stop the soldiers from firing, he then folds his arms across his chest as a gesture of peace and walks towards some of the soldiers.]

Running Fox [frantically gesturing and yelling]: Wait! Wait! Stop! Look, see the white flag! See the American flag! See that we are not hostile Indians! Look! White Antelope walks forward with his arms folded across his chest! This is a symbol of friendship! This is a gesture of peace! Soldiers! Soldiers! Stop firing! Stop firing! We are for peace!! [Black Kettle raises his arms to show that he has no weapons.] Look! See! Black Kettle is unarmed! See the white flag! See the American flag! Soldiers, stop firing!

[White Antelope who has been walking forward with his arms across his chest in a gesture of peace and friendship is shot down dead. Black Kettle kneels by his limp body and places his arm under White Antelope to raise his torso from the ground. Black Kettle is then wounded with a bullet and falls gradually to one side still struggling to let down gently the torso of White Antelope. Running Fox is hit in the back of the head with a rifle butt. Rabbit Ears picks up Running Fox and runs of the stage. Fiendish cries are heard from the soldiers which rise in the demonic chorus: "No Mercy!" "Kill for our raped white women!" "Kill for our tortured children!" "Kill for the Hungate family!" "Kill . . . kill . . . kill! As the rifle fire continues, a few soldiers put down their guns, take out their knives, and begin scalping and mutilating Indian bodies. While this is occurring, three soldiers grab a screaming Indian woman, throw her on the ground, and hold her down as the fourth soldier starts to rape her. The screaming, mutilations, gun fire, merciless battle cries, and atrocities continue as the lights fall.]

ACT FIVE

[Dr. Ben Goodwill's office. Dr. Ben Goodwill is almost drunk. He is sitting with a bottle of whiskey on the table and a glass. He takes a few drinks from the glass and refills it. He begins singing loudly to himself. The tune is that of "Onward Christian Soldiers."]

Dr Goodwill:
With the monied interests
moves the mob of God!
Brothers, we are stealing
every inch of sod.

Onward! Christian people . . .
moving through the West.
We've got most of the land now,
and well get the rest.

Like the mighty locust
swarms the cavalry.
Sisters, we are shooting
everything we see.

Onward! . . . U.S. horsemen!
Ride out every day.
Rape and scalp and butcher,
Whatever's in your way.

Break and bleed the Indians
for your precious gold.
Go, and betray Christ's religion.
since your souls are sold.

Like an ugly Judas
moves the mob of God!
Stealing, lying, killing
with pious nod.

[Dr Ben Goodwill laughs sarcastically, continues humming the tune, and pours himself another drink. He sits shaking his head in a negative manner, and then leans back in his chair A knock is heard at the door. Dr. Goodwill gets up. Rabbit Ears enters supporting Running Fox.]

Rabbit Ears: Doctor, you have to help Running Fox. A soldier hit him with a rifle at Sand Creek. I have been carrying him for two days. At times he seems to come back into his body. At other times he seems to be leaving it. Today I waited until evening so that no one would see us. I hope that I did not wait too long.

[Rabbit Ears places Running Fox on the table as Dr. Goodwill removes the bottle of whiskey. Dr. Goodwill takes Running Fox's wrist to feel his pulse. He then places his head over Running Fox's heart. He listens apprehensively for a few moments. Dr. Goodwill then smiles.]

Dr. Goodwill: Running Fox is still with us. [Exploring different parts of Running Fox's head with his hands.] It looks like he's got a bad concussion. But I'll bring him around. [He pours some whiskey in a glass and puts it under Running Fox's nose. Dr. Goodwill then opens Running Fox's mouth and pours in a small amount. Running Fox groggily begins choking and coughing and shaking his head in a negative manner. Dr. Goodwill slaps him on the back a few times. Dr. Goodwill grins good-natured.] That did it. The not-so-famous Dr. Ben Goodwill concussion cure. It works for anyone with brains.

Running Fox [flying to get his bearings]: Where . . . where . . . where am I? What day is it? Where are Black Kettle and White Antelope? [holding his head with both hands] Ohhh . . . my head.

Rabbit Ears [elated]: You're with Dr. Goodwill. At Sand Creek the white men started shooting, you were hit in the head with a rifle butt. I grabbed you. We are in Denver now.

Running Fox: But what . . . what happened?

Rabbit Ears: I didn't stay around to find out. We barely got out of there alive. The soldiers started shooting, and the Indian women started screaming. That is all that I know.

Running Fox [still holding his head]: We'll, we'd better get to Governor Evans and tell him what happened. The Indians were lied to. It's unbelievable. They were told that if they peacefully camped at Sand Creek, they would be left alone. They were peacefully settled in Sand Creek, and they were fired upon. Let's go to the governor right now.

Dr Goodwill [thoughtfully]: I wouldn't show myself in Denver right now, if I were you. The entire town has gone wild. Yesterday Chivington returned to Denver. The city greeted him as a conquering hero. Celebrations are going on everywhere. It's outrageous, absolutely outrageous, but Chivington and his men are considered great heroes.

Rabbit Ears [scowling]: It's a poor group of heroes who fire on sleeping women and children at dawn. We were there. Near the Indians' white flag of peace, the soldiers began killing. At least that is what I saw until I grabbed Running Fox and began to run.

Dr. Goodwill [thoughtfully]: The reports are that White Antelope was killed and that Black Kettle was wounded. Black Kettle has apparently escaped. [There is a silence.] But it is hard to believe the other things. But they are true.

Running Fox: What other things?

Dr Goodwill: The scalpings and the mutilations.

Rabbit Ears: When I left, the Indians were in no position to scalp or cut anyone. They were pleading for their lives amidst screams and rifle fire.

Dr. Goodwill [shaking his head negatively]: I am not talking about what the Indians did. I am talking about what the soldiers did.

Running Fox: What? What do you mean? [There is a silence.]

Dr. Goodwill: You are going to hear about it sooner or later. I am sure that every friendly and hostile Indian in the territory is going to hear about it. Between 150 and 200 Indians were killed at Sand Creek. Two-thirds of them were women and children. The soldiers . . . white men in uniform . . . scalped many of the Indians including the women and children. Some of the women . . . some of the women . . . Indian women . . . the women were raped and then they were scalped below the waist. Last night these scalps and others were put on public display during an intermission of a theatrical production in the Denver opera house. The whole audience went wild with outrageous and joyful cheering! I know of nothing so savage in all the white man's history.

[There is a silence.]

Running Fox [furiously]: What about the governor? What about Colonel Chivington and the promises of peace?

Dr. Goodwill: The only thing that I have heard is from a newspaper which wrote, "This is the only good thing that Colonel Chivington has done all year." The feeling is that there will only be a lasting peace when all the Indians are exterminated. The town has gone wild with blood lust. Speculators see property values going up now that the Indian threat is less. A saloon owner has bought the scalps from Sand Creek and is going to display them in back of his bar. Mining interests want more Indian land for gold exploration. Politicians are positioning for power. [sighing and shaking his head in a negative manner] It is America.

Rabbit Ears: Does no one speak of the killing of the women and the children?

Dr. Goodwill: They are trying to justify the massacre saying that the women began to fight the soldiers.

Rabbit Ears: Of course they fought. They fought to protect their children. They fought because the white man promised peace, and the white man lied.

Dr. Goodwill: They are also trying to justify the massacre by saying that after the battle ten freshly taken scalps of white men, white women, and white children were found at Sand Creek. The scalps were less than ten days old at the time of the massacre. Thus they say that Sand Creek was a war waged against hostile Indians. That is what is being said. [Dr Goodwill pours himself a drink. He then speaks sarcastically.] That is how the white man tries to redeem his sins. He holds an investigation, gets conflicting testimonies, moves his jaws for a while, makes reports, and takes all the land he wants while the public is busy getting confused reading the reports. It is "the American way." It is part of "the manifest destiny" of the white man. In the end nothing happens except that the white man owns more land, and the Indian has less land. That is all that happens.

[Dr. Goodwill takes a drink. There is a silence.]

Running Fox [exasperated]: So neither Chivington nor the governor nor the soldiers will be punished?

Dr. Goodwill [sarcastically]: Punished? Punished? Why they are considered heroes!!! Do you realize that the soldiers were allowed to keep any and all of the Indian ponies and Indian possessions from Sand Creek? One soldier is starting a horse ranch from his stock of captured ponies. Who is going to bring these people to justice when the judge and jury would all be white men? What kind of justice would that be? The Indians are to be exterminated. That's all.

[There is a silence. Finally, an exhausted Rabbit Ears speaks.]

Rabbit Ears: Running Fox, do you feel well enough to go? We cannot stay in the white man's town of Denver. We will die if we remain here.

Running Fox: I am well enough to go. We must go . . . [Running Fox breaks into a great rage and his frustration shakes his fists at the sky.] But it will not end here! IT WILL NOT END HERE! After Sand Creek I no longer want to be part white. I would cut out the white within me if I could! But I will cut the white man away from Indian land! I will return to my people, the Sioux! I go to tell our great warrior chiefs, Sitting Bull and Crazy Horse, about what happened at Sand Creek! I go to warn the Indians! I go to arm the Indians! I go to fight with the Indians! HOKAY HEY! IT IS A GREAT DAY TO FIGHT! HOKAY HEY! IT IS A GREAT DAY TO DIE!

[Rabbit Ears and Dr. Ben Goodwill stare at Running Fox as the lights fall.]

EPILOGUE

[After a few seconds of darkness, Major Wynkoop appears on the stage. With the deepest melancholia, he speaks to the audience.]

Wynkoop: Because of the Sand Creek Massacre, Native Americans could no longer trust the promises of the white man. Every hope of peace was destroyed. Historical consequences came to include the defeat of General Custer and the deaths of over 225 of his men at The Little Bighorn River in 1876, as well as the massacre of over 200 Native Americans at Wounded Knee Creek in 1890.

[The lights fall.]

EGMONT AND THE THEOLOGIAN
A Vision in the Dialectic of Hope

CHARACTERS

CLOWN
THE CHORUS IS SPOKEN BY A CHILD
EGMONT
DIETRICH BONHOEFFER
CHILDREN, WOMEN, AND MEN OF THE CONCENTRATION CAMP
1ST SOLDIER
2ND SOLDIER
STOCKBROKER
INVESTOR
RINGMASTER
POPCORN SELLER
LION TAMER
SWORDSWALLOWER
WOMEN AND CHILDREN OF THE CIRCUS

Stage Directions

Beethoven's "Incidental Music to Goethe's Egmont" should be playing as the people enter the theater and as they leave at the end of the fourth act. If one wishes to read the play alone or with others, the same music should also be played.

The Prologue and quotation from Goethe should be read in that order by the clown.

The Chorus should be read by a child.

PROLOGUE

[Both the Prologue and the quote from Goethe are to be read by a clown on a darkened stage with half-light on the clown.]

Count Egmont of Flanders was executed by the Spanish Catholic forces of Phillip II in 1568. Dietrich Bonhoeffer, a Christian theologian, was hanged by the Nazis in 1945. Both men died trying to safeguard the human right of freedom of conscience.

Yet each of these individuals acted from different reasons and motives. Egmont was a nobleman by birth and resented foreign invaders in his country. Bonhoeffer believed it was a Christian's duty to remove from authority any leader like Adolph Hitler who would take the place of God. Bonhoeffer was also actively involved in the plot to kill Hitler.

Thus we have different individuals acting from different motives. Yet both are adamantly opposed to tyranny and dictatorial power. It is lamentable that two such individuals could not meet. It is lamentable because the interchange of thought between the two would be illuminating and instructive to most of us.

Be that as it may, lamentations do not instruct us. Consequently the author has seen fit to bring Egmont and Bonhoeffer together. This has been done primarily to juxtaposition the highest form of romantic humanism with an active form of Christian witness.

Egmont remains a man of his century, but he is summoned to Bonhoeffer's era through the power of our reflective imaginations.

And that God, whom in their rage they have insulted, sends down his angel from on high; at the hallowed touch of the messenger bolts and bars fly back; he pours around our friend a flood of splendor, and leads him gently through the night to liberty.

Goethe, EGMONT, Act V.

ACT ONE
Scene One

CHORUS [This is spoken by a child on a darkened stage with full light being on the child.]:
Egmont –
Thou, the thunder crash
and earth's resounding
shudder.
Nobility arising before
wantonness,
and the standing of one of scorn
in mockery of the Spanish born –

Thy spirit again upon us.
Thy blessing again to us.
As now we talk,
as now we balk –
no defiance now
where once thy challenging brow.

Is defiance no more?
Does striving for the highest
fall by the wayside of rhetoric?
And will all-too-clever men always
march forward in their wanton procession
as those satisfied with another's transgression?

Do not forget us, Egmont.
Do not scorn too much
this shallow, blighted
world.
It does not seem as it once did then,
when courage cried out for action.
Now a mechanized civilization

belittles the glory of individual
struggle.
Now the "fearless" press their buttons,
and children's lives are the food of gluttons.

Egmont, where thou once wept for a country
now beweep the world,
and seek again within the heart of hearts
another man of thy persuasion,
who mocks the tyrant
and claims our liberty!

Scene Two

[As the lights come up slightly, a prison cell is seen. For a few seconds the stage is dimly lit. Dietrich Bonhoeffer is a heavy set man of medium height in his late thirties. He is partially bald and wears wire glasses. He is attired in gray prison garb. Egmont is in his mid-forties and attired in the dress of a nobleman of the 16th century. He has greying hair and a refined, attractive appearance. The bars in the background display a rope with a hangman's loop on the other side of the bars. There is a table, a chair, a Bible, notes, letters, and writing materials. There is a copy of Albrecht Durer's "Apocalypse" on the wall. Bonhoeffer has his head cradled in his arms upon the table. The stage is dimly lit. Egmont places his hand on Bonhoeffer's shoulder. As Egmont speaks the lights gradually increase.]

EGMONT [gradual tempo and force increasing in strength]:
I know, I know this world is but a show.
Seek thy harbored glory first.
And if there be a tyrant's gloom
that defies thy will and proclaims thy country's doom,
then stand as I and shout thy fierceness.
No one, no power shall endure
the spirit we rebellious men procure.
No wealth, no lady, no art, and no religion
stand before freedom's decision:
   to die in the quest of all,

to defy and thus affirm,
to denounce that infringement.
which leads to imprisonment.
They cannot kill thy spirit!
They cannot touch thy life!
What is matter if it does not matter?

Up my friend – climb the scaffold floor
and let those in eternity sing thy hymns.
The stars are the symphony.
Thy death – a theophany.

What did it offer thee, this life
of finitude and strife?
What was its meaning
while now thy heart is beating?
For thy glory is for thy nation,
and thy life is a proclamation
of man beyond himself.

Mock their hanging rope!
Decry their sentence!
Show them not repentance!
Thou hast made sublimity.
Thou hast scorned servility.
Thou hast denounced the manacle
of invader, plunderer, and betrayer.
Heaven's gate becomes thy harbor –
Thee – a shipwrecked vessel ever looking starward.
Look up, eternity's thy mother,
and I – thy brother!

BONHOEFFER:
Your thoughts rise beyond the stars,
but they speak of an honor which is not ours.
The world of churches and men of scrolls
often times fail freedom to extol.
Their interpretations and sacred rites
often denounce the sphere of valor's might.
Still, I do not die for honor's title.
I do not face the rope of condemnation

for solely a wordly proclamation.
It is true I am your brother,
but we are one beneath an Other.
It is for Him; I go.
It is for Him; I defy the tyrant.
It is not for heroic edification.
Rather, it is a witness to His Proclamation.

EGMONT:
But the struggle for the right beckons me here.
It has always been history's denunciation I fear.

BONHOEFFER:
I do not denounce right.
I do not denounce courage.
I do not denounce honor.
That which you have scorned; I have scorned.
Yet there is great mystery in that you
and I were born
Life is significant in all its aspects.
I have believed in the depths of things
I have cared; I and He have shared
the many thoughts of time and distance.
We have known each other.
We have lived each instant.

EGMONT:
Then thou hast found meaning beyond the forces of history?
There is more than the history of man's noble repertory of deeds and feats of wonder?

BONHOEFFER:
Yes, far more . . . far more.
What it all is, I cannot say.
And if I could then only language
would have its day.
But you are correct in a belief in wonder.
One came who tore false gods asunder.
He showed me that the world was good,
but nothing was so good as
His coming.

He showed me the meaning of faith
through the preaching of His word.
He unfurled meaning more than you and I,
and yet without us what He showed
would be a lie.

EGMONT:
That is fine; I suppose . . .
Regardless, I see the military movements
of a tyrant,
necessary rebellion,
and <u>man-willed resurrection</u>.

BONHOEFFER:
Many of the things you see;
I see.
Yet I still hope for things I cannot see.

EGMONT:
What are we discussing?
There is justice, and there is injustice.
One must choose justice.
It is that simple.

BONHOEFFER:
Yes, but there is still time in
other dimensions.
Time to weigh the fine points
of argument,
time to see again the reasons
which move with the ages,
time to recount again the
endless pages.
Let us not hurry.
Soon enough we meet death surely.

EGMONT [somberly]:
Unfortunately the lovers of
justice have too little time.

BONHOEFFER:
Regardless, there is no need to
hurry if one only believes.
Many have thought and argued about the
place of God in history and men who
would make themselves "gods" of history.
I would show you that history's
meaning begins with Jesus Christ as
history's center.
It is through Him that death is
conquered.
It is through Him that we hope
not only for life eternal,
but we also hope
for a better world for
future generations.
I have believed and taught this.
And without a belief in such things
my life would have been so much
theological play.
What I am discussing is not merely a
topic for scholarly contemplation,
logic and recitation.
It is not merely a question for
sharp-witted assessors
and
quick-tongued professors.
It is a question of all time:
whether there is a meaning in each breath;
whether life itself is more than death.

EGMONT:
But history could be just so many
recurring events before the void.
I have never worried about such things.
In my time the hero was as God.
Courage said all. Each day looked forward to
grandeur.
Nobility rode the wind of thought.
Heroism was what we sought.
I do not understand these times

of cheap wealth and a lack of verse.
I do not comprehend the growing
mechanisms of the earth.
Regardless, let me for one week watch
men in action,
and see if my times were so very different.
[Egmont exits.]

BONHOEFFER:
Such a spirit as Egmont's comes to me!
I who am bound to this cell's confinement.
I who often wonder if my thoughts for assassination
were to God an abomination.
Egmont, Egmont, the man of total independence
comes to praise me and announce my greatness.
I, I the one of dependence –
yet to be dependent on God . . .
It is difficult to explain to Egmont
life's need for its Center.
It is difficult to discuss the ends
of sin.
To him this makes no difference.
What matters in his eyes is resistance.
However, the consequences of <u>man-willed resurrection</u>
he will surely come to know.
[The lights fall.]

ACT TWO
Scene One

[Concentration camp. Stage right are eight to ten Jewish men, women, and children dressed in rags, with the Star of David on the left breast. Stage center are two Nazi SS men watching the Jews proceeding off the stage. Between them the control lever for the poisonous gas is situated. Egmont, stage left, is barely visible. There is a low chant among the Jews as they march off the stage.]

FIRST SOLDIER:
Is this the nobility of the Reich?
We hurl its people from our sight.
We deceive them; we do not tell them
that their singing breath
is the last before the face of death.

SECOND SOLDIER:
Silence! You know better than to question
our orders and High Command decisions.
What they have said is absolute
it admits of no revisions.

FIRST SOLDIER:
Then with the throwing of the lever
you and I have ceased to be,
and it will matter little
what we're forced to see. . . .
Yet they all have lives.
Each one with his own
beliefs and sudden yearnings. [He hesitates a moment.]
<u>It is we ourselves we're</u>
<u>burning!</u>
Are we men to stand and let pass by

commands through which a leader lies?
Let them go, we cannot pass judgment.
They were born to be;
it's for us to set them free.

SECOND SOLDIER:
And what is it that we free them to?
A life in the market, a time
for amusement, a few children?
Surely that will not alter the world.
It is now our sacred mission
to rid the world of its division.
There must be only Germany.
All else is infamy.
We must destroy; we must destroy!
There is no concern for girls and boys!
We cannot take account
of common lives of no account.
We give them death and their God.

[He moves to the lever.]

FIRST SOLDIER:
Wait!
What then had you and I?
We've lived.
We've watched the passing of the seasons.
We've talked of war and wives and reasons.
It was something to us both.
And now because of black uniforms
and the blind uniformity of new regime,
have we only become the servants
of a death machine?

SECOND SOLDIER:
Enough of this!
Because I have been commanded;
I obey.

[The switch is thrown. Light is now on Egmont. All other lights are extinguished.]

EGMONT:
What has become of thee, oh world?
There is no longer passion in death.
These people die like flies.
Death, oh wonder and enchantment,
somehow, somewhere your significance was lost.
Wholesale slaughter – to trick a people
and swindle life from them . . .
And the swindler would blame the "High Command."
Well, the "High Command" is
no command at all.
And "obedience" to a madman
is madness itself.

And once the Germans were
a tortured people.
Ravaged by "civilized"
invaders not so long ago.
Burdened, trying to survive,
they willed themselves back
upon history's stage.

Men resurrected a country.
and threw off the yoke
of foreign tribute.
How fine!
How noble!
Only to be besmirched
with death camps.
Senseless death camps.

Is it then that human power unchecked
and without limitation
resurrects more evil than good?
Is it under the thoughts of lofty
struggle,
that the monster quietly
enters to torture,
burn, and kill?

[The lights fall.]

Scene Two

[The same prison cell as Act One.]

PRISON GUARD [cheerfully and with admiration.]:
Letters, Doctor. I hope that your confinement will
soon be over.

BONHOEFFER [smiling]:
Thank you. I hope and pray
your hopes are heard.

[The guard exits. Bonhoeffer picks up the Bible, ponders and reads aloud slowly.]

BONHOEFFER:
"Behold what I have built I am breaking down, and what I have planted I am plucking up. . . . And do you seek great things for yourself? Seek them not . . . but I will give your life as a prize of war!" [slowly]
Jeremiah . . . Jeremiah, no matter what I do or say
I know the prophet will have his day. . . .
O God, who does call and to whom we respond,
if Thou would answer to the living
tell me now of Thy merciful giving! [He moves to the back of the stage.]
Still, I know that I must wait in turn.
I must wait and have patience.
Yet my spirit has called out in question
the oldest thought of our dimension:

Who am I?[*] They often tell me
that I walk from my cell

---

[*] Dietrich Bonhoeffer. <u>Widerstand und Ergbung</u>. München: Chr. Kaiser Verlag, 1959, pp. 242-243. This translation as well as the others that will appear in this play are my own.

deliberately, calmly, firmly,
like a nobleman from his castle.

Who am I? They often tell me
that I speak with the jailers
freely, friendly, clearly,
as if I were the one in command.

Who am I? They also tell me
that I bear the days of misfortune
quietly, cheerfully, proudly,
as one who has lived for victories.

[Egmont returns and is barely visible. Bonhoeffer does not notice him.]

Who am I really? What the others tell me?
Or am I only that which I know of myself?
turbulent, longing, sick, like a bird in a cage,
grappling with life's breath as it strangles me,
hungry for colors, for flowers, for the
singing of birds,
thirsting for kind words, for human surroundings,
trembling with rage over both despotism
and paltry insult,
spun 'round in expectation of great events,
powerlessly fearing for friends at an infinite distance;
exhausted and empty at praying, thinking, and creating,
lifeless; and ready for the final leave-taking.

Who am I? This or the other?
Am I this one today and tomorrow the other?
Am I both together? Before men – a hypocrite
and before myself – a scorned and wretched weakling?
Or yet, is there still something within me resembling a beaten army,
which is already retreating from hard-won victory?

Who am I? They mock me, these lonely questions of mine.
Whoever I am, Thou knowest me, O God, I am Thine.

[Silence. Bonhoeffer turns and sees Egmont. Egmont is melancholic.]

EGMONT:
Who we are at this time, I am afraid to say.
I have tried to understand this world
and I have been lost to sorrow
that this world has learned to live
on the price of the lives it borrows.
Let us quickly pass away from this to another place,
Any other time or space.

BONHOEFFER [fiercely]:
This is no answer!
We cannot forsake this world
for another.
We cannot say that we are chosen
and must not bother
with those who will be
left and torn and scarred
by this, our generation.

EGMONT:
What else can be done?
You are powerless and
are living in a world gone mad.

BONHOEFFER:
Regardless, did you find,
since last we met,
the daring thoughts of
<u>man-willed resurrection?</u>
Did you come to know the
demonic tortures
of such "resurrected men"?

EGMONT:
I saw . . . I saw what I fear
can only add to the world's despair.

BONHOEFFER:
Speak! What is it that you have come to know?
Does this world still seem "a show"?

EGMONT:
I went to the concentration camps.
I saw the children
being paraded to a cleansing
which was itself their ending.
And the guards spoke to one another
in an argument concerning death's lever
of who was to blame
for the horrid shame
as that which man has done.
And in those deaths there was
no passion.
They were tricked and swindled.
They were treated as so much meat
before the butcher.
I felt the guilt in that I am
man.
I see no hope of expiation now
that I have come again.
Let us quickly go; a week here
is a week too long.
Let us both depart; for me my
world is forever gone.

BONHOEFFER [slowly]:
It is now the other lives that we must treasure,
and weep for as we watch
the motions of the clock.
And know that we have become
helpless but have tried.
We have attempted to unmask evil,
but it has not stopped the
brutal onrushing
of man's Satanic plunging
into a formless world.
And I have said that man was
coming of age,

that he was turning a final page
for his own fulfillment.
But now he has become so strong
that he will not accept any
limitations of life.
He has made so much and he has
solved so much that
his strength becomes his weakness.
He forgets the gentle thoughts of meekness.

EGMONT:
It is true. . . . Still, I must go out
again and attempt to find
the noble thoughts of daring
which once bespoke a higher life
than evil acts and strife.
It cannot all have passed away
since last I met the day. [Egmont exits.]

BONHOEFFER:
I am afraid he seeks again a noble aristocracy
and will find more readily a cheap hypocrisy.
I am afraid he seeks a romantic sensitivity
and will only discover a feverish activity.

[The lights fall.]

ACT THREE
Scene One

[Stockbrokerage office. Tickertapes. Desk stage right with investor and stockbroker. Entire American bourgeois atmosphere. Egmont, stage left, is barely visible.]

STOCKBROKER:
The war, ah, the war, it has relieved our oppression.
Thanks to it we've conquered the depression.
Our investments in armaments and supplies
have aided the administration
and made sound again the nation.

INVESTOR:
Yes, we prosper
on what becomes machine-gun fodder.
We sit and take our coffee.
We speak of our investments.
Still, there is something shocking
in how I make my profits.
Something sudden grips me
each time I touch my pocket.

STOCKBROKER:
What is that to us?
If you want to make a killing,
and you want the dollar-safety
then support the war and country.
ACT NOW.
Surely the war is soon to end.
Best make money now and
leave your conscience to attend.

INVESTOR:
Certainly we make a killing,
each penny buys a round
each cent another bullet
each dollar fills the mud
with gallons of another's blood.

STOCKBROKER [irritated]:
Look, my time is filled.
Do you want to invest or debate?
I cannot force the war's conclusion.
I can only offer you a taste for action,
for quick wealth and security.

INVESTOR:
I invest; I invest.
I am no different than the rest.

[Stage darkened. Light only on Egmont.]

EGMONT:
In my time there was more time
to discuss in a market place
the movings of our race.
Today this present market
of symbols and usury,
of points and investments,
gives man no time for reassessment
of whom he has come to be
of how he measures to his measure.
He only measures wealth
and his soul hangs on a
figure's dance.

I used to ride at full gallop
to the place of commerce
and stop and listen and parley for a while.
Yes, then transactions seemed worthwhile.
Persons met and persons listened
of who was born or died or christened.
Now, there's only a mechanical watching

of a board of gain or losing.
Man and world have moved so fast;
there's little left that's meant to last.

                    Scene Two

[The same prison cell as in Act One.]

BONHOEFFER [recollecting]:
Egmont, the romantic Count Egmont.
Once, before his execution,
he loved Clara.
He would know the heaviness of my
sorrow that I must lose
Marie.
Oh, that again she and I walked
the fields and the long, lush
grass played its melody
in the winds.
The freshness of my memory of those
times,
when earth and Thou and she were one
and mine . . .

[Stricken with the gravity of knowing life's depths and the possible loss of everything, Bonhoeffer speaks anxiously.]

Egmont, hasten quickly!
Egmont, you are courage:
the hope for all the living and the greatness
of the race
which will live . . .
which will last.

[Egmont is again seen by the audience. Half-light is on him. He is not seen by Bonhoeffer.]

Egmont knows this tale of loneliness,
of the staleness of the prison,
of the thoughts once born

which have risen giving voice
to Freedom;
and Freedom listens but will
not respond.

[He notices Egmont.]

EGMONT:
Listen, thou knowest there is never
one side without the other.
If there is misfortune then there is also fortune.
One never was without the other.
Thou knowest these matters well.
Listen to me, express thy thoughts on the matter;
bring forth thy spirit, unbind thyself.
Speak of Occurrence and despair.
Speak of the spinning and The Care.

BONHOEFFER:
Fortune and misfortune[*]
vanquishing they overcome us;
and, like heat and frost
at first contact,
they can scarcely be distinguished.

As meteors
hurled from unearthly heights,
shining and threatening they mold
their path above us.

Confounded and afflicted we stand
before the wreckage
of our dull, commonplace lives.

Huge and ominous,
devastating, destroying,
are fortune and misfortune
– requested or unrequested
they add to

---

[*] Ibid., pp. 223-224.

the convulsions of men
changing and re-making
the wreckage
with severity and dedication.

Fortune has its terror
Misfortune has a sweetness,
Indistinguishable they shine forth from eternity
and come to all.
Both are great and terrifying.

Men, far and near,
rush hither and look,
and gape
half envious, half terrified
into the Vortex
where the Eternal
creates and destroys,
confusing and entangling
this earthly drama.
What is fortune? What is
    misfortune?

Only time decides between the two.
When the incomprehensible excitement
of sudden Occurrence
changes our exhausting and torturing tedium,
when the weary, insidious hour of day
first discloses misfortune's true appearance,
then do most of us,
disillusioned and bored,
turn away from the
weariness of lifeless unhappiness.
[Bonhoeffer hesitates and catches his meaning.]
But that is the hour of truth,
the hour of the mother and her children,
the hour of friends and brothers –
the true hour which illuminates
all misfortune
and gently hides it
in a quiet,

unearthly splendor.

EGMONT [after a few moments]:
"The hour of truth . . .
and unearthly splendor . . . "
It is to that hour the world
must be recalled.
I say this because I have been
to the market in America.
There I have seen a
sophisticated bandit culture.
It is a place where
all is permitted
provided investments are successful
and MAMMON is the judge of success.
It is a place where
they also steal
the daily "hour of truth"
from themselves.

BONHOEFFER:
To strive to succeed is
always necessary, yet
too much is always
made of it.
And as for sophistication,
it practically rules the world.
And from sophistication
come the sophists with their
"gods" –
"gods" which are far too human
to be in any sense divine.

EGMONT:
Yes, iconoclasts have destroyed some gods,
but the most important one that they forgot
is the one which has brought this world to naught.
The one of public admiration;
the one which is called "sophistication."
There is only insipid tedium
in the shallow world

of what we are to wear,
where we are to eat,
what is "the thing to do"
and whom we are to meet.
Most have forgotten heaven's oldest remittance.

BONHOEFFER [highly amused]:
Which is?

EGMONT:
The principle of indifference!
Each moves too fast before the clock
and spends his life in idle talk.
Each looks and fails to see
that he has forgotten first to be.

BONHOEFFER:
Then you've seen the fall of dignity
and the laughing at nobility
which now adulterates the world.

EGMONT:
Yes, but dignity and nobility
and the love of the good
must still survive.

BONHOEFFER:
It is precisely the love of dignity,
nobility, and the goodness which must be
sought, found, and nurtured.

EGMONT:
But where to look?

BONHOEFFER:
Seek the single one striving
for the highest.
Seek the one who knows his
own time must end.
He will be your guide
as you cross to Freedom's side.

[The lights fall as slowly as possible.]

ACT FOUR
Scene One

[Circus trailer. Posters of the circus cover the walls. There is a bed on which a clown is lying. Egmont is barely visible. Solemn attitudes on the faces of the ringmaster, lion tamer, swordswallower and other performers. Children and women who are a part of the circus are also seen. A popcorn seller who is new to the circus is scanning the ceiling.]

RINGMASTER [hastening popcorn seller, lion tamer and swordswallower to the clown's bed]:
Quickly! A clown is dying.

POPCORN SELLER:
Only a clown?

LION TAMER [fiercely raising his whip to the popcorn seller]:
Back off!

SWORDSWALLOWER [irritated with popcorn seller]:
Keep silence!

[Ringmaster, popcorn seller, swordswallower, lion tamer, women and children move towards the bed. The women and children are weeping softly.]

CLOWN:
Be not sorry brothers;
I have destroyed the fears
– if only for an instant –
of those who came and watched
with the passing of the years.
For those who came to laugh awhile,
I brushed away their tears.

I have conquered death and loss
through my pranks and foolish wit.
I have sanctified our laughing
much more than those of Sacred Writ.
And the children! Yes! The children!
They always beckoned near –
what more could I or God Himself
ask of life throughout the years?
I am not worth a great amount
In the ages that will pass.
I do not have a legacy that
shall be counted as very much
in the eyes of those who pass
on very little.
My name is not one for history
and this is always good
for history has never recorded
precisely what it should.
Yet I came to know in my own time
the weeping and the laughing,
the jeering laughter,
the sighs,
the cries,
and the why's of why
I was put here.
It was only for an instant . . .
to dance awhile, to sing,
and pace upon the ground.
Yet before me now the children all
are laughing,
and many hands are clapping,
and . . . and . . .

[Lights fade gradually on the clown. Now there is only half-light on Egmont.]

EGMONT [sadly but with strength]:
For this sudden passing
the circus is something less
 – more so –
the world is a great deal less.

Those who had gathered saw
the passing on of goodness.
Other clowns will come it is true.
But none will be as he.
None again will have <u>his</u> touch of wonder
and his laughing spirit.
And few will say as he did
to the inner command which
calls all clowns, "Yes, I'll be it!
I will continue!
I will continue despite the laughter
of the cynics
for it was I who willed to even
make the cynics laugh!
It was I who stopped the hopeless
from their plunging if only for
an instant!
It is I who have come to know
THE ETERNITY OF THE MOMENT
for all laughed, yes, for a second!"
[Egmont ponders his thought. Then he speaks
slowly and deliberately.]
So then it is not just "the few"
who receive
God's call
or "the great men" only.
It comes to all.
But none so well respond
as the laughing jokings of clowns.
Nothing greater rises to God's ear
than the buffoon's mockery of fear!

Scene Two

[Same prison cell as in Act One.]

BONHOEFFER:
Soon enough surely my life is fulfilled.
And what have I come to know
since now I will be set free from this prison's odor?

Is it that there are stations
on Freedom's road?
Yes, but no one can speak for all.
Each one must discover for one's self
the holy meaning of The Other.
Yet there are stations on
Freedom's road.
Discipline, Action, Suffering
and Death
are for us
guides.

Discipline[*]

If you go out to seek Freedom, then learn
at the beginning
to discipline your perceptions and your mind, so that
the wild desires of your body do not lead you
into bondage.
Your mind and body must be undefiled
and totally under your control,
so that obediently they will seek after the
goal which is set for them.
No one ever learned the secret of Freedom
except through discipline.

Action

Not what is pleasing.
but what is right you must
dare to do.
Not by soaring on the wings of possibility,
but by boldly grasping the actual,
not in the flight of thought
but only in action is there Freedom.
Turn from your doubts and go out
to the storm of Occurrence,
sustained only by God's command and your faith;
and Freedom, rejoicing will receive your spirit.

---

[*] Ibid., pp. 250-251.

Suffering

There is a sudden transformation.
Your strong, effective hands are bound.
Powerless and alone you see the end of
your activity.
Still, you hope, laying your cause
in Stronger Hands which comfort and console.
Only for an instant you touched upon Freedom,
then you gave it over to God
in order that He would will its perfection.

[Egmont again returns.]

Death

Come now, highest feast on the road
to Eternal Freedom.
Death – destroy the base bondage of
chain and wall,
destroy our ephemeral bodies and
our deluded senses
that we may finally behold what
temporally we are unable to see.
FREEDOM, we have sought thee
in discipline, in action, in suffering;
dying we now know Thee as THE PRESENCE OF GOD!

[There is a silence for a few seconds.]

EGMONT:
The hour hastens to the FINAL FREEDOM.

BONHOEFFER [smiling]:
Yes, but will "the striving for the highest" continue?

EGMONT:
It will. I am sure that it will.
After the struggle for the highest
has been attempted,

and we have done what we could,
I am sure that God draws near.

BONHOEFFER:
Acceptance, yes, acceptance
for what it is, for what is was
that we have done in honesty,
of whom we've come to be –
of what we now call free.
And still there is always dignity
despite our place or what we face
in the hour which will come.
[There is a knock at the prison door.]
Let us go in silence. [solemnly]
Stay with me as I walk
those final steps to heaven's door.
Let us not rush nor be too far behind.
Patiently I've lived and patiently I'll die.
No sound they'll hear nor complaint.
[He turns to Egmont.]
And now we've said what must be said
for those who will live on after –
that nations which forget Mystery
must meet their own disaster,
that "sophisticated" investment killing
will have its henchmen willing,
that still for all there's hope
despite the swinging rope.
[The light is now only on Bonhoeffer. He stares at the audience and then seems to see something above the people.]
O God,
Who punishes sin and willingly forgives,
I have loved this people.
I have born its disgrace and its oppression
and seen its Redemption – that is enough.
Hold me, contain me! My staff is sinking.
O faithful God, prepare my grave.

[The lights fall.]

REMEMBER TORRES!

CHARACTERS

GOMEZ
GONZALES
ELENA
CARDINAL
ISABELLA
CAMILO TORRES
PEDRO
MIGUEL
COMMUNIST
NIHILIST
SOCIALIST
CARDINAL'S SECRETARY
STUDENTS
SOLDIERS AND PEOPLE OF THE REVOLUTION

ACT ONE

[The setting is a living room in a Colombian hacienda. There are protective bars on the windows. The entire room is extravagantly decorated with elegant Spanish furniture and silver candle fixtures. Persian carpets, glass bookcases of polished wood, and expensive art objects are to be seen. A portable bar is situated in front of the large and comfortable sofa in the middle of the room. The sofa is directly facing the audience. To the right and left of the sofa are individual, expensive, large, soft chairs. Gomez is sitting in one chair, and Gonzales is lounging on the sofa. They are both overweight, greasy men in their mid-fifties. Their hands look like small soft pillows. Both appear remarkably identical in their pampered dress and bearing. As the act begins both are drinking whiskey.]

Gomez: Would you like some more whiskey?

Gonzales: Yes, I would! It is excellent. Where did you get it?

Gomez [going to the bar in front of the sofa]: I had it imported from the United States. It is from Kentucky.

Gonzales: Yes, Kentucky is a great country.

Gomez: I believe they call Kentucky a state.

Gonzales: Yes, you're right: a state part of the United States. That great land of beauty, industry, war, and . . .

Gomez: . . . and gold!

Gonzales: Yes, and gold.

Gomez: Besides, it is an aristocratic country. Their symbol is the eagle.

Gonzales: From what I have heard recently, it should be the buzzard.

Gomez: Why do you say that?

Gonzales: Because the Americans have a tendency to live off dead countries.

Gomez: No . . . no. That is not true. The eagle is the right symbol because the Americans swoop down, give <u>us</u> money, and secure <u>our</u> power.

Gonzales: Yes, but then we buy their whiskey, guns, and machinery. However, I will agree to the symbol of the eagle. Nevertheless they should take the olive branch out of its mouth and replace it with a silver dollar.

Gomez [laughing]: Very good. And they should find a way for the eagle to bite the dollar to see if it is still good.

Gonzales [laughing]: But why are we complaining?

Gomez: I don't know.

Gonzales: Why should we discuss this matter so lightly? Have not the Americans done <u>us</u> a lot of good?

Gomez: They have! They have!

Gonzales: Still, one should be sensitive to world problems if only for the feeling of nobility.

Gomez: Yes, we must have all the luxuries. [Both laugh. Elena, the attractive twenty year old daughter of Gomez, enters the room.]

Elena: Father, the Cardinal is here and would like to see you.

Gomez: Show him in. [Elena exits.]

Gonzales: I had better go. I am in too good of a mood to give my confession . . . or hear the Cardinal's.

Gomez: Don't leave me with him . . . I . . . [The Cardinal enters, he is extremely fat and bears a striking resemblance to Gomez and Gonzales. He is dressed in a scarlet cape and wears the pectoral crucifix which is attached to an elaborate gold chain. One expensive ring is seen on each hand.] Your Eminence! How wonderful it is to see you. [Gomez bows and kisses the Cardinal's ring.]

Gonzales [greeting the Cardinal and kissing his ring]: Your Eminence! A pleasure to see you. Excuse me, but I must return to my hacienda.

Cardinal: Could it wait a few moments? This is rather important. I would like to speak to the two of you together.

Gonzales [obsequiously]: Why certainly, your Eminence, certainly.

Cardinal: I trust that both of you are well.

Gomez: Yes, your Eminence, I never felt better.

Gonzales: Yes, your Eminence, but I have missed our past conversations concerning our infallibility. [All three laugh.]

Cardinal: Yes, yes of course.

Gomez: And how are you, your Eminence?

Cardinal: Well, I feel fine I must say. [glancing at the bar] Ah . . . do you have any . . .

Gonzales [taunting him]: Ah . . . any altar wine, your Eminence?

Cardinal [annoyed at first]: That's enough . . . [But he reconsiders.] or on second thought [smiling] that really isn't quite enough.

Gomez: Perhaps some American whiskey?

Cardinal: Since you offer it. [Gomez goes and gets a drink for the Cardinal. Gonzales also gets a healthy drink for himself. By now Gonzales is starting to slip into a very euphoric state.]

Gonzales: And what brings you to the Gomez hacienda?

Cardinal [sipping the whiskey]: Excellent . . . excellent.

Gonzales [smiling with the slack-jawed look of an imbecile]: It's not just another hacienda, your Eminence.

Cardinal: No, I mean the whiskey.

Gomez: But that goes along with the hacienda.

Cardinal [putting down his glass]: Which brings me to the reason for my visit. Do both of you like things the way they are?

Gomez: They were never better.

Gonzales [He has been drinking steadily and is now almost completely drunk. He laughs.]: Of course we need your blessing now and then to take care of us both in this world and the next. But then . . .

Cardinal [He is now quite serious.]: I know . . . I know. But listen . . . if things are to remain as they are, we are going to have problems.

Gomez [startled]: Certainly you don't advise a change?

Cardinal: Hardly, but a young priest does.

Gonzales: Simple. Excommunicate him.

Gomez: Exactly.

Cardinal: Not quite so simple. If I excommunicate him, the common people will look upon him as a martyr for the cause of social justice, and then we will really have a problem on our hands.

Gonzales: Who is the priest?

Cardinal: Father Camilo Torres.

Gomez: Can he be bribed?

Cardinal: Not this one.

Gonzales: Can he be threatened?

Cardinal: No.

Gomez: Is his mother living? She is probably able to influence him. If you as a Cardinal got in touch with her, perhaps . . .

Cardinal: No . . . no, it wouldn't work.

Gonzales [boisterously drunk]: There have been radical priests before. Let him have his say. Things will die down, and we will be sitting here a year from now calm and secure again.

Cardinal: I hope you are right. However, this one is educated. He has a degree from the University of Louvain in sociology. He is brilliant and has already begun to effectively organize segments of the population against us.

Gomez: What are we supposed to do?

Gonzales: Yes, what could we possibly do anyway?

Cardinal: I was thinking that you and the fifteen other major land owners could make a gesture.

Gonzales [drunk and enraged]: You don't mean give up something?

Cardinal: It would only be a small gesture. It would not be lasting. If you gave some extra money to your workers periodically, things would calm down. I and the bishops as well as some trusted priests could turn the people away from Torres and lead them back to our way of thinking.

Gonzales: Impossible! Impossible! Your Eminence, I barely have enough for the necessities of life.

Gomez: I must send my daughter to a foreign university, preferably in the United States. She must have a British sports car and all the luxuries. If she does not have these things how will she find a husband who suits me! No, it is impossible to give anything at this time.

Gonzales: Impossible!

Cardinal: But . . .

Gonzales: But if we give our workers more money now, they will only demand more in the future. No, leave things as they are.

Cardinal: You don't understand. If you don't give them something now you may have nothing to give them in the future. That is a definite possibility.

Gomez: There may be some other way. You say this Father Torres is educated. What kind of degree does he have in . . . what was it? Socio . . .

Cardinal: Sociology.

Gonzales: What's that?

Cardinal: A study that could aid Torres and his people in destroying us.

Gonzales: Oh . . . well . . . why, he shouldn't have been allowed to study that in the first place.

Gomez [irritated]: Gonzales, would you shut up!

Gonzales [totally drunk and slurring his words]: All right, but I don't see . . .

Cardinal: Gentlemen, gentlemen, let us not argue among ourselves. We have a common enemy to be gotten rid of.

Gomez: You're right, your Eminence. What kind of a degree does this young priest have?

Cardinal: A master of arts degree.

Gomez: And are there higher degrees?

Cardinal: Yes, the University of Louvain offers a doctorate.

Gomez: Ah-ha!

Cardinal: What are you saying?

Gomez: And where is this university?

Cardinal: In Europe . . . Belgium.

Gomez: Perfect!

Cardinal: I think I see what you're getting at.

Gonzales [helplessly drunk]: What? What? See what?

Gomez [ignoring Gonzales]: It's simple. Agree with Father Torres.

Gonzales: What? What are you saying?

Gomez [still ignoring Gonzales]: Listen, your Eminence, tell Father Torres that you agree with his program of social reform. However, ask him if he would not like to study a little longer at Louvain in order to get a "higher" degree. After he has completed his education he can return to Colombia and continue his work with the people. While he is away we can work out a new strategy for ourselves.

Cardinal [reflecting]: It might work. Yes, [smiling] yes, it might work. I could . . . so to speak . . . use my power for his best interests.

Gomez [smiling]: I should think, your Eminence, that your power would not only work for his best interests but also for our own.

Gonzales [slurring his words]: Excellent . . . excellent!

Cardinal [thinking out loud]: Yes, I could touch his vanity in the name of God.

Gomez: What was that?

Cardinal: Why, I could say to him that the Church might more readily delegate greater authority to him if he had a doctorate in his field.

Gomez: Precisely.

Gonzales [by now unaware of everything]: Precisely!

Cardinal [finishing his drink]: Well, I had best be going. Thank you for the whiskey and . . . the advice. [Gonzales and Gomez stand. Gomez has to help steady Gonzales.]

Gomez: Good-bye, your Eminence, and good luck.

Gonzales [really not knowing what he is doing]: Good luck, your Eminence, and say some Masses for the patron saint of Kentucky. Bill me at your convenience. [The Cardinal tries to understand him, but Gonzales falls back into his chair and shuts his eyes with his head leaning to one side.]

Cardinal [to Gomez]: Take good care of our friend. [The Cardinal exits. Gomez studies Gonzales for a few seconds.]

Gomez: Gonzales . . . Gonzales, you ass, wake up.

Gonzales [half-groggy]: How much did it cost us?

Gomez [laughing]: Nothing. Not even an extra glass of whiskey.

Gonzales: Really. Well . . . well . . .

Gomez: I'll get you some coffee. [calling off stage] Elena . . . Elena. [Elena enters.]

Elena: Yes, father?

Gomez [Looking at Gonzales, Gomez begins laughing.]: Elena, please tell one of the servants to get Gonzales some coffee.

Elena: Yes, father. Oh father, may I use one of the cars today?

Gomez: Yes, of course, where are you going?

Elena: Into Bogota to do some shopping.

Gomez: Speak to the servants and then you may go. Oh, wait a minute.

Elena: Yes, father?

Gomez: Could you give Gonzales a ride to his hacienda on your way to the city? I don't believe that he will be able to drive.

Elena: Yes, father. [Elena exits.]

Gomez [looking at Gonzales]: Ah, excellent. All is as it should be . . . just as it should be.

[The lights fall.]

ACT TWO
Scene One

[A shack in Colombia. The entire atmosphere portrays extreme poverty. Newspapers cover the windows. A bed with a ragged cover is situated in the center of the stage. A young but exhausted woman is in the bed. She is moaning quietly. Her husband, Pedro, is standing near her. His appearance is shabby. Camilo Torres, a young priest, has just entered. Camilo Torres is thirty-five, intense, and relatively handsome.]

Torres: Pedro, what has happened? What has happened?

Pedro: Not long ago she started screaming that something exploded in the lower part of her stomach. She has grown weaker and paler.

Torres: Did you send for the doctor?

Pedro: I sent for the doctor, but he would not come. [weeping] I have no money . . . and he would not come. [becoming frightened] Father, what is going to happen?

Torres: She is going to die, Pedro.

Pedro: But she cannot die, Father . . .

Torres: God will welcome her. Pedro, He will welcome her. I will hear her confession . . . and give her the sacrament.

Pedro [weeping and anxious]: But she is too weak to speak.

Torres: God will hear her. He will hear her. [He takes a small black case from his coat. From the case he takes out a white wafer.] Isabella, accept Our Lord.

[Camilo Torres tries to give her the wafer but sees that it is useless. He slowly places the wafer back in its case.]

Pedro [anxiously]: She is too weak, Father, and you have not heard her confession.

Torres: It is all right, Pedro, it is all right. She has nothing to be sorry for. She has already paid for everything. You stay with her, and I will find a doctor to see if anything can yet be done. [Pedro moves next to Isabella and takes her hand. He looks at the priest with horror.]

Pedro [weeping with rage]: There is no need for a doctor!

[Camilo Torres starts to come to Pedro. He stops, realizing the futility of present consolation. He leaves. The lights fall.]

Scene Two

[A city street in the slums of Colombia. It is the same day. There are shabby buildings, garbage, and general trash about the place. There is also a bench for those awaiting the bus. Camilo Torres is sitting alone on the bench. His head is bent down in thought. Miguel, a young student who is about nineteen years old, enters. He sees Camilo Torres and approaches him.]

Miguel: Father Torres, how are you?

Torres: Hello, Miguel. I am well, and yourself?

Miguel: I am fine. Are you going to the meeting today?

Torres: The meeting . . . oh yes, I almost forgot. Yes, I will be there.

Miguel: You must come, Father. The communists and socialists have been trying to gain control at each past meeting. They are each defending a purely ideological thesis which often times sounds inhuman.

Torres: What do you mean?

Miguel: I mean they are arguing more for blood than for bread.

Torres [pleased with Miguel's criticism]: I see. Yes, that is certainly the case. The radicals have become too heated with their own thoughts to see beyond themselves. At times I do not blame them.

Miguel [scanning the scene]: Yes, you only have to look around.

Torres: Yes, you only have to look around. [placing his head in his own hands] Do you know Pedro's wife, Isabella?

Miguel: Yes.

Torres: She died not more than an hour ago. I tried to give her the last sacrament, but she was too weak to receive it. [reflecting] Besides what good would that have done? She died of a burst appendix. She would have lived if a doctor, any doctor, would have come to her a few days ago. It is a very simple operation, Miguel, a very simple operation. But no one would help her because her husband had no money! After seeing such things over and over again I, too, become more and more enraged. Of course I will meet the radicals today.

Miguel: And what will you say to them?

Torres [reflecting]: Not a great deal.

Miguel: But I thought . . .

Torres: I know, I know. You thought I would come down on them and accuse them of only being radicals.

Miguel: Yes.

Torres: The time is not ripe for that. The radicals must still be used when and where they can be effective.

Miguel: I see.

Torres: Although I believe that we are all children of God and therefore should be housed, fed, and clothed in accordance with Christ's teachings; I do not expect our fellow revolutionaries to accept all my beliefs.

Miguel: Father, you had better be careful that they do not use you for their own ends.

Torres: That is true; I must be careful. But I must only take care to the extent the primary objective is achieved. The people must have doctors, food, and adequate housing. That is the teaching of Christ, and I am His priest.

Miguel: The communists wish to accomplish the same objective. So do the rest of the radicals.

Torres: Yes. But without reference to Christ. I am afraid if only the radicals gain power there will only be more slavery.

Miguel: What kind of slavery?

Torres: The kind of slavery people impose upon themselves in the name of an ideal. Sooner or later the ideal becomes the devil since people cannot tolerate the reality that they are human in the face of their own ideal. The ideal can make people uncompassionate, self-righteous, and mad with their own power. The ideal can become hard, cold and dead; and those under the ideal lose a living reality which is the true and the good basis of this world.

Miguel [confused]: What is that reality?

Torres: The reality and the power is the same reality and power that was in Jesus Christ.

Miguel: But the Church has done little to help the poor.

Torres [with quiet bitterness]: The Church is not always Christ!

Miguel: Be careful, Father. You are right, but the hot blood of our people often forces them to forget all perspective.

Torres: At times my own hot blood clouds my own theological perspective. However I am not allowed the luxury of being only a radical. I am a priest and must always place before me and above me the thought and compassion demanded by Jesus Christ.

Miguel: I do not know if the people can measure themselves as well.

Torres: They must, or else hot blood and destruction will work against us. The rich will crush everyone in the name of law and order. [Miguel and Torres stand up. They begin to walk.]

Miguel: Step carefully, Father . . . carefully.

Torres [smiling and taking a light skip]: But we need not be that careful. Have a little faith, Miguel . . . just a little faith.

[The lights fall.]

Scene Three

[A closed room in a tavern. Three radicals are speaking. There is a communist, age 45; a socialist, age 32; and a nihilist, age 21.]

Communist: Colombia is a key to the world revolution!

Nihilist: Yes, but before the revolution can succeed we must destroy! We must bomb the haciendas of the rich aristocrats. At the same time we must bomb the Cardinal's residence. If we can steal the gold and jewels from the Church, buy guns, and then completely destroy the power of this feudal society, the people will have to turn to us and then we . . .

Socialist: Wait a minute . . . wait a minute! We must have change but gradual change. The people must have power not us!

Nihilist [raging]: But how will the people have power if we do not destroy the present power structure? We must tear everything down and then begin to build!

Communist: Yes, we can be helped afterward by the other communistic countries of the world. They will help us in restructuring a people's government. First the aristocratic and bourgeois swine must be slaughtered.

Nihilist [to socialist]: And the people will live off the bacon! [Communist and Nihilist begin laughing.]

Socialist: All right, but we must keep destruction to a minimum otherwise the people will have nothing on which to build.

Nihilist: We must have __maximum__ destruction or else we will not root out all the diseases of the present system!

Socialist [confused but holding his position]: No.

Nihilist [sure of his position]: Yes!

Communist: Let us destroy it all and then we can appeal to my comrades who will help us rebuild.

Nihilist [raging]: But let us destroy! Let us destroy!

Communist: If we keep anything of the present structure it will only again be subsidized by the United States as it presently is.

Socialist: But we could use the money to hold free elections and aid the people.

Communist: But the purity of the revolution would be marred. No . . . a total overturn of power is needed!

Nihilist: And that means total destruction!

Socialist: No.

Communist: Yes!

Nihilist: Yes!

Socialist: But . . .

Nihilist [waving off the socialist]: Nonsense, that is all there is to it.

Socialist: I am leaving. Both of you want blood and power more than you want reform.

Communist [hedging and trying to contain the socialist]: Wait. We, too, want reform. Not just for Colombia but for the world.

Nihilist [going insane with the thought]: The world! The world! We must destroy!

Socialist [about to leave again]: I am going.

Communist: Stop . . . wait. The priest is supposed to come any moment now. We need him. The people trust him. He is a necessary instrument in bringing forth <u>our</u> plans.

Nihilist [reflecting and calming himself]: Please wait. If we are not united, he will lose confidence in us.

Socialist: I cannot unite with you.

Communist: Wait! [The socialist is in the process of leaving.] Wait! [There is a knock at the door.] Come in. [Torres and Miguel enter.]

Socialist: Father, there is no possibility of . . .

Communist [interrupting him]: There is no possibility of coming to an agreement without you. We need your help, Father.

Torres [sensing that he is about to be played into their hands]: What is the difficulty?

Communist: We cannot find a unifying theme.

Torres: What is the trouble?

Communist: I am afraid we have among us a moderate who wishes to betray the revolution.

Socialist: Not at all. I only wish that the power remains in the hands of the Colombian people and that the country does not become so ravaged that the people will only be governing a desert.

Nihilist: Ha! Half measures and too much wind. Let's do all or nothing. We must destroy before we can rebuild.

Torres [with authority]: That is enough! Look, do you want to overthrow the powers which make our people live like diseased animals, or do you want to argue forever among yourselves? Nothing is going to happen without a united front.

Nihilist: But we must destroy the present government.

Socialist: Not in the way you want it destroyed.

Communist: You see, Father, we have a moderate and thus a traitor.

Socialist: A traitor! At least I do not want a foreign power to control my people.

Communist: Neither do I.

Socialist: But you just said before Father Torres arrived that a foreign communistic power would have control of Colombia. I only want the Colombian people to be able to govern themselves and raise their standard of living.

Communist: By a foreign power I meant a power controlled by the workers . . . that is, a power forging to the present system.

Socialist: You're lying.

Nihilist [to Torres]: No, he isn't.

Torres: Look, if we cannot work for a united front among ourselves, I am leaving.

Communist: The Father is right. Let us work together.

Socialist: All right . . . against the present power system.

Torres: Exactly.

Nihilist: Against the privileged class and their indifference to the people.

Torres: Exactly. But we must use effective and measured tactics. We must remember that the prime objective is to get power into the hands of our people.

Communist: Exactly.

Torres: This means that more pamphlets and speeches must be made so that the revolution will come from the people. If enough pressure is exerted by them, the present regime will fall. This is the present concern. Let us trim all our ideologies to fit the immediacy of the hour. Only in this way can we unite for the present.

Socialist: And the future?

Torres: A socialistic government established through free elections will be the new life of the Colombian people.

Nihilist: But the present feudal regime will be destroyed.

Torres: Of course.

Nihilist: Bravo! Let us continue our work.

Communist: Precisely!

Torres: Remember that the people must be united. I will do what I can at the university and through the Church. You must all start to mobilize your groups for the final overthrow, but move carefully. The secret police and the army are ruthless. They could destroy the entire movement before we could gain a satisfactory foothold. Keep things directed toward the people. If enough pressures can be exerted by present social needs, and our showing a way to alleviate such needs, the revolution will succeed.

Socialist: Long live the revolution!

Communist: Long live the revolution!

Miguel and Nihilist: Long live the revolution!

Torres: But first let us make sure that it is given a satisfactory birth.

Communist: I must be going.

Nihilist: I will come with you.

Communist: Good-bye, Father. We will continue our work. [The communist and nihilist leave.]

Socialist: Thank you, Father. I agree with what you have said. I will tell my friends of your proposal. [He exits.]

Miguel [after a few moments]: Well done, Father, but . . .

Torres: I know . . . but we cannot really trust any of them.

Miguel: Yes, that is true.

Torres: But we need them for the present.

Miguel: And afterwards?

Torres: We must have unity now. If we cannot have unity, we will only fight among ourselves. Once the people have been united and mobilized and the revolution has succeeded, then we will be in a better position to discover what is best for the people. Until then we must use our friends.

Miguel: Do you think if the revolution succeeds the people will trust you?

Torres: We must have some faith in the goodness of the people. I must believe that they trust me now and that they will trust me in the future. We are fighting for them, Miguel, and the people are not ungrateful.

[The lights fall.]

ACT THREE
Scene One

[A city street.]

Torres: Miguel, it is time we parted company. I have an appointment with the Cardinal for which I am already late.

Miguel: I will see you tomorrow, Father.

Torres: Fine. Speak with your friends. Get together four or five of those you can trust. I will speak with them soon. [Torres leaves. Miguel waits a few seconds and starts to leave in the opposite direction. A girl's voice is heard.]

Elena: Miguel . . . Miguel. [Elena enters.] There you are. I have been looking for you.

Miguel: Elena. [They kiss each other.] Does your father know where you are?

Elena: Of course not. I told him I was going shopping. Where have you been all day?

Miguel: I have been with Father Torres.

Elena: The radical priest?

Miguel: Yes, and a real priest.

Elena: And what have you been saying?

Miguel: Very little. I should have been speaking to him about us, and our wedding.

Elena: But my father would never permit that.

Miguel [smiling]: I know and that is why I often participate with a radical priest for reasons closer to me than politics.

Elena: Do you think he would really marry us without my father's consent?

Miguel [laughing] I am sure he would. It would be part of the revolution.

Elena: The revolution?

Miguel [There is a brief silence. He then speaks with helpless bitterness.]: The revolution which will destroy the shame of being poor. [brief silence]

Elena [concerned]: You should not feel shame. It is the rich who deserve the shame. [brief silence] Do you know Gonzales, the landowner?

Miguel [bitterly]: No, but I know of him.

Elena: This afternoon he became drunk again at our hacienda. Father asked me to drive him home. Gonzales, between periods when we had to stop so that he could vomit, kept mumbling something about your friend, Father Torres. Something about education as bribery.

Miguel: Education as bribery?

Elena: Apparently they want to get Father Torres out of the country. The Cardinal was also at the hacienda today. Apparently my father, Gonzales, and the Cardinal are going to send Father Torres to Europe for more education.

Miguel: And frustrate his work?

Elena: I suppose that is their plan.

Miguel: Then everyone is against him . . . everyone.

[The lights fall.]

Scene Two

[The Cardinal's office. His "Eminence," is seated at a large desk in a swivel chair. A huge Bible is on the desk. His office is elaborately decorated. A gold crucifix hangs on the wall. There are polished wood bookcases. Behind the desk is a Renaissance painting in which a plump and smiling Christ is depicted changing water into wine. On either side of the painting is a picture of John XXIII and Pius XII. The room exudes elegance, having the same type of rugs and candle fixtures as Gomez's hacienda in Act One. The Cardinal is seated and is looking at his official papers. His secretary, an overweight and puffy priest, enters.]

Secretary: Your Eminence, Father Torres is here. [The Cardinal stands up and straightens his robes and pectoral cross.]

Cardinal: Show him in. [The Cardinal remains standing. Torres enters.]

Torres: Good afternoon, your Eminence.

Cardinal: Father . . . Father, how good it is to see you. How good it is to see you. Please sit down. [The Cardinal escorts Torres to a seat at the left of the desk. The Cardinal picks up a cigar box and goes to Torres.] A cigar?

Torres: No thank you, your Eminence.

Cardinal [Sitting behind his desk and leaning back in his swivel chair, he lights and puffs on his cigar.]: Well, Father, what have you been doing since we last saw each other?

Torres: Your Eminence, you know that I have been teaching and serving the Church as a priest.

Cardinal [narrowing his snake-like eyes]: And what else?

Torres [blandly]: That is more than enough for anyone.

Cardinal: There have been many reports that you have been engaging in revolutionary activities.

Torres: Those activities have not been so much revolutionary as Christian.

Cardinal: But they have not been done through Holy Mother Church's authority.

Torres: That is true in some cases.

Cardinal: However, the Church has begun to admire your zeal in these pursuits.

Torres [surprised in a guarded fashion]: Really?

Cardinal: Yes, Father, yes indeed.

Torres: Would the Church be willing to aid me with finances to help the poor?

Cardinal [thinking and puffing smoke]: It would.

Torres: Excellent. Then the Church should begin by building more hospitals, homes for orphans and the aged. It should sell its gold chalices, emerald rings, and immense land holdings. It should use the proceeds to help the poor. We should all work for a living like everyone else. Now priests are supported financially by the people. We should be helping the people with our financial contributions to them. No poor man should ever be asked for money!

Cardinal [taken aback but remaining the negotiator]: You are very progressive, Father, very progressive. However, you realize that it will take Holy Mother Church time to adjust to such changes.

Torres [annoyed]: The people cannot wait for the Church to "adjust." Every day people are dying from the needs of bare necessities. The rings on your hands could buy enough food to feed an entire village for a month. Yet the rings will remain on your hands just as the Church will remain speaking the word "adjustment."

Cardinal [resenting the attack]: Now just a minute, Father. Just a minute. I agree that changes should come. However, the Church is not ready for such drastic changes as you are advocating. And I, as one of the Church's leaders, do not believe that you are, yourself, prepared to take the responsibility for the consequences of such changes.

Torres: Whether I am prepared or not, the people <u>are</u> prepared to undertake such action and be responsible for the consequences.

Cardinal: But who will control the people if not leaders like ourselves?

Torres [cringing at the last statement]: Your Eminence, the people do not need to be controlled. They need to be freed from poverty and disease.

Cardinal [conciliatory]: I agree, Father, and you are one of those who must help to free them. However, I do not know if you are sufficiently prepared to do so.

Torres: What do you mean?

Cardinal: Simply this. I have been sufficiently impressed by your efforts thus far to place more power in your hands. However, Father, you are very young. You have not completed your education. I have decided that it would be for your own best interests, Colombia's best interests, and the Church's best interests, if you returned to the University of Louvain and earned your doctorate in sociology. Then we could both see more clearly what would be the best attitude to assume for both Colombia and the Church.

Torres: And how long should I stay at Louvain?

Cardinal: Until your studies are completed.

Torres: That would take at least three years! All that I have done thus far would be ruined.

Cardinal [putting down his cigar and looking heavenward]: Father, you have no faith in me and your fellow priests. You as a priest should know that the Church's care of souls is an absolute spiritual responsibility. All our power is from God and is based upon our beloved Lord's statement; "Thou art Peter and upon this rock I will build my Church, and the gates of Hell shall not prevail against it." You know this, Father, and you also know that all right, all power, all charisma, as well as all spiritual and all temporal gifts both in heaven above and on earth below are delegated to that Holy Catholic and Apostolic Church and Her divinely ordered structure.

Torres [becoming infuriated]: I know, your Eminence, and this is all that I know: I cannot go up to the altar of God as a priest when my brothers and my sisters are dying from hunger, from disease, and from statements like you have just made!

Cardinal [taken aback, but measuring himself]: Father, certainly you cannot go against our beloved Lord's statement to the founder of the true, holy, and apostolic Church.

Torres [furious]: The Church is that place where the poor are fed and justice is enacted on behalf of the needy. There and only there is Christ's Church! I can't find anywhere in the Bible where Jesus said to Peter: "We'll live off the poor until we're so fat and weak that we'll be forced to look at the sky since we'll be unable to see over the top of our bellies."

Cardinal [becoming enraged]: I suppose you're making a reference to me.

Torres [with mockery]: So the snake of conscience can even strike at a Cardinal!

Cardinal: [trying to control himself]: All right, Father, all right. Perhaps I am overweight.

Torres [laughing out loud]: That's not the point.

Cardinal [red in the face and blurting out the question]: Father, will you go to Louvain or won't you?

Torres [knowing when to stop but unable to control himself entirely]: Your Eminence, I must have time to consider your request.

Cardinal: Please take a few days to consider my proposal. I trust you will complete your studies or else.

Torres: Or else what?

Cardinal: Or else severe measures must be taken.

Torres: Oh, I see. [He pauses for a few moments and then stands up.] Good day, your Eminence. [Torres goes to the door. The Cardinal bows but looks up and realizes that no one is there to acknowledge his bow. As Torres opens the door the secretary, who has been listening at the door unseen by the audience and who has had his weight pressed up against the door, falls on the floor. Torres turns to the Cardinal and points to the secretary on the floor.] Your Eminence . . . your servant. [Torres leaves laughing.]

Cardinal [furious and raging at his secretary]: Get up, you fool.

Secretary: But, your Eminence . . .

Cardinal: I said get up! [He picks up his cigar, takes a puff and begins choking. The lights fall.]

Scene Three

[A university classroom. Torres has just completed a lecture. He is standing near a table with a few books on it. The students have surrounded him.]

1st Student: Father, when will we move?

2nd Student: Next month or at the end of the year?

3rd Student: Yes, Father, when?

Torres: We need more people before we can act as a united front. Go to the villages and speak with the farmers. Go to the factories and speak with the workers. The time is growing ripe for an all-out revolution. But we need more people. Be careful. You must all use discretion. More and more I am forced to speak in public. But each of you can be effective by speaking to workers and farmers. You can also be effective by listening to their sufferings and their questions. Be gentle with the people. Explain yourselves clearly and show them that you are sincerely trying to bring about a better life for them and for their families.

1st Student: Long live the revolution!

2nd and 3rd Students: La Revolucion!!! [The students leave. Torres sits down on the table and Miguel enters.]

Miguel: The students look as though they are ready.

Torres [sternly]: They are not ready yet. We need more people behind us. The students will need more patience and will have to become more acquainted with the people.
[Miguel reflects a moment.]

Miguel: Father, I have some news for you.

Torres: Oh?

Miguel: I was speaking with Elena, the daughter of Senor Gomez. She mentioned that the Cardinal was at her father's hacienda and was speaking about bribing you with more education. Does that make any sense to you?

Torres: Oh yes, yes it makes a great deal of sense. Yes, everything is much clearer now. [He picks up his books and begins to leave.]

Miguel: What is it, Father?

Torres: I have an appointment with the Cardinal.

Miguel: May I walk with you?

Torres: Certainly, come along. [stopping] Miguel, do you know what they are trying to do? They are trying to take my work away from me by holding out some abstract degree and many false promises. I realize exactly what they are trying to do. Perhaps I should be quiet and let them toy with me a little longer. However, I am sick of their sordid, cheap, and underhanded maneuvers. It is time I confronted them directly.

Miguel: If you do that, they will not allow you to speak at the university.

Torres: They will also deny me the privilege of saying Mass and other rites which a priest may use to comfort the poor. Still, I have waited too long. Soon they will begin to tell lies about me. They will invent lies to try and destroy the people's trust in me and the revolution. [Torres notices that Miguel has become quite anxious.]

Miguel: But if they silence you, what can you do against them?

Torres [attempting to sort out many thoughts at once]: Miguel, whatever will happen in the future I do no know. I only know that whatever means are available I will use to crush the evil that is all about us. You and the others must carry on the work that we have begun at the university. Try to understand that many students at the university mean well but they, too, are of the privileged class. Many simply want to rebel for purely psychological reasons. Their rebellion is therefore unstructured and very temporary. It is simply a type of non-conformism which offends the workers and the farmers. You must work to unite the students with all segments of the population.

Miguel: I will try, Father. But what will you do?

Torres: I will meet with the Cardinal first. After I have spoken with him, I will then know which course to take. I will probably join the army of liberation in the mountains. That will be the only effective means left for me to aid the revolution.

Miguel [terrified]: But, Father . . .

Torres: Shh, Miguel. We are friends now. Call me Camilo before we part for I will not be a priest in the eyes of this world much longer.

Miguel: But what if you are killed? And what if I fail? And what if the army of liberation is destroyed?

Torres [quietly and with simple dignity]: We shall not fail. Whether the revolution succeeds completely now or later is not so important. And Miguel, remember this: even if both of us are killed and many armies of liberation are destroyed, others will rise up again to attack the indifference of the privileged classes. Many need only look at the people's suffering and their consciences as well as the consciences of many others as yet unborn will rise up to demand justice. The High Spirit of Christ Himself will aid them in their struggle just as It has aided me. [He stops for a few seconds and tries to control his emotions.] Miguel, have faith in Jesus Christ and in the revolution; that is all you need. And now we must part. [They stand up, shake hands, and embrace each other.]

Miguel [on the verge of tears]: But, Father . . .

Torres [smiling]: Shh, Miguel. Remember . . . Camilo. [He leaves quickly. Miguel starts to follow him but stops. He looks around the classroom as the lights fall.]

Scene Four

[The Cardinal's office. The secretary is now occupying the chair next to the desk formerly occupied by Camilo Torres. The Cardinal is seated behind the desk.]

Cardinal [furiously]: Write a letter to Senor Gomez. Tell him that the plan is not working. Tell him also that if Father Torres does not go to Louvain, I will deprive him of the right to say Mass. I will also forbid him to lecture at the university or speak in public. Gomez must use his influence with the secret police to see that my commands are enforced. [sounding more and more like a dictator] Tell Gomez that Torres's insubordination will not be tolerated! [There is a knock at the door. The Cardinal yells at the door.] Come in!

Torres: Your Eminence.

Cardinal [trying to control himself]: Come in, Father. [turning to his secretary] Get out of here!

Secretary: Yes, your Eminence . . . Yes, your Eminence. [Grabbing his papers, he hurries out.]

Cardinal: Would you like a drink?

Torres [smiling]: No, thank you, your Eminence, but please help yourself.

Cardinal: I believe I will. [The Cardinal looks puzzled for a moment as though he had misplaced something. He then remembers what he was looking for. He opens the large Bible on his desk which is actually hollow. He takes out a large bottle of Kentucky whiskey, the same brand of whiskey used by Gomez and Gonzales in Act One. Torres begins chuckling.] I see that you are in a good mood.

Torres [baiting a trap]: Oh, I am, your Eminence. I am.

Cardinal: And have you reached a decision? [The Cardinal leans back in his plush swivel-chair, holding his drink.]

Torres: I have. [a brief silence]

Cardinal [imperiously]: And what is it? [He leans forward looking intently at Torres.]

Torres [smiling]: I have decided to agree with you.

Cardinal [leaning back again]: Oh, excellent, excellent. And when do you plan to leave for Louvain? [He takes a sip of his drink.]

Torres: Oh, in about five years. [The Cardinal chokes on his whiskey. He spills half of his glass on his scarlet cape. He stands up and begins coughing. Torres stands up and goes over to assist him. He slaps the Cardinal on the back with great enthusiasm.] There, there, your Eminence. Something went down the wrong way, didn't it?

Cardinal: It certainly did. Thank you . . . thank you. [The Cardinal is puzzled. He realizes that something has gone wrong. He slowly remembers.] Why is it that you have decided to wait five years?

Torres [realizing that the fun is over]: Because in that way I could better study our Colombian problem. In that way I would be better prepared to make the most of my studies at Louvain.

Cardinal [desperate – changing to a more hostile tone]: But you are prepared well enough now. If you left now your most important work could begin sooner. [imploringly] Please go to Louvain now, Father. Let us not make things difficult for each other.

Torres [realizing that the end has come]: Your Eminence, I cannot see how things will be made difficult by my staying here.

Cardinal [fiercely]: You know what I mean.

Torres [matching him in fierceness]: No, your Eminence, what do you mean?

Cardinal [He takes a sip from his glass and puts it down. He folds his hands on his desk. During these gestures he is trying to gain control of himself and the situation.]: Look, Father, you are backing a revolution. You as a priest have no business doing such a thing. You should mellow in mind and spirit, yourself, before you try to change such an ancient society as this.

Torres [sarcastically]: Very good, your Eminence, but when some men mellow, they rot!

Cardinal [slowly]: Father, if you remain in Colombia for another month, I will have to deprive you of the privileges of saying Mass, preaching and lecturing. I am sorry, but my hands are tied.

Torres [staring at the whiskey bottle]: By the rich!

Cardinal [jumping to his feet]: What? I'll . . . we'll . . .

Torres [He also stands. He speaks with total passion.]: All right, your Eminence, you'll stand there and lie over the top of that crucifix which lies on your chest. Well, I am tired of listening to you and your petty threats. You sound like a dying man who has sold his soul for a soft chair and a glass of whiskey. [He rips his own Roman Catholic collar off and throws it at the Cardinal.] Here, take your "official" symbol. Before I ever again go up to the altar of God, I will be sure my brothers and my sisters are fed first. That is Christ's teaching and I am His priest. I need neither your threats nor your consent to serve God and my neighbor. [He starts to leave.]

Cardinal [shocked and seeking any phrase]: It will hurt you to fight against the Church of God.

Torres [turns and stops]: I will not be fighting against "the Church of God." I will only be fighting against a few lazy, rich men who live off the labor and the misery of the poor. [He leaves. The Cardinal is left standing. The lights fall.]

ACT FOUR
Scene One

[A jungle camp of the army of liberation. Four soldiers are dressed with bandoliers and are holding rifles. Torres is with them. He has a bandolier of bullets across his chest and his rifle is lying close to him. The general mood is one of brief relaxation between battles.]

1st Soldier: It looks like it's going to be brutal.

2nd Soldier: How many men did we lose last night?

3rd Soldier: Fifteen.

4th Soldier: And the night before?

1st Soldier: Five.

3rd Soldier: It is not good. The army of the rich has plenty of supplies, better guns, and the chance of sleeping.

2nd Soldier: Yes, they have everything but honor.

1st Soldier [laughing and slapping his own neck]: And mosquitos. Say Camilo, you look a little sad. Still praying, eh?

Torres [good naturedly]: No . . . not praying – thinking.

1st Soldier: I would think a little more myself before I ran back and forth across the front lines as you did yesterday.

3rd Soldier: Yes, Camilo. If we lose you how shall we explain it to God? Not that He'll listen to me anyway. But you know, if I commit many more sins He will put me in the same place with the rich people.

Torres [smiling]: And then God will have another revolution. [They all laugh and then stop. There is a brief silence.]

1st Soldier: I wonder where our friends are who died.

3rd Soldier [somberly]: What do you say, Camilo?

Torres: They are with God and yet they are still with us. So let us bring God's kingdom to earth! Let us continue the fight for which our friends have died!

1st Soldier: Viva la Revolucion! [The rest chant, "Viva La Revolucion!"]

2nd Soldier: We had better join the rest of the troops. [He leaves.]

1st Soldier: Let us go. [3rd and 4th soldiers leave.] Camilo are you coming?

Torres: I will be with you in a moment. I want to watch the stars in the heavens for just a little while. Then I will join you.

1st Soldier: As you wish, but don't spend too much time. We are soon to fight again. [He leaves.]

Torres [alone and looking at the sky]: It is a strange thing the way seven stars seem to dance upon one another. [He looks about him.] They are saying something to me. Ah, I know. [He looks at his rifle and then picks it up. He stops.] Something pulls me backward and forward at once. [He looks around and then at the sky.] Life would hold me here. Yet it is a higher life for all that calls me onward. Soon we must fight again. [He takes seven bullets from his bandolier. He smiles. Immediately his smile changes to a fierce seriousness.] And I must dedicate each bullet:

One – for Isabella who died unaided. [A bullet is placed in the rifle after each number is announced.]
Two – for Pedro's sorrow!
Three – for Miguel and the united front!
Four – to destroy the rich and give all to the people!
Five – for the Revolution!
Six – for Christ!
Seven – for Christ and the Revolution!
[He places the seventh bullet in his gun and begins yelling with a mad happiness.] Christ and the Revolution! [Facing the audience he moves to the back of the stage with his rifle. He starts shouting wildly.] La Revolucion!!! La Revolucion!!! [His shouts are answered from all the corners of the stage. The other soldiers join him. All are on the stage shouting "La Revolucion" waving their rifles and shouting as they leave the stage. Shots are heard. The lights fall quickly.]

Scene Two

[Two days later. The same closed room in a tavern as Act Two, Scene Three. Elena and Miguel are seated at a table.]

Miguel: This place is very lonely.

Elena: But I am here.

Miguel: Yes, but Father Torres's presence seems to inhabit the room from the last meeting we had here.

Elena: Have you heard from him lately?

Miguel: No. He said he was gong to fight with the army of liberation. Since then I have not heard from him. [The socialist from Act Two, Scene Three enters.]

Socialist: Father Torres is dead.

Miguel [gripping himself]: Let me see. [He takes a newspaper from the socialist and studies it for a moment. He then reads aloud.]

"Camilo Torres, renegade priest and communist, was justly killed by the National Army on Friday. His body and the bodies of other traitors have been buried in a lime pit. This is a just and fitting end for an animal who wished to subvert the peace and security of Colombia. Let this be a warning to all those who wish in any way to attack the sacred truth of our blessed protectress, Holy Mother Church, or in any way change unlawfully the established policies of state."

[Miguel stands up and begins to laugh out loud. He stops. Fiercely, he speaks] What do the other newspapers say?

Socialist: Two other papers describe him as an anarchist and as a traitor. Another paper is not sure whether he ever existed.

Miguel: I thought so. Look, there is no time to lose. Quickly. Mobilize all the factions you can find in the city square.

Elena: But Father Torres is dead.

Miguel [laughing]: No, he isn't. Quickly. We must act before the rich and the Church publish any more reports like this one. [At once the lights fall.]

Scene Three

[As soon as possible the lights come up again. Miguel is standing on crates in the public square. Pedro, nihilist, communist, socialist, and other people surround the crates. By now the impact of Camilo Torres's death begins to show its effect. He begins speaking slowly. He attempts to choose the right words.]

Miguel: Some of you have read the newspapers and you are confused about Camilo Torres and what he has done for you. The Church and the government have already begun to defile his name. Already they are trying to make you forget him. [He hesitates for a few seconds. His voice breaks into a

passionate eloquence. He is no longer concerned with precisely the right words. Rather he wishes to present the images of the priest as they present themselves to his mind. The more he speaks, the greater becomes the force and eloquence of his plea.]
But do not forget, rather remember . . .
Remember Torres
when they shall tell you that God
can be controlled,
and that His men are false.
Remember Torres
when time and man
will tell you to forget him.
Remember Torres's spirit.
Remember that his spirit
is now one with The Spirit of God.
But also remember that
prophets die alone and deserted
so that a child
may have bread.

Did he die in
the Church?
Do not ask such questions.
You know that as the
stars present themselves in the heavens
Torres presents himself to God!
Let the Church fall to perdition
With its articles of retribution.

Torres lives –
his name to thousands.
Torres strives
in Holy Passion.
Will you have him lessened
by the hypocrites who will question?
Damn them!
To the battle against tyranny!
To the altar of justice!
If we are to see God,
then let us feed His children!

Church and State erect
the scaffold
of disease and starvation.
Church and State have made
all our sufferings.

Load the rifle!
Surmount the barricade!
And as the bullets fly
and the blood of innocence
flows –
Remember the cries of the oppressed!
Remember the Spirit against the flesh!
Remember the saint and not the devils!
Remember his sacrifice for our liberation!
Remember his death for our resurrection!
Remember Christ and His servant!
Remember Christ!
Remember Torres!

[There are multitudinous shouts all intermingled of "Christ!" "Torres!" "La Revolucion!" and "Viva la revolucion!" This frenzy continues for several seconds. Shouts are heard. A bomb explodes. The police appear. Workers, students, and police collide as the lights fall.]

MOSES McNUTT

CHARACTERS

MOSES McNUTT
AARON ANATHEMA
THE GOD OF HUMAN SECURITY
DR. TEDDY TIGHTJAW
JASON
STEPHANIE
DR. CHRISTIAN CUNNING
DR. SKIPPER SPACEWASTE
NEWSCASTER
TWO CAMERAMEN
A TELEVISION DIRECTOR

[A high mountain located above a desert in Southern California. It is the early 1980's. Moses McNutt is approximately 39 years old, 6'4" tall, and weighs 205 pounds. He is red-faced and a bit jowly from too much drinking. With Moses is Aaron Anathema, a bearded 57 year old ex-Jesuit, 5'8" tall, 170 pounds. Both gentlemen have gray hair. Moses and Aaron are getting out of an old green, dented Volkswagon beetle which has one pink fender. The front of the car is tied down with a rope.]

Moses McNutt [stepping out of the car]: Son of a bitch! I should have stopped at that last gas station! I wonder how far we'll have to walk. Damn it! The gas gauge is broken, but I thought I had enough gas. Of all the god forsaken places to run out of gas!

Aaron Anathema [shrugging his shoulders]: Well, we'll just have to hitchhike into the next town. [Aaron reaches into his pocket and pulls out a cigarette paper. He then pulls out a small pouch and rolls a marijuana cigarette. He places it in the center of his lips, lights it, and inhales deeply.] Say, what was your name again?

Moses McNutt: My name is Moses, Moses McNutt. That's "nut" with two "t's."

Aaron Anathema [Laughing, he offers Moses his cigarette.]: What a name! Well, Moses, do you want some marijuana?

Moses McNutt: Not really. That stuff hurts my lungs. I have my own remedies for frustration. [Moses goes to the front of the Volkswagon and unties the rope. He can be seen moving blankets and suitcases around in a hurried and impatient manner.] Aha! There it is! [Moses flourishes a pint bottle of scotch whiskey. He unscrews the cap and takes a long drink.

After he is through, he wipes his lips on his sleeve.] Great! White Label Scotch. the scotch that never varies. You can always count on White Label even if you can't count on a damn gas gauge. Man, I feel like getting gassed! I've waited seven years to take a vacation, and what happens? I run out of gas! Well, I'll just have to get myself gassed. that's all. [Moses takes another drink. He offers the bottle to Aaron.] Want a taste?

Aaron Anathema: No thanks, Moses. I can't handle it. It hurts my stomach.

Moses McNutt: Well, just so we each have something.

Aaron Anathema: Yeah, I guess so, Say, thanks again for picking me up. It's hot here . . . no place to be hitchhiking.

Moses McNutt: I picked you up all right, but it looks like we'll both have to hitchhike now [Moses looks down the road.] I don't see any cars out there.

Aaron Anathema [dragging on his cigarette]: Don't worry about it. Someone will come along.

Moses McNutt [wearily]: I guess so. [There is a brief silence.] Say, what was your name?

Aaron Anathema: Aaron Anathema.

Moses McNutt: What kind of a name is that?

Aaron Anathema: A name I gave myself.

Moses McNutt: I thought my name was strange, but I've never heard a name like yours! My mother was Jewish and my father was Scotch Presbyterian. [Moses smiles, looks at his bottle and takes another swig.] I'm mostly Scotch after work and on the weekends. Anyway, my mother was Jewish and my father was a Presbyterian. They got along pretty well, but they always argued about religion. I always thought both of them were nuts. [Moses smiles and takes another swig.]

Come to think of it, they were nuts – McNutts, that is.

Aaron Anathema [laughing and taking another drag on his cigarette]: Well, that's pretty good. A Jewish Presbyterian and a scotch drinker. You're probably one of a kind.

Moses McNutt [shrugging his shoulders]: That could be. But tell me, what nationality is an enema? Is that how you say it?

Aaron Anathema [howling with laughter]: No! My god, no! Not "enema" . . . Anathema. An-ath-em-a.

Moses McNutt [somewhat shamefaced]: Okay, okay. Ana-ath-em-a.

Aaron Anathema [speaking quickly]: Anathema.

Moses McNutt [just as quickly]: Anathema.

Aaron Anathema: Good. Anathema. I gave myself that name. I went down and changed my name when I was forty. Went before a judge. Did the whole thing. You see, I'm an ex-Jesuit priest. My original name was Smith. but you can't get much out of Smith. Rather pedestrian, all said and done. I mean, I like Smiths, and there are certainly a lot of them, but I needed a change.

Moses McNutt [taking a drink]: But why Anathema?

Aaron Anathema: Well, you see, I am an excommunicated Jesuit priest. Long ago I disagreed with the Roman Catholics and they excommunicated me. That is, they kicked me out of their church. When they do that, they pronounce the words "Anathema Sit." They say that, and you're out.

Moses McNutt [scratching his head]: Why, those dirty bastards! It is bad enough to kick you out, but they shouldn't treat you like a dog. I wouldn't put up with that!

Aaron Anathema [perplexed]: What do you mean?

Moses McNutt: I mean, to say "Anathema sit." You're not a dog! You're a man! No one should tell you to sit!

Aaron Anathema [laughing uproariously]: No . . . no. You don't understand. "Anathema Sit" is Latin. It means, "Let him be accursed." That's what they pronounce on heretics. "Anathema Sit" or "Let him be accursed."

Moses McNutt: Oh. [There is a brief silence.] You don't seem to be very upset about it.

Aaron Anathema [still laughing]: No. I'm not upset about it at all. I actually think that is an honor. I stood up for my beliefs, and I was accursed. Besides, nothing really happened to me. Although, there was a time when "Anathema Sit" was pronounced they took you out and burned you at the stake. They used to burn heretics, you know,

Moses McNutt: I really don't know much about these things. I'm a director of social welfare in the city of San Francisco. I graduated from college and got a job with the Social Welfare Department. I wasn't much interested in books after a certain point. I just saw so many evil things in the world, and I felt bad about it. So, I got a job with the Social Welfare Department.

Aaron Anathema: Why that's amazing. Absolutely amazing. I'm in the Welfare Department in Oakland. I'm not a director, just a counselor. It's strange that we've never met.

Moses McNutt: Well, you know, there are a lot of welfare departments and a lot of people in them.

Aaron Anathema: It's still amazing. I've been working in the Welfare Department for about fifteen years. That's what I did after I was excommunicated. [laughing] After they pronounced "Anathema Sit," I really didn't sit. I went out and did the best I could. But, still, I've never met you at any of the meetings.

Moses McNutt: Well, anyway, it's good to meet you. But tell

me, what was it that you did to have them kick you out of their church?

Aaron Anathema: Oh, I don't think you really want to hear about it.

Moses McNutt [drinking from his bottle]: Sure I do. Besides, it will fill in the time. Tell me what happened.

Aaron Anathema [timidly]: Okay, if you really want to hear it.

Moses McNutt: Sure I do. Go ahead.

Aaron Anathema: Well, I was about forty years old. I had been a professor of church history and theology for about ten years. It was the academic year of 1963-64. I was teaching then. Another teacher and I went to Naples for a holiday. I had read a book about Naples. It was called A STREET LAMP AND THE STARS. It was about Mario Borrelli, a priest who worked with the poor people of Naples. It was really a great book. This priest had actually become one of the street people in order to get to know them. He had been a thief and a pimp and, well, many things, so that the poor would trust him. It was his idea to start a type of halfway house, a place where adolescent boys would have a place to stay. You see, there is a very poor section of Naples, a place so poor that children actually sleep with the rats in the alleys. In that same section, there is even a more horrible truth. Believe it or not, 80% of the young girls die at the age of eighteen of venereal disease. I wanted to see that section of town. So, one beautiful autumn day my Jesuit friend and I walked through that part of Naples. It was unbelievable. Children were seen begging on all corners. If they were not begging, they would be scraping a few particles of brown and black tobacco from crushed cigarettes off the sidewalks with their hands or with a knife. You see, the area was so poor there was a dealer in that type of tobacco. The children would spend a couple of days scraping tobacco to get eight ounces. They would then take the tobacco to a dealer who would pay them the equivalent of fifty cents. The dealer would then sell the tobacco on the black market. It was really sordid. The children's eyes were the eyes of tired old people. Exhausted, despairing eyes. Eyes filed with tears that could not flow. Eyes filled with pride and hatred. So, I watched those children and I thought of my own life. You know, men do that when they are about forty. [laughing] I suppose a psychiatrist would say that I was going through the male menopause or something. I really don't care what a psychiatrist or psychologist would say. After all, they don't have to scrape tobacco off the street to have a plate of spaghetti once every two days. [Aaron is silent. He looks up and down the road. He then rolls another cigarette. Moses stares at Aaron. The silence continues. Both men reflect. Aaron inhales a few times on his cigarette while Moses takes another swig of whiskey.]

Moses McNutt: I know what you mean. In San Francisco there are a lot of poor children who have been bitten by rats. There are other children who fish off the docks in the hope of catching food for an unemployed and deserted mother. There are also old people who have worked hard all their lives only to wind up living in a tenement house with more rats, more bills and landlords who either want to raise their rent or evict them. You don't hear about it much, but it's there.

Aaron Anathema: It's in Oakland, too.

[Aaron takes a drag from his cigarette and stares at it. In disgust, he throws it on the ground, crushing it out with his heel. Moses looks at him and takes another swig of whiskey.]

Moses McNutt [firmly]: Well, go on. Tell me what happened next.

Aaron Anathema [in disgusted tone]: All right. I'll tell you. I saw that section of Naples and then all the magnificent villas and churches and, after a day of so, we went back to Rome. The so-called great Ecumenical Council was about to begin and I was to be an aide on church history to one of the cardinals. At the opening of the council, I went early to the Vatican Library to prepare some notes. Somehow, I had misplaced some papers and I was a little delayed in joining the other scholars who were to wait for the cardinals. I was hurrying to make up the time when I dropped some papers in one of the corridors. I stopped to picked them up, and as I did, I just happened to look out the window at the procession of the cardinals approaching the cathedral. You wouldn't believe it! There was a line of at least fifty Mercedes. Big Mercedes. I think they call it the Mercedes Model 600. You must have seen one of them now and then. You know, the big ones with the curtains in the back windows.

Moses McNutt [laughing]: Well, ah, Aaron . . . that's your name, isn't it?

Aaron Anathema [with a furious look on his face]: Yes, Aaron Anathema. [He grins viciously.]

Moses McNutt [Studying Aaron, he speaks softly.]: Well, Aaron, where I work we don't see many Mercedes with curtains in the back windows.

Aaron Anathema [quietly]: Where I work I don't see them either. And there is a section of Naples where you won't see one at all. Anyway, I watched that procession of big black cars. I was absolutely transfixed. I just stood there staring at the grand opulence. And then I began inwardly to see the wrathful and weary eyes of the children of Naples picking up the tobacco specks on the sidewalk. I looked around and then at my watch. I was late. Very late. I then multiplied $100,000 times fifty. You see, I figured one car like that costs at least $100,000 and there were fifty of them. At the top of my church history notes, I did my calculations. The total came to five million dollars.

Moses McNutt [awestruck]: My god!

Aaron Anathema: My god, is right! That's what I thought. Had I been serving God or had I been serving a thing I know not what. I looked at my refined theological and churchly reflections, and then at the sum of five million dollars. [laughing] I think it was one time in my life that I was really proud of myself. You see, I was very lucky. There was a trash can providentially located near the window from which I was viewing the great "Ecumenical" spectacle. In absolute rage and disgust, I threw my notes and calculations into the trash can. I then spent the rest of the day in the Sistine Chapel meditating on Michelangelo's Last Judgment. That night, when I went back to the college, the father superior was, as you can imagine, furious with me. I just laughed at him. Finally, in absolute fury, he said to me, "Father, what is wrong with you? The Cardinal is outraged and you have disgraced us." In sheer mockery, I replied, "In Christ's own words to his disciples, 'Call no man father. You have but one father and he is in heaven. Call no man teacher. You have but one teacher, the Christ.'"* To this, the goodly imbecile said, "Even the devil can quote scripture." To which I replied. "So can an ex-Jesuit." To which the hypocritical bureaucrat said, "What do you mean, an ex-Jesuit?" To which I replied, "I mean myself!"

Moses McNutt [roaring with laughter]: Well, good for you, good for you! [He controls himself] Then what happened?

Aaron Anathema [laughing]: You can well imagine. One thing led to another. There were their threats at which I scoffed. Finally, they excommunicated me. They said, "Anathema Sit." But I said, "Anathema Stand." And I changed my name. By the way, as you can see, I'm still standing.

[Both Moses and Aaron laugh for a few moments. Then, Moses looks at his watch. He drains his pint of scotch, looks at the bottle, sighs, and throws it to the back of the stage.]

Moses McNutt: Well, I don't know as much as you. I only know right from wrong.

Aaron Anathema [laughing]: Then you know enough.

Moses McNutt [also laughing and staring back and forth down the road]: I also know that we had better find some gas. It's getting late, and I don't think there is anyone out there to

---

* The Gospel of Matthew, 23:8-10.

pick us up.

Aaron Anathema [smiling]: Moses, my good friend, we'll just have to pick ourselves up. We might as well start walking.

Moses McNutt [also smiling]: We might as well.

[The lights fall as both men walk off the stage.]

ACT TWO

[At the back of the stage there is a huge mural. First in line on the mural is a huge six-door orange Cadillac limousine which is hitched to an immense chartreuse trailer which is hitched to a smaller trailer pulling a cabin cruiser, which is attached to a trailer pulling a dune buggy. Attached to the dune buggy trailer is another trailer supporting two dirt bikes. Attached to that trailer is another supporting two bicycles. Attached to that is the final wheelbarrow-type trailer in which is seen two sets of golf clubs, several fishing poles, water skis, snow skis, cross country skis, and the latest "grass" skis. In addition to this sportsman's paraphernalia, in the wheelbarrow-type trailer there can also be seen bowling balls, tennis balls, racquet balls, footballs, basketballs, soccer balls, rifles. shotguns, pogo sticks, frisbees, racquetball racquets, squash racquets, and tennis racquets.

To one side of this collection of merchandise is seen a huge gold statue of a sitting 500 pound man. The statue is painted in varying one-inch stripes of gold and silver. The idol's head is that of an enormous gold cow. However, instead of horns, there are two labelless brown see-through beer bottles placed so that the top of the bottles are attached to the temples of the cow, Upon the idol's huge stomach is written in purple letters, "THE GOD OF HUMAN SECURITY." In the general vicinity of the idol's heart are two coin slots with written instructions above the slots.

Upon the chartreuse trailer is written in huge gold letters, "ALL OF THIS BELONGS TO DR. TEDDY TIGHTIAW. HIGH PRIEST OF PERPETUAL YOUTH AND DEFENDER OF THE FACE." As the lights come up, the audience should be given a few silent moments to study this mural of consumerism.

Shortly afterwards, Moses McNutt and Aaron Anathema enter. Both look exhausted. At first, they do not even notice the mural or the idol.]

Moses McNutt: Man, that was a long walk! We had to walk all night long. Not one of those cars would pick us up. I've never seen so many cars! I wonder where they're all going?

Aaron Anathema [exhausted]: Jesus, am I tired! Moses, I'm just not as young as you are. Maybe I got in the way of people picking us up with my beard and all. I'm sorry.

Moses McNutt [disgusted with everything]: Beard? Hell! Half of the people who passed us had beards. I don't know if I wanted to get in their cars! [laughing] Of course, it would have been better than walking all night.

Aaron Anathema [also laughing]: It certainly would have been! [Aaron looks about the stage and for the first time sees the mural and the idol.] Hey, Moses! Look at this!

[Moses looks at Aaron who is now facing the mural and the idol with his back to the audience. Moses turns around and also sees the idol and the mural. Both are transfixed for a few seconds. Aaron goes up to the idol.]

Moses McNutt: Aaron, what are you doing?

Aaron Anathema: I'm studying this . . . this thing. Look at this monstrosity! It even has, why, it even has instructions! Moses, listen to this! [Aaron begins reading.] "I am the God of Human Security. To hear me speak, please deposit sixty-five cents. Any combination of coins will do, and your change will be returned. To stop me from speaking, please deposit eighty-five cents. Any combination of coins will do and your change will be returned."

Moses McNutt [furiously]: You're kidding me! You've got to be kidding me! What kind of scam is this? What's going on?

Aaron Anathema [laughing]: Oh, come on, Moses! Where's

your sense of adventure? [Aaron searches in his pocket.] Say, Moses, do you have any spare change?

Moses McNutt [threateningly going up to the idol]: I wouldn't give this . . . this thing . . . a penny! My god, what is this?

Aaron Anathema [laughing and counting some coins in his hand]: Never mind, Moses. Never mind. I've got three quarters. Besides, the thing makes change.

Moses McNutt: Don't count on it! Believe me, don't count on it!

[Aaron immediately goes to one of the slots and deposits his seventy-five cents. He waits for the change to be returned. Nothing happens. Aaron scratches his head. A few seconds pass.]

Aaron Anathema [becoming furious]: What? What? Not only doesn't it speak, but it doesn't even make change!

Moses McNutt [laughing]: Well, what did you expect?

[At this momemt electric currents are seen flashing in the brown beer bottles, and a recorded voice is heard. The voice is sonorous, loud and pontifical.]

The God of Human Security:
    I am the god of human security.
    You know me and you serve me well.
    You worship me instead of facing absurdity.
    For me, your neighbor you would butcher and sell . . .

    I am the god of human security.
    You know me and you serve me well.
    You worship me instead of facing absurdity.
    For me, your neighbor you would butcher and sell . . .

[The voice continues repeating the same lines over and over. Moses and Aaron look at each other. The same recording continues in the background.]

Moses McNutt [after a few moments]: What in the hell?! What is going on? [Puzzled] I can't figure it out. What does it mean . . . "instead of facing absurdity . . . ?"

Aaron Anathema [laughing and studying the instructions as the voice continues]: Hmmm . . . This program must have been written by an untenured philosopher. Moses, the machine is just saying what we both know. People are afraid . . . afraid of just about everything . . . death . . . the unknown. So, they make the idol of human security – money – and they worship it. To face the absurdity of a life used up in earning and spending is too difficult for them. So they'll worship money and slaughter their neighbors for it. [There is a brief pause. Aaron continues to study the instructions and is finally satisfied. Laughing.] Now I see why there are two slots. Who wants to hear the truth? Good lord, what a device! People will PAY ANYTHING to shut that thing up!

[Moses and Aaron continue listening. Suddenly, a bizarre looking man steps out on the stage. The man weighs about 250 pounds, and is approximately 5'8" tall. Despite his obesity, he has a face-lifted, quasi-youthful visage like that of a demonic joker's face seen on playing cards. He has dyed jet-black hair. He is wearing white patent leather boots into which are stuffed white polyester trousers, The trousers are held up by a white patent leather belt. His silk shirt is bright orange with huge purple flowers printed on it. His huge stomach and small shoulders can be seen as his shirt is unbuttoned to the waist. Several gold chains with gold medallions are hanging from his neck. As he enters the stage, he goes to the back of the idol and turns down the volume. However, a low moaning is heard repeating the same words.]

Dr. Teddy Tightjaw: Good morning, gentlemen. Welcome to Tightface Inc. I am Dr. Teddy Tightjaw [rapturously] and everything you see here is MINE! ALL MINE! Everything is MINE! [He is in such a state of rapture that he almost faints. He manages to control himself and looks somewhat puzzled. He stares at Moses and Aaron.] Say, there must be something wrong. It's still talking . . . our god is still talking. It must be a malfunction. No one lets TGOHS speak too long.

Moses McNutt: TGOHS?

Dr. Teddy Tightjaw [benevolently]: TGOHS are the initials for 'The God of Human Security." Certainly you have heard of this mighty power!

Moses McNutt [angrily]: Yes, I've heard of him. We hear of him a lot these days.

Aaron Anathema [bitterly]: I've heard of him down through the centuries.

Dr. Teddy Tightjaw [perplexed]: Yes, but we try to be merciful to the people. That is why there is the second slot. You see, very few people can stand to listen to him. They know what they are, but they can't stand what they are. Thus, in our great mercy, we have a second slot with which to silence our god.

Aaron Anathema [yawning]: Oh, let him speak! It's simply human nature. Besides, I've been shortchanged. You owe me ten cents.

Dr. Teddy Tightjaw [withdrawing and frightened]: Ten cents?

Aaron Anathema: Yes, your idol doesn't seem to make change. You owe me ten cents.

Dr. Teddy Tightjaw [slyly, pretending to search his pockets]: My, how unfortunate. But we'll put it in the mail for you. Just let my secretary know.

Aaron Anathema [amused]: Just where is this secretary of yours?

Dr. Teddy Tightjaw: Oh, she'll be here sooner or later.

Aaron Anathema [laughing]: You're sure she'll be here?

Dr. Teddy Tightjaw [self-righteously]: Of course! Certainly

you would not doubt the words of Dr. Teddy Tightjaw, High Priest of Perpetual Youth and Defender of the Face?

Aaron Anathema [bored]: Who would doubt such a man?

Dr. Teddy Tightjaw [feeling secure again, he goes to the back of the idol.]: No one. [moving on quickly] Now, who is going to pay to shut off TGOHS? [He turns up the volume.]

Moses McNutt [looking at the mural and the idol]: I wouldn't give you a dime to stop him talking. Let him speak for all I care.

Aaron Anathema: Oh, let him speak. I kind of like him. Maybe I'll get one for my office.

Dr. Teddy Tightjaw [nervously]: But . . . but . . . you can't . . . you can't let him keep speaking!

Aaron Anathema: Oh, sure. Let him speak.

Moses McNutt: Yeah, let him speak . . . turn up the volume! It's guys like you who should listen to your own idols. I hope he drives you crazy.

[Moses moves to the back of the idol and turns up the volume to a deafening roar. Moses and Aaron smile complacently at each other as they watch Dr. Teddy Tightjaw. Dr. Teddy Tightjaw places his hands over his ears and begins to scream.]

Dr. Teddy Tightjaw: Stop it! Stop it! [He tries to get to the volume control but Moses stands in front of him.]

Moses McNutt: No! You just listen.

Dr. Teddy Tightjaw: No, please, no more!

Moses McNutt Then use YOUR money to stop it.

Dr. Teddy Tightjaw: BUT I would have to give up a dollar . . .

a whole dollar! The idol is to make others pay, not me.

Aaron Anathema [smiling]: But the instructions say it only costs eighty-five cents. Your change will be returned.

Dr. Teddy Tightjaw [frantically]: Well, it doesn't . . . it doesn't always make change.

Moses McNutt: Oh, come on. It's NEVER made change, has it?

Dr. Teddy Tightjaw: Well, it used to, but, well, we fixed that.

Aaron Anathema: I'm sure you did.

[Moses turns up the volume to the same deafening level. As he does so, he points to the second slot. Weeping and submissive, Dr. Teddy Tightjaw places four quarters in the machine. Finally, the roaring voice stops and the beer bottle horns cease to flash. Dr. Teddy Tightjaw weeps at the feet of the idol.]

Dr. Teddy Tightjaw [to the idol]: Forgive me! Forgive me! I gave up a dollar! Forgive me! Have mercy! I promise you I'll try and get it back. [He whimpers for a few more moments and then dries his eyes. He stares at Moses for a few seconds, then smiles viciously and stands up. He speaks to the idol.] Yes. I will get it back!

Aaron Anathema [good-naturedly]: Say. I thought you were out of money!

Dr. Teddy Tightjaw [his old self again]: It was my last dollar. But, I assure you that your dime is as good as in the mail.

Aaron Anathema [laughing uproariously]: As good as that?

Dr. Teddy Tightjaw [self-righteously]: As good as that. [He goes over to Moses and stares a few seconds at his face.] You're a little jowly, you know that? Big cheeks do that. Big cheeks and too much booze. A perfect combination for the premature jowls. [Moses stares back at him in a wrathful and annoyed way.]

Moses McNutt: Who gives a damn?

Dr. Teddy Tightjaw: Why, I give a damn! I really care about such things. You see, I'm a plastic surgeon as well as being the President of Tightface Inc. By the way, Tightface Inc. is a publicly-held corporation possessing 1,732 franchises which perform plastic surgery. We're located mainly along the Sun Belt. You see, the Sun Belt – Florida to Texas to California – is where the rich people retire. Consequently, we've done our franchising in that region. Now, if someone like yourself wanted his jowls tightened . . . please, allow me the liberty. [In a very professional medical manner, he goes up to Moses, pinches his cheeks and grabs some skin under his chin.] Yes sir, a little tuck here and a little tuck there, and you'd look great! Absolutely great!

Moses McNutt [staring at Dr. Teddy Tightjaw, then at Aaron, then back at Tightjaw]: So that's what you do, huh? And that makes you a rich man? A man who can buy all this . . . this ... stuff?

Dr. Teddy Tightjaw [complacently]: Well, I don't mind telling you, plastic surgery and the retired rich have been very good to me. Our company's motto is, "A little tuck makes a big buck." And we HAVE made a big buck indeed! If you're not interested in having a tuck of your own, you would still do well to invest in Tightface Inc. It's being traded over the counter at 15-3/4. It's time to buy, I tell you. It's definitely time to buy.

Moses McNutt [annoyed]: Well, I'm sure I can't afford your services or your stock. About all I can afford is gas for my 1955 Volkswagon. You see, my friend and I ran out of gas. We walked all night and we're still trying to find some gas.

Dr. Teddy Tightjaw [slyly]: Oh, sure, I can find you some gas. But first, I want to introduce you to my two children. I want you to see what Tightface Inc. has done for me. Maybe you'll consider buying some stock later on.

[Dr. Teddy Tightjaw goes to the side of the stage closest to the chartreuse trailer. He begins pleading in a whining voice for his children to come on stage.]

Dr. Teddy Tightjaw: Now, Jason . . . Now, Stephanie. Come out and meet the two nice men. Please, Jason! Please. Stephanie! Come out and show the gentlemen what I've taught you. [whimpering] Jason! Stephanie! PLEASE come out! [to Moses and Aaron] They'll be out in just a second. Wait 'til you see them. [in a very whining voice] They are so-o-o cute, and they're real producers!

[Suddenly, two children appear on stage hopping on pogo sticks. Each child has long hair so that it is difficult to tell which is the boy and which is the girl. Both are dressed in the latest sport shirts, sport shorts, and sport/jogging shoes. They bound about the stage on their pogo sticks. With great pride, Dr. Teddy Tightjaw speaks.]

Dr. Teddy Tightjaw: See! What did I tell you! These kids are real producers! [Clapping his hands and shouting in a loud voice, he enters into a very strange sort of ecstasy.] Produce! Produce! You're producers! You're winners! Produce more, Jason . . . more, Stephanie! MORE, MORE, MORE! That's it! Faster . . . faster! [The children are now hopping around on their pogo sticks in an absolute frenzy. Perspiration and great determination are seen on their faces. Moses and Aaron stare at each other in amazement. Dr. Teddy Tightjaw keeps clapping and shouting.] Produce! Faster! Produce! Produce! [Finally, both children begin hopping madly before The God of Human Security. They hop up and down frantically for about ten seconds and then collide with each other. They lay sprawled on the ground for a few seconds. Dr. Teddy Tightjaw goes over and helps them up.] Well done . . . well done, good and faithful Jason. Enter into the joy of thy Teddy! Well done, good and faithful Stephanie. Enter into the joy of thy Teddy! You have indeed produced! [in a very feminine tone] My beautiful, beautiful babies! My sweet, productive, precious babies! Ask Daddy for your reward, and he will give it to you.

Ask for ANYTHING, and Daddy will get it for you!

Jason [Standing up and wiping his forehand, he stamps his foot in a very spoiled manner.]: I want a new silver-grey Mercedes coupe, and I want it NOW! NOW! Do you hear me? NOW! [He stamps his foot again.]

Stephanie [standing up and stamping her foot like her brother]: And I want a baby-powder blue Porsche Targa, and I want it NOW! NOW!
Dr. Teddy Tightjaw [anxiously]: Now, Jason . . . now, Stephanie . . . now, my sweet, cute little darlings . . .

Jason [stamping his foot]: NOW!

Stephanie. We said NOW!

Dr. Teddy Tightjaw: Now cute-ums you know you won't be able to drive for at least another five years, and . . .

Jason: You're stupid, Teddy!

Stephanie: Teddy, you're stupid, stupid, STUPID!

Dr. Teddy Tightjaw [whining]: Now, Jason. Now, Stephanie. Don't say that to Daddy Teddy. I want to give you everything, and you will have everything.

Jason [stamping his foot again]: Oh, you're so stupid!

Stephanie [imitating Jason]: So stupid!

Dr. Teddy Tightjaw: But . . .

Jason [authoritatively]: No "but's," Teddy. We've produced!

Stephanie: Yeah, Teddy. A deal is a deal.

[Aaron laughingly pulls Moses aside.]

Aaron Anathema: It seems that both Jason and Stephanie

want the golden fleece right off the bat. [Moses only looks at the whole scene with disgust.]

Dr. Teddy Tightjaw [imploringly]: Please be merciful to me.

Jason: Mercy? Mercy? To someone like you? You know the Governor, don't you?

Dr. Teddy Tightjaw [confused]: Yes, but . . .

Stephanie: Oh, you're so stupid. You know the Senator, don't you?

Dr. Teddy Tightjaw: Yes, but . . .

Jason: I said no "but's," Teddy. Now, Produce!

Stephanie: Produce!

Jason: Produce! Produce!

Dr. Teddy Tightjaw: But I HAVE produced!

Jason: But you haven't produced driver's licenses for Stephanie and me.

Stephanie [stamping her foot]: I want my driver's license, and I want it NOW!

Jason: YOU get us our licenses NOW! Call the Governor . . . call the Senator!

Stephanie [screaming]: I want it NOW! I want EVERYTHING NOW!

Jason [also screaming]: EVERYTHING! EVERYTHING! EVERYTHING!

Stephanie [still screaming]: NOW' NOW! NOW!

Jason [working himself into a frenzy]: You get us

EVERYTHING, Teddy, and you get it NOW or I'll tell Uncle Skippy about you!

Stephanie: That's EXACTLY what we'll do . . . we'll tell Uncle Skippy all about you.

Dr. Teddy Tightjaw [Holding his ears with both hands, he speaks in an anguished tone.]: Oh, no! Not that! Please don't tell Skippy! I'll call the Governor . . . I'll call the Senator . . . I'll get you everything. I'll get it now. Have mercy! Have mercy!
Jason: But you once told us that there is no mercy where there is production.

Stephanie: Yes, that's what you said, Teddy.

Dr. Teddy Tightjaw: I did, I said that, and look what you have become today. You are producers! You are dealers! You are winners! [He rushes over to them and begins slobbering all over them.] You are my darlings . . . my most precious ones! You are my darling, precious cute-ums. Oh, I love you! I love you! I love you!

[Teddy continues to slobber all over them, hugging and kissing them. Jason and Stephanie stand immobile, pouting, with looks of spoiled disgust on their faces.]

Jason [abruptly]: Okay, Teddy. That's enough. Get us the driver's licenses and get me the Mercedes. You know where the telephone is. Produce!

Stephanie [threateningly]: Yeah, knock it off, Teddy. Get on the phone and produce. I want my Porsche. Uncle Skippy will be here soon. We'll give him a progress report.

Dr Teddy Tightjaw [sheepishly]: But it's Sunday, cute-ums. Both the Senator and the Governor are away. [The children are furious and kick their pogo sticks.] But I'll talk to them tomorrow. I promise you! Tomorrow! I promise!

[Teddy kneels in anguish before The God of Human Security.

His face is hidden in his hands. In a bored and annoyed way, both Jason and Stephanie pick up their pogo sticks. They hold them in such a way that the sticks resemble swords. As Dr. Teddy Tightjaw is kneeling, with his back to the audience, they go over to him. Jason lays the longer part of his stick on Teddy's shoulder. Stephanie lays the longer part of her stick on Teddy's left shoulder. Teddy remains kneeling but he dries his eyes. He appears to have become knighted by his own children.]

Jason: Teddy, this time you are forgiven. Remember, you can do anything. You are a producer. Go Forth! Produce!

Dr. Teddy Tightjaw [weeping with joy]: Oh, thank you! Thank you! Oh, thank you! Good and faithful Jason, thank you!

Stephanie: Go forth, Teddy. You are a winner. Everything is possible if you just wish for it. You can do it, Teddy! Go forth and win!

Dr. Teddy Tightjaw: Oh, thank you, thank you, good and faithful Stephanie!

Jason [lifting his pogo stick and speaking solemnly]: Arise, oh Teddy! The night is passing away.

Stephanie [also lifting her pogo stick]: Arise, oh Teddy! The new dawn is breaking!

Dr. Teddy Tightjaw [with great effort and many groans and belches, he finally stands up.]: Oh, thank you, my cute-ums! Thank you!

Jason [indifferently]: You're welcome, Teddy.

Stephanie: Yep, you're welcome, Teddy.

Dr. Teddy Tightjaw [radiantly]: What beautiful manners you both have.

Jason [hopping on his pogo stick]: Now we have to produce

just as you have to produce.

Stephanie [also hopping on her pogo stick]: Yes, Teddy. We must produce just as you must produce.

Dr. Teddy Tightjaw [beaming]: Produce, my darlings, produce! [chanting] Produce! Produce! Produce!

[Jason and Stephanie begin hopping madly about on their pogo sticks. Dr. Teddy Tightjaw keeps chanting, "Produce! Produce! Produce!" In a frenzied state, the children hop about the stage. Teddy's chanting becomes louder and more frequent as the lights begin to fall. Finally, the frenzy of chanting and hopping becomes so intense that the children exit hopping off the stage. Stephanie exits right; Jason stage left. The lights fall. Teddy's chanting can be heard faintly. The hopping continues offstage until a huge crash is heard. There are a few seconds of silence. All the lights are nearly extinguished. Finally, the children's low moans and weeping are heard as the stage is enveloped in total darkness.]

ACT THREE

[Same scene as in Act Two.]

Dr. Teddy Tightjaw [in a feminine voice]: I'm so glad that you could meet Jason and Stephanie. Now tell me, what did you think of them?

[Moses McNutt has a disgusted and bored look on his face.]

Aaron Anathema [cordially]: Well, I think . . . I think they are real producers.

Moses McNutt [bored]. Say, can we just get some gasoline and get out of here?

Dr. Teddy Tightjaw [slyly]: Oh, I'll get you some gasoline in just a few minutes. But right now, I have to wait for two very important men. They are some of the most influential men in the country. I think you'll want to meet them, too.

Aaron Anathema: Are they producers, too?

Dr. Teddy Tightjaw [adoringly]: They are THE foremost producers in the world!

Moses McNutt [bored] Can they produce a few gallons of gasoline?

Dr. Teddy Tightjaw: Gasoline? Why, that's nothing compared to what these heroes of our culture have done. Certainly you have heard of Dr. Skipper Spacewaste, Nobel Prize Laureate and inventor of the space shuttle garbage ship.

Moses McNutt: You mean the $100 billion project for lifting

America's garbage into space?

Dr Teddy Tightjaw [pompously]: Exactly. The illustrious Dr. Skipper Spacewaste. I don't mind saying that he is almost a member of the family. The kids and I call him Uncle Skippy. He loves the kids and, in many ways, is just like them.

Aaron Anathema [slyly]: A real producer?

Dr. Teddy Tightjaw: A producer of the first order.

Moses McNutt [furiously]: Yeah, he produced a garbage space truck to send U.S. crap into space. $100 billion worth of space garbage, while the U.S. slums produce every form of crime and filth. $100 billion worth of taxpayers' money to be the first in space, while the U.S. stays twelfth in the world in caring for its old people. Why should the United States be twelfth in ANYTHING? $100 billion shot into space, shot right up there so even space will become polluted with our junk. Oh, come on, man! Enough is enough! This garbage rocket is the most absurd device that the world has ever known. Why don't we explore ways to put our own country and our own world in order before we start exploring space?

Dr. Teddy Tightjaw [aghast]: Why, I'm shocked to hear this! Absolutely shocked! Are you a communist or something?

Moses McNutt [sarcastically]: No, I'm not a goddamn communist! Don't toss that word out whenever someone doesn't agree with the standard procedures of U.S. stupidity. I'm NOT a communist. I just happen to know right from wrong, and its wrong not to put your own house in order first.

Dr. Teddy Tightjaw [acting like a frightened child]: Why, why I'm going to tell Uncle Skippy about you, that's what I'll do!

Moses McNutt [laughing uproariously]: Tell "Uncle Skippy" that he can go to hell for all I care. My god! I've never heard of such stupidity. Why don't you go and live in a slum for a while? Go down there and see how many little tucks you can take!

[Dr. Teddy Tightjaw stares sheepishly at a very volcanic Moses McNutt. There is a brief silence. Dr. Skipper Spacewaste enters with Dr. Christian Cunning. Both men are of the same build as Dr. Teddy Tightjaw with the same tight joker face. They are also dressed in exactly the same way as Teddy. As they enter, each is carrying an expensive golf bag filled with gold-headed golf clubs. They lean their golf bags against the chartreuse trailer before they begin speaking.]

Dr. Christian Cunning: Nice game, Skip, but you lost again.

Dr. Skipper Spacewaste: Well, Chris, I just can't get that hook out of my drive. It always costs me a few strokes. I guess it just isn't my day.

Dr Christian Cunning: But the day is young! Of course, it's your day. The space ship is supposed to land here today, isn't it.

Dr. Skipper Spacewaste [officially]: Yes, that's what I heard from Washington. Ifs supposed to land any time now. [Noticing Teddy for the first time.] Why, Teddy. Hello there, you old jaw-moulder! [They shake hands. Moses and Aaron look at each other.]

Dr. Teddy Tightjaw: Why, it's Uncle Skippy!

Dr. Skipper Spacewaste: Teddy, I'd like you to meet Dr. Christian Cunning, archbishop of the Washington, D.C. cathedral and preacher to the President himself.

Dr. Teddy Tightjaw [obsequiously]: Oh, this is indeed an honor, a real honor! I've heard of you and how you built up that Washington congregation! How you preach the good news of production to both the people and the congress. How you . . .

Dr Christian Cunning [laughing]: Well, it's good to meet you, too. One of your doctors took a few tucks from both me and my wife, Doris. You took a few tucks, and you took . . .

Moses McNutt [rudely interrupting]: Mega bucks.

Dr. Christian Cunning [raising his eyebrows at Moses and then speaking condescendingly]: I was going to say you took away many years. You do a great service for God, man and woman. Yes, sir. And Tightface Inc. is one hell of a stock to buy. Right, doctor?

Dr. Teddy Tightjaw [smiling sheepishly]: Well, you know, we have to produce.

Dr. Skipper Spacewaste: We must produce.

Dr. Christian Cunning [excitedly]: Produce!

Dr. Teddy Tightjaw: Produce!

Dr. Skipper Spacewaste: Produce!

[All three "producers" look at each other. They then gather in a row in front of The God of Human Security and bow their heads for a few moments of silence. Dr. Christian Cunning speaks in a low voice to Dr. Teddy Tightjaw.]

Dr. Christian Cunning: Who are the . . . the "undesirables" over there?

Dr. Teddy Tightjaw: I don't know, but they're not like us.

Dr Skipper Spacewaste [in horror]: You mean they're UNPRODUCTIVE?

Dr. Teddy Tightjaw: I really don't know.

Dr. Christian Cunning [pompously]: Do they know who WE are?

Dr. Teddy Tightjaw: Yes.

Dr. Skipper Spacewaste [pompously]: Well, I hope they are sufficiently impressed to mind their manners.

Dr. Teddy Tightjaw [sadly]: I don't think they're impressed.

Dr. Christian Cunning: Well in that case you know what to do.

Dr. Teddy Tightjaw: Certainly, Dr. Christian Cunning.

Dr. Christian Cunning: Just call me Chris.

Dr Teddy Tightjaw: All right, Chris. We'll put them in their place.

[Dr. Teddy Tightjaw exits near The God of Human Security. He immediately re-enters pushing a six-foot by six-foot television screen with control knobs at the bottom. The television is turned on and one of the well-known faces of an overpaid, under-worked national newscaster is seen. He begins speaking in his smooth, authoritarian way.]

Newscaster: Ladies and Gentlemen. At 5:30 PM today, The United States of America is scheduled to witness one of the most productive moments in our national history. Yes, Ladies and Gentlemen, at this very moment America's first space shuttle garbage ship is winging its way home from its first dumping of garbage. [The newscaster is interrupted and handed a piece of paper.] Excuse me, Ladies and Gentlemen. I meant to say that at this very moment America's first space shuttle anti-pollution ship is returning from its first delivery of . . . ah . . . ahem . . . [The newscaster is quickly handed another piece of paper. He wipes his forehead.] . . . its first delivery of waste material in outer space. [The newscaster then lets out with a huge sigh of relief.] Ladies and Gentlemen, this date will be inscribed in our memories and in our hearts with those same noble sentiments which make this great nation what it is. Along with the signing of the Declaration of Independence and Lincoln's delivery of the Gettysburg Address, this historic moment will announce to all the world where we have been and what we have become. Not only are we a nation of garbage producers, we are also a nation that can fling its waste material heavenward and thus begin to fill the infinite voids of outer space. [The newscaster is again interrupted. Suddenly, helicopters can be heard on both stage right and stage left. Two cameramen and a director appear entering stage right.]

First Cameraman: Hey, Joe! Hurry up! There's Dr. Spacewaste.

Second Cameraman: Okay, Harry. Get a close-up on Dr. Christian Cunning.

Director: Right on time, boys. Right on time. We did it!

Newscaster: Ladies and Gentlemen, the television network of IDIOT in Washington. D.C. is proud to be bringing you live via satellite from a desert somewhere in the middle of California the actual landing of the garbage...excuse me...the anti-pollution ship. [He wipes his forehead again.] Come in please. [Nothing happens as the newscaster awkwardly pleads while the vast sea of millions waits.] Come in, please! Please! Please! Please!? [Suddenly, Doctors Tightjaw, Spacewaste and Cunning are seen on the television screen. The relieved voice of the newscaster is heard.] Dr. Spacewaste, can you hear me? [A cameraman places a microphone in front of Dr. Spacewaste.]

Dr. Skipper Spacewaste: I can hear you just fine.

Newscaster: This is Charlie Chatter at Station IDIOT in Washington. D.C.

Dr. Skipper Spacewaste: Good afternoon, Charlie.

Newscaster: I see you have the illustrious Dr. Christian Cunning there with you.

Dr. Skipper Spacewaste: Yes, Charlie. Chris is here to bless the area where the ship will land. [to Dr. Cunning] Say hello, Chris.

Dr. Christian Cunning [looking heavenward, then at the

camera, then heavenward again]: Dearly beloved, we are gathered here in Christ's name... [verbally stumbling]... or in Buddha's name, or in Jehovah's name . . . ,well, we are "ecumenically" gathered here. [wiping his forehead] Well, we are gathered here, I know that much. We are gathered here to bear witness . . . ah . . . er . . . to witness the second coming, or the . . . er...the first coming . . . the . . . ah . . . so to speak . . . incarnation of garbage. [really confused] What I mean to say is that . . . well . . . man and woman were created in the image and likeness of God. And man and woman created garbage in the image and likeness of man and woman. But, man and woman had to be redeemed so man and woman created the space garbage ship so that all garbage might be resurrected. Amen. [a few seconds of "pious" silence]

Dr. Skipper Spacewaste [somberly]: That was beautiful, Chris.

Dr. Teddy Tightjaw [sloppily wiping his sentimental tears]: That was really beautiful, Dr. Cunning. You really moved me.

Moses McNutt [furiously]: The only thing that has been moved around here is garbage.

Aaron Anathema [also furious and unable to take it any longer]: Well said, Moses. Well said.

[Doctors Christian Cunning, Spacewaste, and Tightjaw have shocked looks on their faces.]

Dr. Skipper Spacewaste: How dare you question Dr. Christian Cunning! Who are you, anyway?

Moses McNutt [threateningly]: Oh, shut up! I know right from wrong. Something you seem to have forgotten.

[Dr. Spacewaste cringes in horror.]

Dr. Teddy Tightjaw [whining]: Uncle Skippy, I wanted to tell you about him. He's NOT one of us!

Dr. Skipper Spacewaste [sternly]: No, he certainly is NOT.

Director: Hey! What's going on? We've got a show to produce. We've got to produce! My god, you're on television, do you know that?

[At once, Doctors Spacewaste, Tightjaw, and Cunning kneel before the television set. At the same time, The God of Human Security starts flashing his beer-bottle horns and bellows.]

The God of Human Security:
    I am the god of human security.
    You know me and you serve me well.
    You worship me instead of facing absurdity.
    For me, your neighbor you would butcher and sell.

[The voice continues to bellow. Dr. Tightjaw anxiously turns down the volume, but the voice can still be heard.]

Director: What in the hell is going on?

Dr Teddy Tightjaw [confusedly]: I don't know. I just don't know. Something activated TGOHS.

Director: TGOHS?

Dr. Teddy Tightjaw: The God of Human Security. Something's wrong. Something's very, very wrong.

Moses McNutt: I'll say! Something is very wrong. Very, very wrong.

Dr. Christian Cunning; Who are you? Don't you understand? We are on television. [Moses shrugs his shoulders.]

Dr Skipper Spacewaste [examining TGOHS]: I see what happened. The satellite has empowered TGOHS.

My god! Won't it ever shut up?

Aaron Anathema [furiously]: Don't count on it.

Director [anxiously to Moses and Aaron]: All right, both of you, get out of the picture.

Moses McNutt: I just wanted some gasoline . . .

Dr. Teddy Tightjaw: Oh, no you won't! I'm going to sell them the gas at ten dollars a gallon. [He immediately runs off the stage and comes back with a gasoline can.] All right, old man. Pay me! Fifty bucks for five gallons. No one takes a dollar from me. No one!

Moses McNutt: I'm not paying you anything.

Dr. Teddy Tightjaw: Pay!

Moses McNutt: No!

Dr. Teddy Tightjaw [screaming and stamping his foot]: PAY! PAY! NOW!

Moses McNutt: No!

Director: Oh, stop it! Here, I'll pay you! [He pulls out a huge wad of bills and pays Dr. Teddy Tightjaw.] Now, the two of you get the hell out of here! [to the cameraman] Get them out of here! Use the helicopter! Just get them OUT OF HERE!

[Aaron and Moses are escorted off the stage by the cameraman.]

Director [smiling happily]: Now. Let's produce!

Dr. Skipper Spacewaste and Dr. Christian Cunning: Let's produce!

Dr. Teddy Tightjaw [calling offstage]: Stephanie . . . Jason . . . hurry up! You're going to be on TV! Come on, my cute-ums!

[Stephanie and Jason come bounding forward on pogo sticks. The voice of TGOHS is heard as the director, the one remaining cameraman, and Doctors Spacewaste, Cunning and Tightjaw look on approvingly with insipid smiles. The lights fall.]

Mr. Riccardi is an instructor in philosophy, world religions, and business ethics at various colleges and universities in Southern California. He is also a business broker. His latest dramatic videoed production, THE BURDEN OF CHRISTMAS, has received acclaim from scholars, psychiatrists, theatre directors, and suicide prevention centers.

His other works include:
>CHRIST AND FREEDOM: A CHRISTOCENTRIC ANALYSIS OF SUICIDAL BEHAVIOR. This is an analysis of contemporary self-destructive behavior in relation to the world-views of the Bible, Justin Martyr, Athanasius, Augustine, Luther, Calvin, Kierkegaard, Dostoyevsky, Schopenhauer, Nietzsche, and Camus.
>
>LIGHT IN THE LABYRINTH. This is a study of John Calvin's use of the labyrinthian image as a key to understanding human nature.

www.ingramcontent.com/pod-product-compliance
Lightning Source LLC
Chambersburg PA
CBHW070058020526
44112CB00034B/1581